# SELF-REALIZATION

## *AN OUTLINE OF ETHICS*

BY

### HENRY W. WRIGHT

PROFESSOR OF PHILOSOPHY, UNIVERSITY OF MANITOBA

NEW YORK

### HENRY HOLT AND COMPANY

To

PROFESSOR JAMES EDWIN CREIGHTON

through whose advice and encouragement this study
was begun.

# PREFACE

The writer on Ethics at the present time is fortunate in having at his disposal the valuable results of two important movements in the science which took place in the nineteenth century. The one idealistic, originating in Germany but culminating as far as Ethics is concerned in Great Britain, formulated the clearest conception which human thought has yet attained of the spiritual activities that coöperate in personal development. The other naturalistic, continuing the tradition of English Utilitarianism under the illuminating influence of evolutionary science, furnished us with the most complete description that we possess of the actual conditions, natural and social, under which morality has developed. Now while these two schools are sharply opposed in standpoint and method, their conclusions, in so far as these are well-founded, do not contradict but rather supplement one another. Hence the moralist of to-day, if he wishes to profit by the results of previous ethical reflection, must aim to make his theory a synthesis of these two different bodies of truth. Such has been my aim in the present volume. The form of the Moral Ideal I have endeavored to ground in the essential nature of volition, understood as the controlling agency in personal development; its content I have sought to derive from the actual conditions of human existence as these have been discovered by empirical study. In carrying out this program I was made to recognize anew my heavy obligations to the leaders of the two schools above mentioned. Among idealists I owe most to Hegel, particularly to the pregnant suggestions in the *Encyclopædia* of a moral " dialectic " whereby the

individual through self-negation overcomes the limitations
of his finitude and realizes his greater self, to Green's
*Prolegomena,* and to the works of Edward Caird. The
representatives of the other school to whom my debt is
largest are, perhaps, Leslie Stephen, Herbert Spencer—and
Darwin himself.

In the arrangement of my material I have without doubt
been influenced decisively by the example of a book very
well known and highly esteemed by me—Professor James
Seth's *Ethical Principles.* To introduce the principle of
Self-realization by a preliminary study of the opposing
theories of Hedonism and Rationalism, in which the one-
sidedness and inadequacy of each is clearly shown, has
always seemed to me a logical procedure and one well
suited to the purposes of a text-book. I should be indeed
remiss if I failed to take the opportunity here presented
of expressing my deep gratitude to the author of this book.
As my first instructor in Ethics, Professor Seth rendered
me that high service which is in the power of only the
greatest teachers to perform—he produced in my mind a
conviction of the importance and dignity of his subject
and awakened in me an enthusiasm for its further study
which has never waned.

Of late a growing tendency is noticeable among writers
on Ethics to avoid the abstractly formal, the purely theoretical, and to make their expositions concrete and practical. The desire which thus finds expression, to keep ethical
principles in close and vitalizing contact with the facts of
actual morality, and thus to facilitate their application to
conduct, is in every way commendable and promises well
for the development of ethical science. But this desire,
in itself wholly praiseworthy, should not in my opinion
lead to such neglect of theory as to make the ethical
treatise merely a series of discussions of different moral
problems. Of course the question concerns mainly the

method of presentation; any scientific treatment is bound to be systematic and in order to be systematic must have a framework of theory. How prominent then should the theoretical framework be made in a text-book of Ethics? My belief is that it should be made sufficiently prominent to organize the material presented into a well-articulated body of doctrine which can be grasped in its unity and whose parts are so related that one implies and thus leads on to the others. Such formulation is justified, I think, both on logical and pedagogical grounds. These considerations apply particularly to the treatment accorded to the several virtues. Classifications of the virtues have been out of fashion for some time in ethical literature. The reasons usually given for abandoning the attempt thus to classify the fundamental forms of good conduct are that no classification can hope to be final or help being schematic and arbitrary. Now such objections seem to me altogether inconclusive and whatever force they may possess is in my opinion far outweighed by the advantages which promise to follow from a systematic exposition of the leading virtues. The system of the virtues, each clearly defined in its relation to all the rest, may with truth be said to complete the science of Ethics, since it exhibits principles and ideals in their application to daily conduct and as yielding a program for actual living.

In conclusion, I wish to acknowledge my indebtedness to friends in Lake Forest for helpful suggestion and criticism; especially I desire to thank Professor J. M. Clapp of Lake Forest College for assistance in proof-reading, and my wife whose loyal coöperation in all my endeavors has made this work possible.

HENRY W. WRIGHT.

LAKE FOREST, ILL.,
March 10, 1913.

# CONTENTS

## PART ONE

### ETHICS AS THE SCIENCE OF GOOD CONDUCT

#### CHAPTER I

#### THE SUBJECT-MATTER OF ETHICS—CONDUCT

#### CHAPTER II

#### THE METHOD OF ETHICS—A PRACTICAL AND NORMATIVE SCIENCE

#### CHAPTER III

#### THE PROBLEM OF ETHICS—THE DISCOVERY OF THE SUMMUM BONUM

## Chapter IV

### Knowledge of the Good, or Conscience

## Chapter V

### The Appeal of the Good or Moral Obligation

## Chapter VI

### The Motive of Good Conduct

*PART TWO*

## THE NATURE OF THE GOOD

### CHAPTER I

#### THE NATURE OF THE GOOD—CONDUCT OR CHARACTER

### CHAPTER II

#### THEORIES OF THE GOOD—HEDONISM

### CHAPTER III

#### THEORIES OF THE GOOD—RATIONALISM

### CHAPTER IV

#### VOLITION AS AN ORGANIZING AGENCY

# CONTENTS

## Chapter II

### Self-Realization and the Standard of Goodness

## Chapter III

### Self-Realization and Self-Sacrifice

## Chapter IV

### Self-Realization and the Motive of Goodness

## Chapter V

### Self-Realization and Happiness

### Chapter VI

### Self-Realization and the System of Virtues

## PART FOUR

## THE LIFE OF SELF-REALIZATION

### Chapter I

### The Individual Virtues

### Chapter II

### The Social Virtues

### Chapter III

## PART ONE

## ETHICS AS THE SCIENCE OF GOOD CONDUCT

# CHAPTER I

## THE SUBJECT-MATTER OF ETHICS—CONDUCT

1. **The Meaning of Conduct.**—Ethics may be described as the science of conduct, provided that conduct itself is defined with sufficient strictness. It is natural to think of the term " conduct " as synonymous with the word " action." But action is defined by Psychology as movement having conscious antecedents and concomitants,[1] and evidently is possible with animals as well as men; while the field of morality has always been limited by the common reason of mankind to the sphere of human action. The same difficulty arises if with Spencer [2] we define conduct as the adjustment of acts to ends; since when thus defined it includes the action of all living creatures. If the word is used to signify the subject-matter of Ethics, therefore, conduct must be defined as *voluntary action* and thus limited to the human sphere. For only to such action does responsibility attach and are the moral predicates properly applicable. Ethics is then the science of conduct when by conduct is understood voluntary action.

[1] TITCHENER: *Outline of Psychology*, § 61.
[2] SPENCER: *Data of Ethics*, Chap. I, § 2.

2. **Essential Features of Voluntary Action.**—It will assist us in our present undertaking—that of determining the nature of voluntary action—if we consider ·briefly some of the essential features of this type of action before attempting its formal definition.

In the first place, voluntary action always involves some kind of activity or change. Usually it involves change of position in space, or movement. So generally is this the case as to suggest that movement is a universal and necessary accompaniment of all volition. Yet such is not the fact if *visible* movement is meant. For thinking—the thinking of one who aims to reach a definite conclusion—which is certainly voluntary, and deserves to be classed as conduct, may be unaccompanied by any visible movement. It is true that even here many psychologists maintain that small invisible movements occur within the body of the thinker, and constitute an essential element in his activity.[3] However this may be, it is certain that activity of some sort, a series of changes possessing a measure of continuity and direction, characterizes all voluntary action.

Now a stream which rushes down a hillside, turning away to avoid large boulders, making a quiet pool here and a rapid torrent there, exhibits this feature of activity; it passes through a series of changes which are continuous and all directed towards one result. Yet no one would think of regarding the activity of the stream as *voluntary.* The reason most obvious is that the movement of the water has no conscious conditions or accompaniments. We discover then a second feature which is essential to voluntary action—the presence of *consciousness.* Because they are not conscious, all changes occurring in inanimate objects

---

[3] " We sometimes think of such doing as purely mental. In reality, however, movements are involved in all cases, and even were this not true the general principle of habit so far as this stands for a law governing the transmission of nervous currents would still be valid."—ANGELL: *Psychology,* p. 76.

(and in plants as well) are excluded from the sphere of voluntary action.

Suppose, in the second place, that consciousness of a comparatively simple form should be present and produce activity. A bull, aroused by the sight of a scarlet jersey worn by a man who is traversing the pasture, rushes upon him, goring and trampling him. Here we have activity with conscious conditions and concomitants. The perception of the red object " angered " the bull and prompted him to attack the person displaying the obnoxious color. Yet we should not call the action voluntary or hold the animal morally responsible for it. If asked why not, we should probably reply that the animal did not " know what it was doing," and our meaning would be that while the act had its source in certain images and feelings in the animal consciousness, still it was accompanied by no knowledge which could foresee the suffering and death of the man or understand any of its consequences. Evidently, therefore, foreknowledge involving some ability to generalize upon the past and to anticipate the future is a necessary feature of voluntary action. The addition of this element of foreknowledge to volition rules out of the field of conduct all animal action except possibly occasional acts of a few species of the higher animals such as the dog and monkey, which some authorities believe to be capable of an elementary form of judgment and hence able to act with a limited degree of foreknowledge.[4]

Finally we can imagine activity conditioned by consciousness and accompanied by foreknowledge, which is nevertheless not voluntary. Imagine a motorist turning down the center of a road in the middle of which some children are playing, expecting, if they do not run out

[4] Hobhouse believes that certain of the higher vertebrates, such as those mentioned, are capable of practical (as distinguished from conceptual) judgment. (HOBHOUSE: *Mind in Evolution*, Chaps. VI and IX.)

of the road, to turn his machine to one side or bring it
to a stop. Suppose that the children do not move and
the driver, owing to some break in the machinery, is unable
at the last moment to stop or turn his car. The ensuing
action might with fairness be said to have its condition
in the consciousness of the driver, since he consciously gave
direction to the machine, and was accompanied by a second's
clear foreknowledge of the results on his part. The same
situation would exist if we imagined a prisoner of war
having his finger pressed forcibly by his captors upon a
key which he knew would explode a mine and destroy
one of his own country's ships. We have in both of these
cases—which, to be sure, make somewhat extravagant demands upon the imagination but are quite possible—acts
conditioned by consciousness and accompanied by foreknowledge. We should not dream of regarding them as
voluntary, however; because they are not *intentional*. A
fourth feature essential to voluntary action has been found.
Not merely must the act have its source in a conscious
process, and its results be in a measure foreseen, but the
act and its results must be intended, i.e. they must be
consciously chosen, be preferred and sought after as *ends*.

3. **Voluntary Action Defined.**—At least four factors
then enter into voluntary action: (1) activity, (2) consciousness, (3) knowledge, and (4) intention. In order to
be voluntary an action must have its source in consciousness, its results must be in a measure foreknown, and also
intended. The fourth of these factors of course includes
the second and third; an act can be intended only if it
is conscious and its result is foreseen. When the outcome
of action is thus intended it becomes an end or aim and,
as chosen by the agent, determines the nature and course
of his activity. To the pursuit and attainment of this end
all his action is made a means. Gathering up in a single
statement these different characteristics, voluntary action

may be defined as *action in pursuit of a consciously chosen end.* Let us consider in further detail this mode of activity, distinguishing the steps which enter necessarily into its regular procedure.

**4. In Voluntary Action an Object Is Conceived as an End.**—All voluntary action is determined by the idea of an object conceived as an *end.* This end or aim by which the will is directed in its activity is of necessity a product of thought and imagination. Usually the object which is sought is not present to the senses, and hence must be imagined or thought of. But even when the object desired is present in perception, if it is to act as an end it must be related in an intelligible way to certain ideas. With the object sought, whether perceived or imagined, must be associated ideas of the means or movements necessary to secure it, and some conception of the satisfaction which will result from obtaining it. Ideas of the two classes last named serve to relate the object to the agent himself, make it an object for him, i.e. an end. Because the object has this connection with the needs and capacities of the agent it interests and attracts him. This attractive quality belonging to the end is signified in the consciousness of the agent by a pleasant feeling which suffuses and colors the whole complex of ideas which we have been describing. An illustration will make clearer the nature and relation of these different constituents which go to make up the end. Suppose that after I have settled down to my evening's reading I discover that I have not a needed book in my possession. At once the idea of going to the library for the missing book occurs to my mind. The book in the library thus comes to be thought of as an end of action. The book itself as a specific object is imagined—the image may be reproductive and I see in my fancy the back of the book as it appears on the shelf or feel the roughness of its binding when in my hand, or I may have a verbal image, seeing the words of the title printed out or hearing them spoken. With the idea of the book as thus imagined are associated ideas more or less vague of the movements I must make to procure the book—motor images of the movements incidental upon rising from my chair, leaving the room, walking across the campus, and even of reaching up to take the book from its accustomed place on the shelf. Finally there is added an idea of the result of the action, of the opportunity which the possession of the book will give me to complete successfully my evening's work. The thought of thus finishing my work pleases me and its pleasantness spreads over the whole combination of ideas which thus becomes interesting and attractive to me. This complex of ideas with its pleasant tone, which is formed in much less time than it takes to describe it, may be accepted as a typical end.

5. **Is Distinguished from Present Actuality.**—The end as conceived or imagined belongs strictly to the ideal sphere and thus is set in sharp opposition to objects which actually exist or are in present possession. This opposition of the end as ideal or imagined, to the present and actual, is essential to its nature and office as end; for precisely because it does not actually exist, while it does interest and attract, the thought of the end arouses the agent to action. The opposition between the ideal and the actual, due to the thought of an end unattained, introduces strain and tension into the consciousness of the agent. His present condition is rendered unpleasant or even painful because its continued existence precludes the attainment of the object. He is made restless and uneasy in the actual by the possibilities held forth by the ideal. Thus, in the illustration of the book wanted from the library, the thought of securing it makes me discontented with the facilities of my own library, distracts my attention from other tasks I might perform, and causes me genuine uneasiness and discomfort.

**6. And Chosen in Preference to Other Ideal Possibilities.**—Voluntary action requires that the end be not merely distinguished from actually existing objects but also be chosen in preference to all other ideal possibilities. These possibilities may take the form of several clearly imagined alternatives to the end finally realized. Then deliberation ensues over the desirability of these rival ends, with an attempt to foresee the consequences involved in the various possibilities of action, as when one debates between different possibilities of route and destination in a coming holiday excursion. Or the alternative possibilities may be present only by implication. In many cases of voluntary action there is no debate between conflicting objects; indeed it is often true that only one possibility of action is consciously considered. Yet in all action truly voluntary, the possibility of *not* performing the action, of *not* seeking the end, enters in some form into the consciousness of the agent. His present condition, contrasted as actual with the idea of the end, becomes, in the idea of its continuance into the future, itself an ideal possibility. I am aware, with more or less conscious clearness, of the possibility of continuing to sit in my easy-chair before the study-fire as an alternative to going to the library in the rain for the needed book. Consequent upon this feature of voluntary action, the feelings which accompany it are further complicated. While the idea of procuring the needed book is itself pleasant, the steps which must be taken to attain this end —those of leaving my comfortable chair and going out on an inclement night—are in thought highly unpleasant. And while my present condition of need for the book is unpleasant and irritating, the thought of remaining where I am in contrast to going after the book is very pleasant. Hence arises that baffling confusion of pleasant and unpleasant feeling which is attendant upon hesitation and decision.

Besides being contrasted with other possibilities of action, an end must be chosen or selected from among them if it is to be voluntarily realized. This choice consists in fixation of the attention upon one end, to the exclusion of all other alternatives. Thus to hold attention upon one end requires effort, since it involves a resisting of the attractions of other objects which are often very powerful. Modern psychology has taught us that the effort involved in volition is effort of the attention in holding an idea in the focus of consciousness despite all influences working to crowd it out, and not effort exercised in energizing unwilling muscles and in moving laggard limbs to carry out the fiat of consciousness. Let the idea be attended to, the psychologist tells us, and it will work itself out. This does not mean, however, that only effort enough need be exerted to bring the idea of the end once within the circle of clearest consciousness, thus forcing out for the time being all other attractive possibilities. On the contrary, protracted effort is often required to hold the idea fast in the focus of attention while the steps necessary for its realization are serially thought of and taken—else the idea of a conflicting aim will seize the attention and interrupt the action in its performance. Thus I may have to keep the idea of the desired book in the forefront of my thoughts until well on the way to the library, lest the thoughts of the comforts of chair and fire be sufficient to turn me back before I have passed the door.

7. **Because of Its Appeal to the Character of the Agent.**—Such choice of an end of action must itself have some cause or ground. Selection can occur only where there is some basis or criterion for comparing the different alternatives. In voluntary action choice is determined by the character of the agent, as this is reflected in his consciousness at the time of decision. The conscious processes

which thus represent the character of the agent in determining his choice vary greatly in the degree of their complexity and of their adequacy to the character they express. At the one extreme we have choice determined by the simple memory-image of a past experience in which the individual sought and gained a similar object with pleasant results to himself, as a person might select and purchase a certain kind of fruit because it had particularly pleased his taste on a former occasion. The opposite extreme is given in instances of selection based upon a large purpose or comprehensive ideal which has been built up as the result of years of thought and experience, and whose bearing upon the present situation is discovered after a period of deliberation. The decision of a man to accept public office at a pecuniary sacrifice, because in his ideal of life public service stands higher than private ambition, would be an illustration in point. The important fact is that the nature of the agent determines his choices. Hence if action is really voluntary it is, as Aristotle recognized, an expression of character—of some comparatively permanent disposition or attribute in the nature of the individual who performs it.[5] This is the reason why we are justified in holding individuals responsible for their voluntary acts. If I decide to go to the library in search of the missing book the ground of my choice must rest in my own nature. It may be my interest in the subject I am studying, or a habit I have formed of pursuing to completion a task I have undertaken, or some other trait or disposition which influences my choice, but in any case the act, if voluntary, has its source in myself.

8. **Which Gains Satisfaction Through Its Attainment.**—When the end chosen is attained through action the tension between ideal aim and actual condition is re-

[5] ARISTOTLE: *Nicomachean Ethics*, Bk. II, Chap. III (Welldon's trans., p. 42).

lieved and its unpleasantness allayed. The end which is thought of and desired is made an actual possession of the agent, and thus unity and equilibrium are restored to his consciousness. This state of unity, regained through the inclusion of an object desired and sought for, is itself pleasant and is experienced by the agent as *satisfaction*— the pleasant consciousness of success in giving expression to his character. With such feelings of satisfaction I begin my work again after returning from the library with the object of my quest, pleased that I have not allowed an obstacle which could thus be removed to interfere with the prosecution of my evening's labors.

Finally, it should be observed that the steps just described are not in any sense separable or independent, nor is voluntary action merely the sum or sequence of them thus conceived. On the contrary, each voluntary act is a vital unity within which the different steps or activities just distinguished are joined in close organic interdependence. Each voluntary act is a pulsation in the life of intelligence, a moment in the expression of personality.

9. **Ethics Is Concerned with the Whole of Human Conduct.**—If conduct, thus understood as voluntary action, is taken for the subject-matter of Ethics, then it is obvious that this science will be limited in its scope to the field of human action; for man alone among living species is capable of acting in pursuit of a consciously chosen end. Within the limits of human life, however, Ethics is concerned, not with a part, but with the whole of conduct. It is the comprehensive science of human practice, and, since all intelligent life has its source in will, may be said to be the science of human life itself. In a real sense, then, conduct is not a fraction, but the whole of human life, and all of the activity by which man's personality gains expression falls within the field of Ethics. Necessarily, Ethics is general in its treatment, leaving a detailed con-

sideration of special activities to subordinate sciences and confining itself to the essential characteristics and fundamental principles of conduct.

10. **Objections to This View.**—Objections of two different kinds may arise to this view of the subject-matter of Ethics. According to the first we have made the field of Ethics too narrow in thus limiting it to voluntary action. For, it is urged, we hold men responsible for actions that clearly are not voluntary. Acts done from fixed habit, such as the striking of a blow or the utterance of an oath when angry, might be cited as examples. Certainly such acts are frequently without intention, and hence, when considered in isolation, appear as involuntary. They are not properly understood when thus isolated, however; but must rather be conceived as the outcome of a series of acts, the first of which were intended, and voluntary, and for which the agent was responsible. The habit itself is voluntarily initiated if not the single act, and we properly hold the agent responsible for it and for all the action it entails. Much the same can be said of acts recognized as " accidental " but for which we hold the individual responsible and inflict censure or punishment. While the act itself is strictly unintentional and involuntary, it results from a lack of care and attention which has voluntary origin and for which responsibility is justly incurred.

The second objection is of just the opposite character and rests upon the opinion that not all voluntary action has moral significance. Hence, it is claimed, we make the field of Ethics too broad when we identify it with the sphere of voluntary action. Herbert Spencer was of this opinion, and his illustration of conduct which is ethically indifferent has become classic.

" As already said, a large part of ordinary conduct is indifferent. Shall I walk to the waterfall to-day? Or shall I ramble along the seashore? Here the ends are ethically indifferent. If I go to the waterfall, shall I go over the moor or take the path through the wood? Here the means are ethically indifferent. And from hour to hour most of the things we do are not to be judged as either good or bad in respect of either end or means." [6]

Professor Dewey agrees with Spencer on this point.[7] He believes that when one end is taken for granted and out of its connection with other ends, the question of the means employed in its realization is one of technique rather than of morals. "It is a question of taste and of skill—of personal preference and of practical wisdom, or of economy, expediency." Thus if the matter of the afternoon walk stand alone and have no bearing upon, or conflict with, other aims or interests, then the choice of a path to follow is an affair of individual taste or practical expediency and has no ethical significance. Only when the value of the proposed end is felt to be incompatible with that of another, appealing to a different kind of interest or tendency, do we have a truly moral situation in the view of the latter writer. But, as a matter of fact, ends can be thus considered out of relation to other ends, and to their ultimate consequences, only by artifice and abstraction. All the ends consciously chosen by an individual, along with the activities they call forth, belong together, since they are expressions of a unitary personality and are interwoven by threads of common interest and meaning. Thus, in Spencer's illustration, the afternoon walk gives mental diversion and physical exercise, and these in their turn are necessary to the health of mind and body,— ends of high moral worth. As a means to this end the walk itself possesses moral value and, since it is difficult to imagine, that with a given person and at a certain time, one path would not fulfil the purposes of the walk a little better than any other, we have in the choice of route a

[6] SPENCER: *Data of Ethics*, Chap. I, § 2.
[7] DEWEY AND TUFTS: *Ethics*, p. 206.

question of real, although not momentous, moral significance. Whether I shall have my house painted white or brown seems on first thought merely a matter of taste or economy and to have no ethical bearing whatever. Yet further reflection shows me that the painting of my house contributes in an important way to the purposes, themselves of undoubted moral value, which the house itself subserves, and that the advantage gained by painting is measured largely by my success in selecting the " right " color. As the field of conduct is thus a unity, the different ends being inter-related and the single acts connected in the chains of their consequences with the most inclusive purposes, it is impossible to draw a line within it which shall exclude certain actions as morally indifferent. Of course, it is not meant that ends are never considered out of relationship with other ends nor that in every case of choice we should raise the issues of eternity and try to determine the ultimate bearing of our action. In many cases the bearing of an action upon the attainment of other ends—itself important enough—*is* thoughtlessly overlooked when it should be taken into consideration. But manifestly time alone forbids that the whole field of conduct should be surveyed at every instance of choice. Hence, in selecting a tool or choosing a method for our work, we follow approved technical procedure which, while it is now habitual with us, was first adopted because representing what in the experience of the race was the most effective way of securing the end desired.

REFERENCES

SPENCER, *Data of Ethics*, Chap. I.
DEWEY AND TUFTS, *Ethics*, Chap. X.
SETH, *Ethical Principles*, Introduction, Chap. I, §§ 1, 2.
ALEXANDER, *Moral Order and Progress*, Book I, Chap. I.
ARISTOTLE, *Nicomachean Ethics*, (Welldon's trans.), Book II, Chap. III.
GREEN, *Prolegomena to Ethics*, Book II, Chap. II.

# CHAPTER II

## THE METHOD OF ETHICS—A PRACTICAL AND NORMATIVE SCIENCE

1. **Ethics as a Practical Science.**—The method of Ethics is consequent upon the character of its subject-matter. As the science of conduct, Ethics is necessarily a " practical " science. In order to make clear what is meant by such a practical science we may contrast it in aim and method with theoretical science, although—as will appear later—the distinctions we make are only provisional. A theoretical science is concerned with the knowledge of objects as facts. It investigates the conditions under which they exist, seeking to discover the other objects with which they are necessarily connected. The aim of such science is to ascertain in this way the nature and connection of all existing objects, explaining the existence of each one as a necessary consequence of the existence of another, its antecedent or cause. Geology is a science of this kind. It seeks to know the facts concerning the earth's structure, to discover the order of events in its history. It explains the existence of objects at present observable, e.g. sedimentary rocks, by connecting them with other objects and agencies which preceded them in the past and stand as their causes. A practical science, on the contrary, is concerned primarily with the realization of objects as ends of action. To be sure, purposive action is a fact, the con-

ditions of whose existence may be investigated according to the method of theoretical science. The work of Ethics is greatly aided by a knowledge of the history of the different forms of conduct and of the natural agencies that have influenced their existence and development. But such knowledge is only prefatory to ethical science proper, which is interested in conduct, not as a series of events causally connected, but as a means intelligently employed in the realization of chosen ends. As a practical science, then, Ethics seeks to discover through what actions the ends of human conduct may be realized. With the introduction of objects as ends to be realized a new conception enters, of great importance in all sciences of practice, i.e. *value*. Value is possessed by objects, not in their mere existence, but in their relation to conscious intelligence. Whatever is required to satisfy a need or fulfil a capacity of an intelligent being has value. The fact that an object is chosen for pursuit by a voluntary agent shows he is unsatisfied without it, and that, in promising relief to his want, the object has value. Objects whose realization is sought by mankind in general may, therefore, be regarded as necessary for the satisfaction of the human will and, hence, possessed of value. This value is communicated to all actions which are required as means to their attainment. The work of Ethics as a practical science may then be said to be the discovery of what conduct thus has value or, more definitely (although the criterion of distinction has not yet been supplied), *moral* value. Ethics is a practical science, therefore, whose aim is to discover what conduct has moral value.

2. **Ethics as a Normative Science.**—Upon the distinction between *existence* and *value* hinges the difference in method between the *descriptive* and the *normative* sciences. *Descriptive* sciences are composed of judgments of fact or existence. These judgments are so organized in each sci-

ence that the resulting body of knowledge correctly reflects the nature and connection of objects existing in a certain field of human experience. The " natural " sciences thus aim at a complete description of the phenomena of nature, each investigating the behavior of objects and the order of events in a particular part of the world. *Normative* sciences are composed of judgments of *worth*. Their aim is to evaluate, to appreciate. They are concerned, not with what *is*, but with what *ought to be*. They imply the possibility of a choice between objects differing in value, with consequent obligation to choose the best. Now it is possible to estimate the worth of objects or actions only when we have some standard to which they should conform, by which their value may be measured. Indeed, when the true standard of value in a field is once clearly defined its application is comparatively easy. Hence the first and most important task of any normative science is to discover the standard or norm by which worth may be estimated in its field.

Ethics belongs in the group of normative sciences. It has work of description to accomplish, to be sure, in describing existent practices and beliefs of human society and explaining the manner of their evolution. But this work is of minor importance as compared to the task of *evaluating* conduct, which falls to the duty of Ethics. When the normative method is thus accepted as proper to Ethics, the question of the standard of value in the field of conduct is immediately raised to the greatest prominence. For conduct cannot be evaluated without some standard or criterion by which the worth of different actions may be tested. As that to which all actions should conform, such a standard must itself be some form of conduct, or end, realized in action. An end of action in order thus to act as a standard must itself possess full value, that is, completely satisfy the will which seeks it.

That end, which in its realization possesses full value, and hence may be used as a standard for evaluating conduct, is called the Good. To discover what action or end of action may be accepted as the Good or standard of value in the field of conduct, and then to apply this standard, judging those actions which conform to the standard to be good and those which do not to be bad, is the task of Ethics as a normative science. In brief, it is the *science of good conduct*. This conception of the task of Ethics is essentially the same as that reached when we considered it as a science of practice. It has been suggested that there is a real difference between the two methods, inasmuch as the normative science is occupied exclusively with discovering the ideal or standard, while the practical science is concerned only with the conditions of its realization. But this difference is simply one of emphasis; the two kinds of inquiry cannot be separated. It is impossible to determine how human conduct shall achieve its end unless we have adequate knowledge of the end itself, and a complete understanding of the end includes knowledge of the actions involved in its realization.

3. **The Human Will the Ground of Moral Value.**— Ethics is a practical and normative science, and its business is to determine what conduct satisfies the human will and hence is good, and what conduct fails in this respect, and is therefore bad. Moral value thus attaches to all voluntary action and is grounded in the will itself, the source of all such action. It should be recognized, however, that when in this way we base moral value upon the demands of the human will we do not, as might appear, prejudge the whole question of what conduct is good. Good action may be action which promotes social welfare, or increases selfish pleasure, or glorifies God, for all that is known at the present stage of the investigation; the fact which we now emphasize is the fundamental psychological one, that if

any of these objects is to become an end of action it must appeal to the human will. All value, that is to say, in the whole field of conduct refers back to that capacity of intelligent volition of which conduct itself is the expression. Now we have knowledge of this power of volition only as it is manifested in our own human experience. Hence any scientific investigation of moral value, all empirical study of Ethics in fact, must be based upon an analysis of the needs and capacities of the human will and of the conditions of its expression in human life.

4. **Other Practical Sciences: (a) Technical.**—In describing Ethics as a practical science we put it in the class of such sciences as agriculture and medicine, generally recognized as practical. It will throw further light upon the task of Ethics if we consider its relation to these other sciences which are more obviously practical, or even technical, in their method.

Since Ethics is concerned with the whole of human conduct, it is evident that the other practical sciences must have their fields within the inclusive domain of Ethics. Such is the case, each of these sciences being occupied with a certain department of human conduct and attempting to determine what actions are necessary in order that the ends peculiar to this department of life be realized. Indeed, the fields of all the well-known practical sciences fall within one large department of conduct—that of '' practice,'' in the narrow meaning which excludes both the intellectual and the emotional, or æsthetic. It is in this sense that we use the word when we speak of a person as eminently '' practical.'' We do not mean that such a person is equally skilled in all departments of life, in the activities of thought as well as outward performance. Our reference is rather to a particular kind of conduct—to skill in a certain mode of activity—that of adapting means to the ends of intelligence. It will prevent confusion to call this mode of conduct the *technical* rather than the " practical." Technical activity consists, not in thinking of ends or ideals, nor in enjoying them in contemplation, but in devising methods, in inventing instruments, for their attainment. It is exercised chiefly in the outer world in adapting the objects and forces of nature to the uses of human intelligence. The prominence of this kind of activity in human life has been so great that it has seemed to cover the whole field of conduct itself—" action " and " practice " being identified with outward performance, visible execution. But even technical activity—not to mention conduct itself with its still greater scope—cannot be limited to the manipulation of material objects and physical forces in the external world. It is exercised in the political and social as well as the mechanical spheres. A plan for workingmen's compensation or a system of life-insurance is as much a product of intelligent technique as a steam engine or a mining process.

There are many practical sciences concerned with the use of technical skill in the different special fields of human experience. These sciences aim to prescribe in detail the rules which must be followed, the methods which must be used, the agencies which must be employed, in one special field or another, if the purpose appropriate to that field is to be realized. Thus the science of bridge-building tells of the material which must be employed and of the plan which must be followed in construction, in order that a bridge may be built adapted to the purposes of human intercourse and commerce. Any plan or device required as a *means* or *instrument* in a special field—whether it be a tool, or machine, a medicine, or a political institution—has, of course, technical value. As technique is a branch of conduct, so technical value is a species of moral value. In fact they are not distinguished in name, and we speak of a *good* engine or a *good* remedy,—that the cantilever, say, is a *good* bridge for this situation, when we mean that the device in question is an effective instrument for accomplishing its end. It would contribute to clearness if we adopted a term distinctive of technical value, such as *efficiency,* and spoke of an efficient engine, remedy, law, etc. The technical sciences fall into groups in accordance with the fields to which they are applied. In the inorganic sphere, the world of matter and motion, we find many technical sciences, all concerned with the conquest of nature and the employment of its forces in the service of man. The science of mining prescribes the methods which must be followed if ores are to be extracted from the earth most efficiently. The science of agriculture tells how the soil must be treated if it is to yield the largest returns. The sciences of engineering are discovering how materials may be utilized, and natural forces employed, for the increase of man's convenience and comfort. Besides these, there are others in the same group too numerous to mention, such as carpentry, bridge-building, etc. Coming into the organic or animate sphere we find the practical sciences of animal husbandry, which tell how animals must be housed and fed and bred if they are to be most serviceable to man as sources of food, carriers of burdens, etc. In the closely related field of human life are found the sciences, of hygiene which prescribes the rules which man must observe if he is to retain his health, and of medicine, which indicates the remedies he must use to cure disease. Going on to the still higher fields of society and politics, we find still another group of technical sciences—those of trade and commerce, of the practice of law and government, of education, etc.

5. **(b) Intellectual.**—Another department of conduct is that of thought, or intellectual activity. We so frequently contrast the theoretical with the practical that it is difficult

to think of thought or theory as a branch of practice. Yet, if by conduct is meant voluntary action, it is certainly such; for ends are chosen and pursued in the field of thought and imagination as well as in the field of technique. The work of the scientific investigator, who spends years of thought over a problem with the purpose of discovering the truth about it, and thus adding to the sum of human knowledge, is sufficient proof of this. The aim of intellectual activity is to gain ideas which " agree with reality," i.e. are *true*. The end of thinking is always the discovery of truth. A practical science of thought is needed, therefore, which shall state the requirements to which thinking must conform if it is to reach true conclusions. We have such a science in Logic, the science of correct thinking. Moreover, all of the special sciences, commonly designated as theoretical or descriptive, are in a sense practical, inasmuch as each tells the conditions under which facts may be experienced in a particular field. Thus such a science as Chemistry, which has been termed theoretical in contrast to a practical science like Ethics, because its aim is to describe existent objects rather than to tell how objects may be realized as ends, may itself be regarded as a practical science in so far as it seeks to discover the ways in which material substances must be regarded in order to reveal the facts of their constitution. There are, of course, as many of such sciences as there are different parts of the experienced world, each concerned with the discovery of truth in its field. The distinction between theoretical and practical as applied to the method of the sciences now appears neither absolute nor final. Theory turns out to be a department of practice, and the theoretical sciences to be themselves practical sciences concerned with the attainment of a distinctive end—Truth. The difference between Ethics and the theoretical sciences is not, consequently, that Ethics is concerned with the realization of ends while these sciences are not, but rather that Ethics is concerned with all the ends required to satisfy the will in every department of its activity, while they are interested in the attainment of one special end alone.

6. (c) Æsthetic.—A third department of conduct is the æsthetic. The aim of æsthetic activity is the production of a type of feeling—not that pleasure which always accompanies the attainment of desired objects, but pure or disinterested pleasure. Such " disinterested " pleasure —and it is the only case where pure feeling is made an end—is produced through the contemplation of certain objects which set the perceptive and imaginative faculties in free and harmonious play. Perceptions and images (mostly of sight and sound) able to effect this end and produce the enjoyment in question are recognized as having æsthetic value and are judged beautiful. In order that æsthetic pleasure may be experienced it is necessary that objects of a definite character be present and that their presence be accompanied by such subjective conditions as interest, attention, etc. The practical science of Æsthetics endeavors to determine the conditions, both objective and subjective, which must be fulfilled if the " sense of beauty " is to be awakened. Thus on the side of the object Æsthetics investigates, for example, what proportions figures must have to please the eye, and how tones may be combined to give pleasure to the ear; while on the subjective side it studies the effect that psychic conditions, such as love for the object and intimate knowledge of it, have upon the æsthetic experience. Besides the general science of Æsthetics there are many particular sciences, which prescribe the rules which must be followed if the effect of beauty is to be produced in various special fields. Such are the sciences of Drawing, of Music, of Architecture, etc.

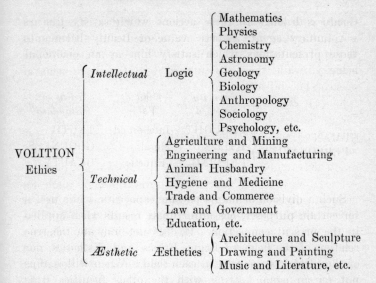

VOLITION
Ethics

Intellectual   Logic
- Mathematics
- Physics
- Chemistry
- Astronomy
- Geology
- Biology
- Anthropology
- Sociology
- Psychology, etc.

Technical
- Agriculture and Mining
- Engineering and Manufacturing
- Animal Husbandry
- Hygiene and Medicine
- Trade and Commerce
- Law and Government
- Education, etc.

Æsthetic   Æsthetics
- Architecture and Sculpture
- Drawing and Painting
- Music and Literature, etc.

**7. Other Normative Sciences.**—The fact that thought
and feeling are fields of conduct in which ends are chosen
and attained is witnessed by the classification of normative sciences which is generally adopted. Besides Ethics
two other normative sciences are recognized—Logic and
Æsthetics—Logic seeking to discover the requirements of
Truth as the intellectual ideal and to evaluate modes of
thinking by this standard; and Æsthetics in a like manner
attempting to define the ideal of Beauty and, with this
criterion, to pass judgment upon natural objects and artistic products. This classification of normative sciences is
somewhat misleading, however, since it places Ethics upon
an equal footing with Logic and Æsthetics, and makes the
ideal of Goodness coördinate with the ideals of Truth and
Beauty. Thus man, as an intelligent being, is said to
possess three capacities, those of Thought and Will and
Feeling; intellectual value or Truth belongs to those ideas
which satisfy him as a thinking being, moral value or

Goodness belongs to those actions which satisfy him as a voluntary agent, æsthetic value or Beauty belongs to those presentations which satisfy him as an emotional being.

| | Capacity Satisfied | Kind of Value | Ideal or Standard |
|---|---|---|---|
| HUMAN PERSONALITY { | THOUGHT | Intellectual | TRUTH |
| | WILL | Moral | GOODNESS |
| | FEELING | Æsthetic | BEAUTY |

Such a division of man's psychic capacities, while useful for certain purposes, has unfortunate results when applied in the present connection. It does not indicate the true relation of the fields of Logic, Ethics, and Æsthetics, nor of the ideals that govern in each field. When will is thus put on an equal footing with the other faculties it is necessarily taken as exclusive of thought and feeling, and hence made identical with action in the narrower sense. The sphere of Ethics then becomes that of outward perform- ance, of what we have called technical activity—adjustment and adaptation—and, in consequence of this limitation, its ideal of Goodness loses all authority over the intellectual and æsthetic fields. Now the truth is that will is the inclusive factor; value attaches to objects only as ends of volition, and this applies in the spheres of thought and feeling as well as that of " action." Hence all value is primarily moral value or Goodness. But volition is exercised in different departments of life, in the pursuit of various classes of objects; there are, consequently, spe- cial kinds of value, included within, and subordinated to, moral value. In the intellectual sphere ideas are sought which agree with reality and, to such ideas, intellectual value or truth is attributed; in the technical sphere agencies are sought which subserve the purposes of intelligence and, to such instruments, technical value or efficiency is attributed; in the æsthetic sphere objects are sought which in mere contemplation awaken the feeling of pleasure, and, to such objects, æsthetic value or beauty is attributed. But in each case the value is also, and primarily, *moral* value because it attaches to the objects as ends chosen and pursued by will. Goodness belongs to all objects which as ends satisfy the capacity of volition; truth to those ends which satisfy volition in its intellectual sphere, and beauty to those ends which satisfy volition in its æsthetic sphere.

| | *Capacity Satisfied* | *Kind of Value* | *Ideal or Standard* |
|---|---|---|---|
| HUMAN | VOLITION | MORAL | GOODNESS |
| PERSONALITY | Thought<br>Action<br>Feeling | Intellectual<br>Technical<br>Æsthetic | Truth<br>Efficiency<br>Beauty |

Ethics as a normative science is not coördinate with Logic and Æsthetics, therefore, but comprehensive of them; and the ideal of Goodness not of equal authority with those of Truth and Beauty, but supreme over both.

8. **Conclusion.**—Our brief survey of the practical and normative sciences other than Ethics has served to emphasize its inclusive and fundamental character. Special practical sciences cover, as we have seen, nearly the whole field of conduct in its three departments of thought and feeling and action. The need and importance of Ethics is not due to the fact that its subject-matter is new and unexplored, therefore, but to the fact that to Ethics alone belongs the task of investigating the field of conduct as a whole, of discovering its governing principles, and making clear the relation of its essential parts. Ethics is the comprehensive science of human life itself.

## REFERENCES

SETH, *Ethical Principles*, Introduction, Chap. II.
WUNDT, *Ethics* (English trans.), Vol. I, Introduction.
MUIRHEAD, *Elements of Ethics*, Book I, Chaps. II, III.
PAULSEN, *System of Ethics* (English trans.), Introduction.
THILLY, *Introduction to Ethics*, Chap. I.
SIDGWICK, *Methods of Ethics*, Book I, Chap. I.
MACKENZIE, *Manual of Ethics*, Introduction, Chaps. I, II.
MEZES, *Ethics, Descriptive and Explanatory*, Chap. I.

# CHAPTER III

## THE PROBLEM OF ETHICS—THE DISCOVERY OF THE SUMMUM BONUM

1. **How Determine What Is Good Conduct?**—The aim of Ethics as a practical and normative science is to determine what conduct is good—or, as we now understand, what conduct will completely satisfy the human will. Through what line of inquiry may this aim be most effectively achieved? At the outset it should be noticed that ethical science is not compelled to invent or imagine forms of conduct that may possibly meet the requirements of goodness. Human experience presents many types of conduct or (since actions are distinguished by the ends they seek) many ends of action, and it is the business of Ethics to scrutinize these existing ideals and practices. Certain ends have been pursued by men in all periods of human history; others are characteristic of particular races and times. Among these latter sharp rivalry has frequently existed and one set of ideals has replaced another only after a bitter struggle, as when the ideals of Christianity replaced those of classical antiquity. But while Ethics should thus draw its material from the facts of human experience, it is by no means limited to a description and classification of the various forms of conduct and ideals

of action that have figured in human history. Its work is to criticise these different ends, and such criticism requires some knowledge of the nature and demands of that power of volition which is seeking satisfaction through them—requires the presence, at least implicitly, of some standard of moral value. As it becomes more explicit, this standard of Goodness will take shape as the end or ideal which in its realization completely satisfies the human will; and although the elements which enter into the constitution of this ideal may all be drawn from existing human conduct, they may be so combined as to acquire a new meaning and a supreme importance.

2. **Many Ends Actually Sought Are Good only as Means.**—If we look out on human life we see men engaged in the pursuit of ends which appear infinitely diverse. A closer look will show, however, that of chief ends, of leading purposes, a comparatively few, as Aristotle observed, hold the attention of the majority of mankind. Such popular ends are money and reputation and pleasure. Yet these ends prove upon examination to have value not in themselves, but only as means to something else. Take money, as an instance. It is good only for what it will buy, and not in itself. This is apparent to every one except the miser, to whom his gold seems an end in itself because his thoughts have been perverted by ceaseless efforts at money-getting. Nor is it otherwise with reputation, in the sense of fame or popularity. To be widely known in society, to be favorably spoken of by one's fellows, is good only if it bring more real and substantial benefits. Otherwise it is but a hollow sham, an empty mockery, as many who attain it have testified. In the same class are most of the objects which we behold men pursuing. Here a man is bending all his energies to secure a home for himself and family; there one is working early and late to win professional success. But all such things are good

only as means to other things and not at all in themselves. Hence while ends of this class may well be a part of the good, their attainment can never represent the whole of goodness: they can of themselves never satisfy the human will, because they ever point further on to other ends more satisfactory than themselves.

3. **To Satisfy the Will an Object Must Be an End in Itself.**—In contrast to the ends just mentioned stands another class of objects which, although not sought by a large proportion of mankind, are nevertheless earnestly pursued by a few. These objects do not appear as means to further ends, but as ends in themselves—or if they do serve as instruments in the attainment of other objects, then these latter turn out to be only fuller and more complete expressions of themselves. Examples of this class of ends are the knowledge pursued by the scientific investigator, and the welfare of country as sought by the patriot. In both these cases the end seems to possess value in itself; it is difficult to imagine a further good which would demand the subordination of truth or of the public welfare. Where the interests of truth appear to be thus subordinated, as in the telling of myths to children or the deception of sick persons, it is really done for the sake of a more complete truth. And a sacrifice of national welfare is demanded only when necessary for the good of humanity with which the larger interests of the nation are identified. This contrast between different classes of ends brings to light an important characteristic of the end which is *entirely* good. It must be an end in itself, existing for the sake of no other end, and so complete as to require the addition of no other object. For only such an end can in its realization afford full satisfaction to the human will. All other ends, while they may afford a partial satisfaction, direct the will on to the pursuit of other objects to which they are merely instrumental.

⨍    4. **The Problem of the Summum Bonum.**—This object, which is an end in itself, and hence able to satisfy the human will completely, is called, in distinction from all lesser or lower goods, the Highest Good, or the *summum bonum*. Now the discovery of the *summum bonum* may be taken for the chief problem of Ethics. For only conduct which realizes this end is *good* conduct, and all conduct which does realize it is entirely good. Moreover, a thorough knowledge of this end must include a knowledge of the means necessary for its realization; since the supreme end, like all other ends, is an end of action, and can exist only as it is realized in conduct. Hence in discovering the *summum bonum* we solve the problem of what conduct is good, and thus fulfil the aim of Ethics. It is not strange, therefore, that ethical inquiry should have centered on this problem and that most discussions of morality should, since the beginning of ethical reflection, have borne more or less directly upon the question, " What is the *summum bonum?* " The fact that the problem, not finally solved after many centuries, is still discussed, testifies both to its great import and many difficulties. For besides other difficulties the problem of the Highest Good has this one, peculiar to itself, that while the value of other ends is proved by reference to the further ends to which they contribute, the *summum bonum* is a means to no further end and its value can be proved only by a reference back to the will which is its source, and a demonstration of its power to satisfy completely this capacity of intelligent volition.

5. **The Summum Bonum as the Moral Ideal.**—Since the *summum bonum* represents the maximum of human attainment and thus the goal of moral development for man, it has seldom if ever been realized in human experience. It is frequently realized in part, and hence one may, by a study of the different achievements of many

individuals, observe in actual existence a large number of its constituent elements. It is also in process of realization by a multitude of lives which, while they never attain their end in the world of our experience, have discovered the direction of the goal, besides traveling a long distance towards it. The *summum bonum* in its completeness, therefore, does not exist actually, but only in thought and imagination—is thus *an ideal*. An ideal is a conception of what is most desirable in life. It is an end the thought of which arouses feeling and enthusiasm because promising largest satisfaction. Now while there are ideals in every department of human experience; yet supreme over them all is the Moral Ideal, the idea of the *summum bonum*. By the Moral Ideal we mean that type of conduct or character which represents the highest attainment for man, the most complete fulfilment of his nature, the fullest satisfaction of his will. As such it is none other than the Highest Good and identical with the standard of moral value. Consequently ethical inquiry is often described as a quest of the Moral Ideal.

6. **The Formation of the Moral Ideal.**—Every end is, as we know, a product of thought whose existence depends upon the ability to judge and generalize. But many ends chosen for pursuit are particular objects limited both in time and in place to the present environment; hence they call only for the most elementary activities of cognition, such as those involved in perception and the perceptual judgment. Ideals, on the contrary, are of a universal or typical character, and are projected into the distant future; their formation, therefore, requires a degree of intellectual grasp and some constructive imagination. One might expect that as a consequence of this fact ideals would be restricted in their existence and influence to a comparatively small fraction of mankind, as alone possessing the intellectual power requisite to their formation. Yet

such is not the case; it appears rather that the majority of men possess at some time during their lives moral and religious ideals—forecasts of future attainment, visions of excellence they hope to attain. Proof of this is furnished by the method which revivalists and mission-workers among the submerged classes frequently adopt and find effective as a means of moral betterment. They seek by devices of rhetoric and music to awaken in the minds of their auditors memories of old ideals—boyhood dreams of noble achievement, youthful aspirations for honor and integrity. With many, these " ideals " seem, to be sure, scarcely more than passing fancies, fleeting visions. Yet they indicate the presence in the normal human being, particularly during the period of youth and early maturity, of imaginative and intellectual ability sufficient to the formation of ideals which can give direction to life and conduct. Authorities in genetic psychology [1] tell us that the period of adolescence is the time in human life when ideals are most readily and frequently formed. It is at this time, when the higher powers of intelligence at first develop, that they play most freely and spontaneously—that imagination wings its loftiest flight and thought makes its widest sweep. At this period the individual first becomes conscious of the present in its relation to the past ever receding behind, and the future stretching away before. Awakening also to a sense of his own selfhood in its connection with other selves, he is led almost inevitably to project into the future an idea of himself achieving what he most desires, and thus attaining his Highest Good. Then it is that the boy sees himself in possession of great wealth and owning houses and lands, yachts and horses; or as a statesman influencing the policies of nations; or as a physician, alleviating the ills of thousands of his suffering fellow-beings.

[1] STANLEY HALL: *Adolescence*, Vol. II, Chaps. XI-XVI.

**7. Characteristics of the Ideal.**—An ideal in order to be effective in moral development must be an expression of what is latent in the character of the agent and within the range of his possible attainment. It must appeal to the individual as the legitimate outcome of his own nature, the realization of the possibilities inherent in his own situation, the fulfilment of his own deepest desires. If these conditions are not fulfilled, the ideal will either prove unattainable and the agent in his discouragement will abandon all endeavor, or its attainment will fail to bring the expected satisfaction and he will be rendered skeptical of all moral values. For these reasons it is necessary that each individual construct his own ideal. While he may be assisted in this task by information given and influence wisely exerted, yet when this influence extends so far as to cause him to adopt as his own an ideal which is not rooted in his own nature and capacities, it does far more harm than good. The ideal should always represent the unrealized possibilities of the actual. As Professor Dewey says with truth: " To set up ideals of perfection which are other than the serious recognition of the possibilities of development resident in each concrete situation is in the end to pay ourselves with sentimentalities, if not with words, and meanwhile it is to direct thought and energy away from the situations which need and which welcome the perfecting care of attention and affection." [2]

Although it is true that the ideal should be based upon the actual abilities of the agent and be relative to the existing circumstances of his life, it is equally true that in order to awaken enthusiasm and inspire effort the ideal must be raised far above the actual and represent a height of attainment which appears impossible enough to all save the enraptured idealist. It is this height of the ideal above the actual with all its negations that invests it with

[2] DEWEY AND TUFTS: *Ethics*, p. 422.

such fascination and glamor—that makes the pursuit of it a romantic adventure. It is indeed unfortunate when a human being stakes his life upon the realization of an ideal which is altogether beyond his capacity to attain if he had a dozen lives to live; for then a bitter disappointment, a crushing sense of failure, are the reward of his life's endeavor. But the fact never to be forgotten is that we cannot predict what is possible or impossible with a human individual before he actually tries it. The greatest of human achievements have been due to the promptings of ideals which sensible, practical people would have denounced as visionary and absurd in their first adoption. If man is really to attain, therefore, he must have the courage to venture; he cannot afford to wait until assured of success before making his endeavor. Emerson's familiar maxim, " Hitch your wagon to a star," is sound, both psychologically and ethically. A lofty ideal, even when accompanied by no knowledge of how it is to be realized, may provoke enthusiasm and effort sufficient to devise new methods, overcome old obstacles, and finally to place the agent upon a level of attainment far higher than he would have reached had he chosen a lower ideal, the road to whose realization lay open before him.

8. **Source of the Power of the Ideal.**—No intelligent student of history can doubt the tremendous influence of the Ideal upon human conduct. The ancient ideal of civic virtue led large numbers of Greek and Roman citizens to devote their lives wholly to their country's welfare. The Christian ideal of service and self-sacrifice has inflamed the hearts of later thousands with missionary ardor, causing them to dedicate themselves to a life of labor for humanity's good. The modern ideal of loyalty to Truth has prompted a multitude of men to pursue scientific investigations with unflagging zeal, and in the face of hardship and persecution, in order that, as the result

of their efforts, man's store of available knowledge should be increased. The secret of the power of the Moral Ideal over the lives of men lies in its appeal to the larger possibilities of man as a spiritual being—ultimately, in these higher psychic capacities themselves, which enlarge man's horizon beyond the limits of his present situation and organic needs and bring him into touch with Universal Reality. The Ideal attracts and inspires because it represents the complete fulfilment of man's powers as a voluntary agent—the attainment of the highest human good.

## REFERENCES

ARISTOTLE, *Nicomachean Ethics* (Welldon's trans.), Book I.
MACKENZIE, *Manual of Ethics*, Book I, Chap. I.
SETH, *Ethical Principles*, Introduction, Chap. I, §§ 3-7.
PALMER, *The Nature of Goodness*, Chaps. I, II.
GREEN, *Prolegomena to Ethics*, Book III, Chap. I.
LESLIE STEPHEN, *Science of Ethics*, Chap. II.

# CHAPTER IV

## KNOWLEDGE OF THE GOOD, OR CONSCIENCE

If the Highest Good is to be realized in human conduct, it must (1) be known as an object of thought, and (2) appeal as an end of action, under which conditions it will (3) constitute the motive of good conduct. We shall, therefore, consider in the three chapters following: first, knowledge of the Good, or Conscience; second, the appeal of the Good, or Obligation; and, third, the Motive of Goodness.

1. **Conscience Not a Separate Faculty but a Species of Judgment.**—Men were for long supposed to receive knowledge of good and evil from a special faculty, *Conscience*, implanted in human nature for this purpose. To Conscience was assigned the supreme place among the cognitive faculties of man, as the final arbiter in all matters of conduct—a kind of oracle, in fact, revealing the mind of God upon all questions of right and wrong. Such a view was possible only so long as mind was understood as an assemblage of different faculties, and Psychology remained a general account of the achievements of these faculties. When, however, Psychology undertook a close, detailed analysis and description of mental processes, no evidence was found of the existence of conscience as a

separate faculty. Our thinking upon moral subjects involves the same processes and follows the same laws as does our thinking upon other matters. Conclusions which pertain to questions of morality are subject to the same requirements of consistency and proof as are imposed on other conclusions. Indeed, moral judgment differs from all other judgment only in referring to a particular subject which possesses distinctive qualities. By conscience we mean, therefore, simply a species of judgment—judgment of moral value.

2. **Conscience as Judgment of Moral Value.**—We have now to study as carefully as possible the working of conscience or moral judgment. Let us begin by analyzing a concrete instance of moral judgment, or the action of conscience.

Suppose that a person, sitting by a window facing the street, sees a group of boys approach a corner fruit-stand kept by an aged and decrepit woman. While one of the party engages the attention of the woman with questions concerning the price of the fruit, others put a number of apples in their pockets, and then the whole party goes off laughing and shouting. The observer at the window, who has seen the performance, exclaims indignantly, " How wrong! " These words give expression to a moral judgment. The subject of this judgment is the conduct of the boys. Since moral value attaches only to voluntary action, the subject of all moral judgments is conduct. It is always upon the conduct of self or the conduct of others that conscience delivers its verdict. The quality attributed to the conduct of the boys in the above example—that of " wrongness "—is a kind of moral value. Here again we may generalize and note that the quality which as predicate is affirmed of the subject (conduct) in moral judgment is always a kind of moral value—moral judgment thus being an *evaluation of conduct*. Now moral value is of two opposite kinds, and hence the words which signify it fall into pairs of contraries, as good and bad, right and wrong, etc. The deliverances of conscience thus take the form of judgments in which the subject is conduct and the predicate some quality drawn from the class of moral values.

| | | *Subject* | *Copula* | *Predicate* |
|---|---|---|---|---|
| Particular Illustration | { | Conduct of boys | is | wrong. |
| General Statement | { | Conduct of self or others | is | good, or bad. right, or wrong, etc. |

The moral judgment possesses the same characteristics as other judgment.[1] When seriously affirmed moral judgment will not admit itself to be mere individual opinion, but claims to be *true,* to hold universally. As in the case of all other judgments, the universal validity claimed by moral judgment appears as a consequence of its *necessity*— that the particular judgment made *had to be* thus and so, and could not have been different, because certain other facts (themselves expressed in judgments) *compelled* it to take just this form. Thus in all our thinking our conclusions seem to be necessitated by antecedent facts or conclusions whose truth has been accepted. Now these antecedent facts or propositions upon which the truth of a judgment appears to rest are known as its *grounds.* Hence we are accustomed to challenge a judgment with the question, '' What are its grounds? Its reasons? '' This question is as legitimate with the moral judgment as with any other, and conscience must be prepared to answer satisfactorily, if its conclusions are to be accepted as true.

Imagine, then, that we asked the onlooker in our example, who judged the behavior of the boys to be wrong,

---

[1] In further explanation of the essential features of judgment, *cf.* CREIGHTON: Introduction, *Logic,* Chap. XXII, '' Main Characteristics of Judgment.''

the question, Why? "Why do you think their conduct wrong?" He would probably answer, "Because it is stealing, of course." The ground of his judgment would therefore be another judgment which, completely expressed, would be, "All stealing is wrong." The instance is again typical. The ground of a particular moral judgment is usually one of a set of judgments of a more general nature whose truth is already accepted, and which assign moral values to certain classes of actions. Of such nature are the familiar judgments, "Stealing is wrong," "Murder is wrong," "Kindness is right," etc. If it is true that the moral values mentioned belong to these general classes of action, then of course they will attach to all particular actions that fall within the classes. Now a conclusion taken in connection with the grounds on which it rests is known as an inference. So moral judgment, becoming conscious of the other judgments which constitute its ground, expands into moral inference or reasoning. Referring again to our example, and using James's well-known formula,[2] the behavior of the boys represents the subject-matter of thought, S. From this behavior as a whole the onlooker singles out one feature that appears to him essential and most important—the feature, that is, of stealing, M. Now this feature enters into many forms of conduct and is recognized to possess certain properties, among them that of being wrong, P. Since P attaches to M and M belongs to S, P is attributable to S. The feature of theft is thus the connecting link or middle ground between the behavior of the boys and the quality of wrongness.

$$S \ — - \ M \ —— \ P$$
This act is stealing and therefore wrong.

Or, putting the inference in the traditional form of the syllogism.

[2] JAMES: *Psychology*, Chap. XXII, "Reasoning."

$$M \longrightarrow P$$
$$S \longrightarrow M$$
$$\overline{\phantom{S \longrightarrow M}}$$
$$S \longrightarrow P$$

All stealing is wrong.

*This act is stealing.*

(Therefore) This act is wrong.

3. **The Ground of the Moral Judgment Is Usually Emotional Rather than Rational.**—But the question of the ground of moral judgment is by no means settled when we explicitly refer the particular act to a class of actions previously judged to be good or bad.  This prior judgment itself needs support and the question is quite legitimate, on what ground do we hold general forms of conduct such as lying, stealing, courage, or kindness to be right or wrong? For these judgments if true must themselves be necessary consequences of other facts or considerations.  Suppose now that we asked the observer at the window, who had indignantly pronounced the conduct of the boys to be wrong because it was stealing, the further question, " Why is stealing wrong? " If he exemplified the average man he would probably show signs of surprise and impatience at the question, and reply, " Why is stealing wrong?  Why —because it *is* wrong! " or in some such words.  That is, the great majority of human beings do not carry their reasoning on moral matters back further than the judgment that certain forms of conduct, such as *e.g.* courage and honesty and kindness, are right, and other forms, such as stealing and lying and murder, are wrong.  Actions belonging to these recognized classes excite strong feelings— of approval in the former group and disapproval in the latter.  Hence whenever an action is encountered which falls within such familiar class, it is greeted immediately by feelings of approval or the reverse, and thus its moral value, whether good or bad, appears self-evident.  The

binding force of conscience, Mill says, " consists in the existence of a mass of feeling which must be broken through in order to do what violates our standard of right, and which, if we do nevertheless violate this standard, will probably have to be encountered afterwards in the form of remorse."[3] These moral feelings seem to justify themselves and to require no further explanation. It is true, therefore, that with the greater number of mankind *the ultimate ground of moral judgment is emotional rather than rational.*[4] Of course this is not the case with the moral judgment alone. The average man has reasons for comparatively few of the conclusions he maintains. He nevertheless regards them as true, since they awaken the sentiment of belief in him. In this way the uneducated man *feels* that the claim of his political party or the doctrines of his church are necessarily true, and resents the challenge to furnish proof. Perhaps the facts with reference to the moral judgment are most concisely stated when we say that in the minds of those who have never reflected upon questions of morality and who make up of course the great bulk of mankind, the ground of all moral judgments is a set of *moral sentiments.* By a moral sentiment is meant a judgment of moral value, accompanied by feelings of pleasure if the conduct is judged good, and displeasure if found bad.[5] A group of such sentiments, approving of some forms of conduct and disapproving of others, is present in the minds of most men, and constitutes the basis of their moral judgments.

4. **Intuitional and Empirical Theories of the Origin of Moral Sentiments.**—The existence of moral sentiments similar in character among civilized peoples, and hence

[3] MILL: *Utilitarianism*, Chap. III.
[4] THILLY: *Introductory Ethics*, Chap. III, pp. 77-79.
[5] For a good description of the various sentiments, intellectual, moral, and religious, in their relation to other mental processes, *cf.* TITCHENER: *Primer of Psychology*, Chap. XII.

familiar to us all, has now to be explained. Two conflicting theories as to their origin have arisen in the course of ethical reflection. The Intuitional theory regards these sentiments as fundamental intuitions of mind. They are, the Intuitionist maintains, a part of our innate mental endowment—a property essential to the mind itself. Some Intuitionists have emphasized the intellectual factor in moral sentiment, declaring that we have an inborn ability to distinguish good from bad, whose deliverances bear the mark of self-evident truth. Other Intuitionists have considered the emotional element as more important, and have held that man possessed an innate " moral sense," a faculty which reacts with feelings of liking and approval to certain forms of conduct, and with feelings of dislike and disapproval to others. The Empirical theory, on the other hand, explains existing moral sentiments as wholly the product of experience. This experience is both racial and individual. The results of the experience of the race in discovering that certain kinds of action are advantageous are inherited by the individual in the form of a sentiment approving of this type of action. The experience of the individual himself—the circumstances of his life, the influences to which he has been subjected—is also a cause for the moral sentiments which he possesses, according to the Empirical view.

Of these two positions the Intuitional is the more difficult to maintain. The Intuitionist proposes an explanation of the origin of the moral sentiments which is clearly inapplicable to other sentiments of a similar character. For of course it is not his *moral* judgments alone that the ordinary man feels to be necessary, without adequate reasons. The case is exactly the same with the most of his judgments on social, political, and religious matters. No one would think of asserting, however, that sentiments on these subjects, no matter how widespread among the inhabitants of a country, were fundamental intuitions of the human mind. On the contrary, it is a commonplace observation that most men derive their political opinions, their religious belief, and their social outlook, from their parentage and early training. The Intuitionist proposes now to make an exception of the moral sentiments, and because these possess a strength and authority which cannot be justified on rational grounds, to assign to them a unique origin, as innate properties of the mind itself. It is consistent with this general standpoint to conceive of the moral sentiments as " divinely implanted " in human nature, after the same manner of thinking that regards conscience as the voice of God in the human soul. In fact, the theory that the moral sentiments are intuitions innate in the mind of man is closely affiliated with the ' special faculty ' view of conscience, both leaning toward a supernatural explanation of morality.

Moreover, the Intuitional theory has an important implication which we cannot at present accept. If the moral sentiments are an essential part of the mental endowment of man we should expect to find them present in the minds of men of all races and times. Or even if we admit that the higher sentiments are at first present potentially, and only come to clear consciousness in the course of human history and development, it is nevertheless a necessary implication of the Intuitional view that the existing sentiments of mankind as they concern such fundamental forms of conduct as murder and stealing and lying must agree. Intuitionists soon recognized this implication and felt the crucial importance of the point which it raised. Hence the defense of Intuitionism has consisted largely of an attempt on the part of its advocates to prove that there is an agreement in the moral sentiments of mankind. Champions of the opposing school summoned all the facts at their command to show that not unanimity but radical disagreement has prevailed among different peoples in matters of morality. Thus the controversy continued. Now it is not difficult to prove that there is a substantial agreement in moral sentiment among men, if we confine ourselves to civilized or comparatively civilized peoples of our own time. As long, then, as continents containing savage or barbarous races remained unexplored and there was little or no knowledge of the early history of human society, the Intuitionist was able to uphold his side of the controversy with a fair degree of success. But since the world has been thoroughly explored and its various peoples studied, and in particular since the discovery of evolution has given such an impetus to all ethnological and anthropological investigation, a mass of facts relative to human morality has been collected which makes the Intuitional view utterly untenable. Such studies of the evolution of human morality as those recently made by Westermarck [6] and Hobhouse [7] show a disagreement in moral belief and practice among different peoples and periods which cannot be reconciled with the theory of moral intuitions. If there is a duty that is fundamental it would seem to be that of respecting the life of fellow-man. Yet we find that in early stages of human society no rights at all attach to the human being as such.[8] The stranger may be killed or tortured at pleasure, and the life of fellow-clansman is respected not because he is recognized as possessing any rights as a human individual, but because his interest is identified with that of the agent. A moral sentiment which is widespread and might seem to be universal is that disapproving of stealing; yet among some peoples theft is not regarded as dishonorable, and among others is even admired as a clever trick.[9] The disapproval of lying is sufficiently general to

---

[6] WESTERMARCK: *Origin and Development of Moral Ideas.*
[7] HOBHOUSE: *Morals in Evolution.*
[8] HOBHOUSE: *Op. cit.,* Vol. I, p. 240.
[9] HOBHOUSE: *Op. cit.,* Vol. I, p. 334.

suggest that it is based upon an intuition inherent in the human mind; yet in certain tribes, authorities inform us, a successful lie is a matter of popular admiration.[10] In fact, we find diversity almost without limit in the moral sentiments of mankind. To be sure, the same investigations which have revealed such widespread divergence in the opinions and customs of men in matters of morality, have also shown the presence in human conduct of a tendency to *develop*—of an evolution in morals, in fact, which has a definite goal and is governed by universal principles.[11] But such tendency toward a consistent and regular development indicates that human morality is the expression of a single unitary power or capacity rather than that it rests upon a set of ready-made intuitions.

5. **Experience as the Source of Moral Sentiments.**— We are forced by these facts to believe that the moral sentiments of the vast majority of men have their origin in experience, as the Empiricist has maintained. They are in a true sense the product of conditions of life, of influences of environment, as these have acted upon the individual and the race. Of course the presence in man of an ability to adapt himself to the conditions of social existence, and that with constantly increasing intelligence, must be presupposed. But the special beliefs and customs called forth by the requirements of social life under human conditions find their explanation in the particular circumstances that evoked them rather than in this general capacity of voluntary intelligence. The fact that the moral

---

[10] WESTERMARCK: *Op. cit.*, Vol. II, p. 72.

[11] Hobhouse believes that "Thus, amid all the variety of social institutions and the ebb and flow of historical change, it is possible in the end to detect a double movement marking the transition from the lower to the higher levels of civilized law and custom." This ' double movement ' is that in which humanity both in the sense of the whole human race and of the human nature in each one of us is progressively realized.—HOBHOUSE: *Op. cit.*, Vol. I, Summary, pp. 367-68.

sentiments which exist at any time are the result of the experience of the race, or of a considerable fraction of it, acquired during ages previous, is of great importance in explaining the agreement of moral sentiment among different members of human society and also the authority which these sentiments possess over the individual. Indeed, Spencer thinks that when we see our moral judgments, as the result of the experience of remote ancestors transmitted to their progeny by physical heredity, and thus become part of our native endowment, we both recognize the large amount of truth contained in the view of Intuitionism that the moral sentiments are innate properties of mind, and at the same time reconcile this view with that of Empiricism.[12] Spencer himself finds no difficulty in believing that opinions and practices acquired by the human individual during his life-time may be inherited by his descendants and finally become ingrained in the stock or race as fixed instincts. But since his time biologists have found good reason for disbelieving that such acquisitions are ever transmitted through the channels of natural inheritance. Hence we cannot depend upon physical heredity to explain the perpetuation of moral sentiments, nor is it legitimate to consider them as instincts formerly acquired but now inborn.

It is quite possible to account for the development and conservation of the moral experience of the race through the operation of another factor, however—" social heredity." By social heredity is meant the transmission through the instrumentality of language, imitation, and suggestion,

---

[12] " For as the doctrine of innate forms of intellectual intuition falls into harmony with the experiential doctrine when we recognize the production of intellectual faculties by inheritance of effects wrought by experience; so the doctrine of innate powers of moral perception becomes congruous with the utilitarian doctrine when it is seen that preferences and aversions are rendered organic by inheritance of the effects of pleasurable and painful experiences in progenitors."—SPENCER: *Data of Ethics*, § 45.

of the accumulated experience of the race to each successive generation of individuals. Through this channel, by means of instruction and training, the moral tradition of a society is communicated to its youthful members. This explanation makes it evident that the individual's own experience is the source of his social and religious sentiments—the home and the school existing as special agencies for influencing him during his earliest and most susceptible years, and producing in him those beliefs and convictions, those habits and dispositions, which are approved by the society of which he is a member.

We are hence reduced to the individual's own experience —the circumstances of his early life, his home training, his education at school, his associates and friends, and the other numberless influences, social and economic, that have acted upon him during his formative period—as the main source of his moral sentiments. This explanation may seem utterly inadequate when we think of the absolute authority claimed by the deliverances of conscience, of the peculiar dignity and even sanctity they possess, of the sense of reverence they awaken. Yet if we consider for a moment the character of this experience,—how well it is adapted to produce just such results,—it will not seem so insufficient as a source of authoritative moral sentiment. The child has the current moral distinctions brought home to him at a very early age. Every device is used to impress his sensitive feelings and imagination.[13] Parents and nurse agree in regarding certain acts with frowns and looks of horror, while others are greeted with smiles and expressions of pleasure. Punishments begin to follow actions of the former class—with threats of penalties still more dire for one who persists in striking or lying or stealing. The growing love of the child is appealed to, he being told that parents can continue to love and cherish only children

[13] THILLY: *Op. cit.*, Chap. III, § 8, "Genesis of Conscience."

who are obedient, truthful, etc. Then the religious factor
is often introduced, and God is alluded to as a Mysterious
Being who is particularly interested in these matters of
right and wrong, and Who, having an eye which is all-
seeing, and a power which knows no limit, will finally
inflict dreadful penalties upon those who continue to do
wrong, and bestow corresponding rewards upon the good
and obedient. The terrors of the law are frequently in-
voked, and the prison referred to as the place where the
dishonest, the untruthful, the violent, are confined. In
the school the boy or girl encounters another authority
able to enforce the same set of distinctions by sanctions
of its own. Finally he meets the all-powerful influence
of public opinion which visits social opprobrium and ostra-
cism upon the head of the individual who dares to disregard conventional standards or transgress approved customs. Small wonder, then, that the moral sentiments traditional in a society acquire an almost hypnotic power over
its members—such principles as " Stealing is wrong,"
" Lying is wrong," having acquired through early associations, vague memories, and a bias given in childhood to the
whole nature, a greater power over the attention than
objects which awaken the strongest natural desires.

6. **The Idea of the Highest Good as the Rational
Ground of Moral Judgment.**—Are we to conclude, because
the moral sentiments of most human beings have their
source in experience and not in reflective reason, that,
therefore, the moral judgment *can* have no rational ground?
By no means. The moral judgment can have as secure a
basis in reason as any other judgment and may lay claim
to the same objective validity. For the moral judgment
is essentially a judgment of *value*—a particular kind of
value called moral. Now this value is possessed by all
objects capable of fulfilling the demands of volition. But
the *summum bonum* is by definition that end which is able

to satisfy completely the capacity of human volition. Hence when the Highest Good is discovered it will furnish the rational ground of moral judgment; since whatever action can be shown to be a means to its attainment will be proved to have positive moral value or goodness, while every action which hinders its attainment will in a like manner be proved bad. To be sure, the connection between a particular act and the attainment of the Good is not always apparent. At this point, then, deliberation must enter; the consequences of the proposed action must be followed out in imagination until its bearing upon the attainment of the Good is ascertained. Thus a number of considerations are introduced which serve to connect the moral judgment finally rendered with its ultimate ground. Reverting to our previous illustration and assuming for the sake of argument that Social Welfare is the Good, moral reflection might take the following course: " This act is stealing; stealing violates the rights of private ownership; the institution of private property is necessary to social welfare; this act is thus opposed to social welfare, and therefore wrong." In this way the reasons for any moral judgment are exhibited in full and, granting that the *summum bonum* is correctly understood, the argument is valid and the conclusion true for all persons.

Inasmuch as the *summum bonum* constitutes the ultimate ground of moral judgment it may be said to furnish conscience with a standard or criterion of moral value. It stands for perfect goodness in human conduct, and by reference to it, consequently, the pretensions of any act to be good can be tested. We secure in this way no magic oracle of right or wrong, however; for after the Good is discovered its use as a standard of moral value will be beset by many difficulties. Its relation to a particular action may be very hard to make out, the situation calling for most painstaking analysis and careful study. Suppose that the act under consideration is that of telling a friend of certain faults he possesses. In the present circumstances, will it be right or wrong, my duty or not? Let us say further that the Highest Good is, in our opinion, the Well-Being of Humanity. This, then, must constitute our standard of moral value. Is it easily applied? Is it a simple matter to ascertain the bearing of telling my friend a disagreeable truth—upon human welfare? Obviously not, yet it is a task which reason must undertake and discharge to the best of its powers. The possibility of wounding my friend's feelings, destroying our friendship, and thus perhaps lessening the social efficiency of us both, must be considered. But, on the other hand, it must not be forgotten that a word from me may lead him to overcome his fault, with great increase of his own happiness and his serviceability to his fellow-men. Then the effect of candor in social relations generally might be considered, and account taken of the help which an individual derives from the frank and kindly criticism of his fellows. To be sure, the same opportunity for slips and errors exists here as in all other reasoning, and the individual who thinks out moral problems for himself is liable to frequent mistake. At least, however, he is determining his conduct in a manner befitting the dignity of an intelligent being— freely, and in accordance with conclusions of his own reason.

7. **Moral Enlightenment.**—Thus to substitute rational insight as the basis of moral judgment, for feelings produced by experience and training, is to enlighten conscience and rationalize morality. It is, as we know, just the aim of Ethics to evaluate conduct rationally, i.e. in accordance with the demands of the Moral Ideal. The necessity for constant exertion to secure means of subsistence has left the vast majority of mankind—up to the present—neither the time nor the strength for ethical

reflection. Doubtless, for a long period in the future as well, most men will be compelled to receive their moral sentiments ready made through various influences of custom and tradition. Yet an increasing number are gaining the education and leisure requisite for systematic reflection upon the problems of conduct. With such, the conventional moral sentiments inculcated in childhood are sure to lose their authority. The individual will challenge the right of the accepted moral code to rule over him and summon it to appear for examination before the bar of his own reason. Then indeed is the crisis, when the traditional moral sentiments must justify themselves to reason or suffer entire repudiation in favor of some plan of life original with the individual. It is at this juncture that Ethics may be especially useful in guiding the thought of the individual when he endeavors for himself to evaluate different forms of conduct and alternative ends, and, the larger grow the numbers of individuals undertaking to think for themselves upon matters of morality, the more general will be the need of ethical instruction.

Fortunately, however, moral enlightenment does not necessarily, or even frequently, entail the wholesale abandonment of conventional beliefs and practices. Nor should we expect that it would, when we remember that conventional morality expresses, in general at least, what the experience of mankind has found to contribute most to the welfare of human society. Moral enlightenment does not mean, therefore, that all moral judgments previously accepted should at present be abandoned, but rather that they should now gain a new and higher authority—the authority of reason in place of that of custom and tradition. The duties of current morality are seen to derive their authority from their relation as means to some end of attested value, and not to be ends in themselves, both arbitrary and

absolute. Thus in the case of telling my friend a disagreeable truth about himself, conventional morality would
exact a rigid and mechanical obedience to the rule, *Tell
the truth,* with the result that the friend might become
estranged from me, while his fault remained uncorrected.
Rational morality, on the other hand, is more flexible and
can be adapted to the requirements of differing cases; it
would permit me to study the case of my friend and
would pronounce good that action which I concluded would
be for his best welfare and the promotion of the highest
human good. But while moral enlightenment thus requires us to establish our morality upon a new foundation,
it by no means renders valueless the early training in
approved moral practices or the acquisition of the conventional moral sentiments. For, after these beliefs and
practices have secured a new basis in reason, it is still of
incalculable benefit to have them already ingrained in the
nervous system in the form of fixed habits. It is this
tremendous boon that moral training confers upon the
individual, and that makes this training worth all the
efforts which parents and teachers can put into it. What
if moral enlightenment does lead the individual to re-
nounce one practice out of ten learned in early childhood?
Surely less effort is required to break this one habit than
to form the other nine entirely new.

8. **Importance of Conscience in Human Life.**—Since
Conscience represents man's Highest Good, either as discovered by him through reflection or expressed for him
in the customs of his race, it is not strange that it should
have been given an exalted position among human faculties.
Conscience is only a particular manifestation of the power
of human intelligence, to be sure; [14] but it is human in-

---

[14] In his *System of Ethics*, Eng. trans., pp. 363-68, Paulsen
protests eloquently and effectively against the idea that the adoption of the historico-psychological in place of the supernatural
theory of conscience will destroy its authority and sanctity.

telligence in the most important of its many fields of exercise, when it deals, not with this interest or that, but with the satisfaction of the whole of man's will, latent as well as actual—the fulfilment of all his possibilities as a voluntary agent. As Professor Royce says: "Your conscience is simply that ideal of life which constitutes your moral personality. In having your conscience you become aware of your plan of being yourself and nobody else. Your conscience presents to you this plan, however, in so far as the plan or ideal in question is distinct from the life in which you are trying to embody your plan. Your life, as it is lived, your experiences, feelings, deeds,— these are the embodiments of your ideal plan, in so far as your ideal plan for your own individual life as this self, gets embodied at all." [15] If conscience is not the voice of God in the mind of man it at least speaks for those powers in human nature which raise him above the animals and link him to what is highest in reality—his comprehensive intelligence, his free will.

The insight which we have gained into the function of conscience in human life compels us now to qualify somewhat the statement formerly made that in most human beings conscience is determined in its decisions by custom and training and not by any real understanding of the Good. While it is true that the moral sentiments which direct the conduct of the majority must be referred to these sources rather than to their own intelligent understanding of the issues involved, it is also true that the operation of these sentiments is accompanied by a consciousness, more or less vague, that they stand for the larger good of the self. Even when the particular moral judgments of an individual are wholly determined by custom, the compulsion which he feels to bring his acts under general rubrics for purposes of moral evalution is itself a dim

[15] ROYCE: *Philosophy of Loyalty*, p. 175.

recognition of the existence of a Good authoritative over all actions because representing the satisfaction of man's larger will. Then there are the suggestions of the Ideal, confused but never forgotten, and hopes inarticulate but ever-stirring, which, even in the least intelligent and aspiring of men, connect themselves with the duties of conventional morality and cause them to appear as means to a higher personal good.

9. **Remorse.**—After performing the action which conscience pronounces right, particularly if it be in the face of strong opposing inclination, a sense of profound satisfaction is felt. For the wrong desire, expressing a merely temporary need, has in retrospect lost its appeal, while the relatively permanent good secured by conscience continues to give satisfaction. Contrariwise, when conscience is thwarted for the sake of present desire, a feeling of great dissatisfaction may arise. For the Good, as represented by Conscience, is enduring in its appeal, and thus while momentary desire once gratified is destroyed, this appeal of Goodness, disregarded and unrealized, continues, and awakens in the consciousness of the wrongdoer an overwhelming sense of guilt and misery. This feeling of sorrow and distress, which frequently follows the doing of evil, is called *remorse*. Darwin, who finds the beginning of conscience in the phenomena of remorse, explains the origin of this latter experience in biological terms.

" At the moment of action man will no doubt be apt to follow the stronger impulse; and though this may occasionally prompt him to the noblest deeds, it will more commonly lead him to gratify his own desires at the expense of other men. But after their gratification, when past and weaker impressions are judged by the ever-enduring social instinct, and by his deep regard for the good opinion of his fellows, retribution will surely come. He will then feel remorse, repentance, regret, or shame; this latter feeling, however, relates almost exclusively to the judgment of others. He will consequently resolve more or less firmly to act differently for the future; and this is conscience; for conscience looks backward and serves as a guide for the future." [16]

While the conception of instinct as here used by Darwin to explain the beginnings of morality is clearly inadequate, yet as far as the relation of the factors involved is concerned, his explanation of remorse is fundamentally true. Conscience has charge of man's larger social and personal good, and one who violates its dictates in order to gratify momentary desire or to further selfish interest, betrays himself, is a traitor to the larger possibilities of his own nature as a man. He sells his birthright as a rational being for the pottage of present pleasure. Because wrongdoing is thus a betrayal of the whole human self, an evil deed, in itself appearing trivial, may awaken in the agent a sense of degradation that seems to affect his whole nature. Literature gives us many examples, imaginary but not exaggerated, of such soul-rending remorse with its agony over lost opportunities for good and its torment by evil that cannot be undone—suffering so great that the unfortunate individual is driven to sacrifice his life in an attempt at expiation or to destroy himself in the depth of his despair.

## REFERENCES

THILLY, *Introduction to Ethics*, Chaps. III, IV.
ALEXANDER, *Moral Order and Progress*, Book II, Part I, Chap. III.
ROYCE, *Philosophy of Loyalty*, Chap. IV.
MARTINEAU, *Types of Ethical Theory*, Part II, Book I, Chap. I.
LESLIE STEPHEN, *Science of Ethics*, Chap. VIII.
MACKENZIE, *Manual of Ethics*, Book II, Chaps. V, VI.

[16] DARWIN: *Descent of Man*, Chap. IV.

# CHAPTER V

## THE APPEAL OF THE GOOD OR MORAL OBLIGATION

1. **Objects Appeal to the Will Through the Feelings They Arouse.**—Knowledge that an end is good does not insure its choice and pursuit. We may know that an action is right and still not perform it. To be realized as an end of action an object must make a certain appeal to the self. It must engage and hold the attention—i.e. be attractive, possess interest. Now the interest or attractiveness of an object is measured by the feelings which it arouses. These feelings color or tone the object when thought of, and, as they endue it with life and influence, are sometimes called its dynamic or motive-power. The character of these feelings seems to vary considerably. When very hungry, the idea of food which attracts me, as an end to be sought, is altogether pleasant. The feeling aroused is one of simple, although very intense, pleasure, and I should describe my feeling as one of strong liking or desire for food. The idea of having a tooth filled, which as an end prompts me to go to the dentist's, is not thus simply pleasant. Of course the idea of having the tooth repaired and thus saved from further decay pleases me,

else it would have no power over my attention, no attractive influence. Yet there are closely associated with it other ideas of the discomfort and pain of the filling process, which are very unpleasant. These fears and apprehensions will divert me from my original intention unless by continuous effort I hold my attention on the course decided upon. Such effort involves strain, which is unpleasant. Hence the feeling aroused by the end in question is one of mingled pleasantness and unpleasantness, which I describe as a feeling of compulsion, saying that I do not like to go to the dentist's, but *feel that I must*. Again when an audience at the close of an address is led to rise and join in singing the national anthem it is impelled to the deed by still another emotional complex of which the feelings of " enthusiasm " and " reverence " are perhaps the chief components. Since such variation exists in the feelings which propel us to action it is next in order to ask what constitutes the interest or appeal of good conduct.

2. **Appeal of the Good as Inclination.**—First let us take a simple case. A man who is thinking of how he shall occupy several hours of leisure happens to remember a friend who is ill and whom he has not seen for several days. " It is only decent that I should go to see him and cheer him up a bit on this holiday," he says to himself. No reason why he should not go occurs to his mind, nor does any contrary impulse arise. He thereupon takes hat and coat and sets out for the friend's house with a thoroughgoing sense of spontaneity, of " doing just what he likes." Evidently, then, conduct which conscience pronounces good sometimes arouses simple feelings of pleasure and its appeal is the appeal of inclination.

Besides action of this kind which proceeds from a moral judgment, although of an abbreviated type, are others which result from unreflecting impulse and seem to involve no activity of conscience whatever. I might act thus in purchasing a paper or magazine, the illustrated cover of which catches my eye when passing a shop window. Many of these acts of thoughtless inclination must be considered as in their own slight way good. Often a moral judgment is implied in a recognition, dim but present in the margin of consciousness, that the conduct in question does not fall within any of the prohibited classes of actions. The agent if challenged would immediately state this fact and then perhaps go on to show how the action contributed to some approved end. Again, an inclination is followed without thought because it has been so often followed in the past—its immunity from criticism or disapproval during that time constituting a kind of moral validation. Habit of course enters as an important factor here. It causes actions, at first performed only after careful thought and long deliberation, to be done with the promptness and simplicity of mere impulse. It even makes conduct, which at first was exceedingly difficult and opposed by urgent desire, as easy and effective as the expression of natural inclination.

3. **Appeal of the Good as Obligation.**—But such a case as the first mentioned, where conscience and inclination are in perfect agreement, impresses one as the exception rather than the rule. More frequently the appeal of goodness is opposed as *obligation* to *inclination,* as what one *ought,* in contrast to what one *inclines,* to do. To keep our thought in close touch with the facts of moral experience, let us take another commonplace illustration. Suppose that a young man employed as a clerk is left for several weeks in charge of his employer's business while the latter is away from home. He promises his employer that he will be faithful in his attendance at the office during the stated hours. But on a warm summer's afternoon, when there is no prospect of a client's appearing, he is urged by friends

to accompany them to see a ball game or boat race. Being very fond of sport he is exceedingly anxious to go, but is restrained by the thought that such action, in violating a promise made to his employer, would be wrong. There is no doubt in this instance, which certainly exemplifies a large class, that inclination and conscience are in sharp conflict. He inclines " with all his heart " to join in the afternoon's sport, yet is deterred by a feeling still stronger than his inclination which enforces the conduct judged right by conscience. This is the feeling of obligation or " oughtness," which stands contrasted to that of inclination as a feeling of constraint, of coercion. The individual who feels moral obligation feels constrained to certain acts by a power or authority external to himself. The Good in this guise of authority over the inclinations of the individual is known as the Moral Law, a rule imposed upon the actions of all individuals. But while obligation differs thus widely from inclination on the one hand, it differs as widely from real compulsion on the other. For since the individual is always conscious of freedom to choose or not to choose the right, he recognizes that in another sense this is not an external authority, but one created by himself. He describes his experience after this manner, " I wanted to do thus, but *my* duty required me, *my* conscience compelled me, to do otherwise."

As far as its essential characteristics are concerned, the feeling of moral obligation is the same whether the conduct to which it attaches is judged good on rational or on emotional grounds. In conventional morality this feeling is aroused by those forms of conduct which the individual has learned through his training and experience to approve, —to the familiar " duties of life " in fact. The tendency to feel the deliverances of conscience as the exactions of a foreign power is increased by their association in customary morality with the commands of authority—divine, civil, parental. The moral law is thought to have its source in the highest of all authorities, the will of God. Yet even here, a consciousness of freedom to obey or disobey, leads men to distinguish the requirements made by conscience from the actual compulsion exercised by the forces of nature or the civil authorities. In rational morality the feeling of obligation attaches primarily to the idea of the Good itself, and secondarily to the actions believed to be means to its attainment. It would perhaps appear that Goodness must lose somewhat in authority through the enlightenment of conscience—being dissociated from thoughts of the Divine Omnipotence, and the Day of Judgment with its rewards and penalties, and associated only with the satisfaction of the human will. But while unenlightened morality may, through its appeal to the instinct of self-preservation, arouse the intenser emotions of fear and dread, rational morality, through its appeal to higher interests and capacities, awakens feelings of inspiration and enthusiasm more permanent and reliable as the motive-power of conduct. On this point Mackenzie says, with true ethical insight: "The more we advance in the development of the moral life, the less possible does it become to point to any single rule that seems to carry its own authority with it, to any law that stands above us and says categorically, You must do this. What we find is, more and more, only the general principle that says, You ought to do what you find to be best. And what is best may vary very much in its external form, and even in its inner nature, with changing conditions. But this does not in any way destroy the absoluteness of the moral standard. It remains as true as ever that we are bound to choose the right 'in the scorn of consequence,' though it may be more difficult for us to say at any given point what precisely is right. The authority, indeed, must come home to us with a far more absolute power, when we recognize that it is our own law, than when we regard it as an alien force." [1]

## 4. Conditions Under Which the Feeling of Moral Obligation Arises.

—It is not difficult to explain why so remarkable a feeling as that of moral obligation, which is at once a feeling of coercion by an external authority and of attraction by a desired end, should arise in such cases as we are now discussing. As far as present action is concerned, the agent is faced by two alternatives, one pleasant and attractive, the other unpleasant and hence unattractive. The youth in our illustration is confronted by the alternative possibilities of an afternoon of sport and pleasure in the open-air or one of monotony and discomfort in a hot and dusty office. Now had the two possible courses of action no further connections or consequences in the conduct of the individual, he must perforce choose that which in itself is pleasanter and more desirable. Our clerk would not hesitate a moment to abandon the routine of his employer's office for the freedom of the water and the field. Yet he does hesitate, and finally resolves to remain at his post. It is a fact of moral experience familiar to us all that we *do* often select the unpleasant alternative, the hard and unattractive course— that we *do* select what we do *not* like or desire. Now this undoubted fact that we choose the less pleasant course shows—paradoxical as it may sound—that it is not the less but the more pleasant after all. Since it does not possess interest and attraction in its own right, it must derive them from other sources. This is precisely what it does. While the idea of being shut up within the four walls of an office during a bright summer's afternoon is not attractive, that of fulfilling the pledge to the employer, or of rising in business or profession is so, and these future ends, these more remote interests, transmit some of their

---

[1] Mackenzie: *Manual of Ethics*, Bk. II, Chap. VI, § 8.

attractiveness to the action which is seen to be the present means to their attainment, more than counter-balancing its own unpleasantness. Thus constantly does the pleasure which attaches to the thought of performing the recognized duties of conventional morality, or attaining the Good discovered by moral reflection, communicate itself to actions in themselves unpleasant and make possible their performance " contrary to inclination." But in such cases the agent identifies himself with the object of present desire and treats these larger ideal considerations enforced by conscience as external influences, the exactions, in fact, of a foreign authority which he must obey. When, therefore, Goodness requires the pursuit of some larger end extending to the future or including the welfare of others, and this contrary to present inclination or selfish interest, its appeal is that of obligation.

Our view must encompass still another case in which moral obligation is felt before we can hope to reach any generalization concerning its essential significance which will apply universally. Again let us avail ourselves of the help of an illustration. A man is giving his afternoons to the systematic study of a certain subject with the intention of writing a book about it eventually. He hears of a series of concerts to be given two afternoons a week in his town. He has no particular liking for music and is disinclined to spare two afternoons a week from his study. Yet he feels that he ought to cultivate his taste for music and to develop a liking for it if possible. Hence, led by a sense of duty, and with a consciousness of contrary desire, he purchases a ticket and attends the concerts. Now in this case—and there are many resembling it—both of the conflicting ends are in the future; if there is any difference the end of inclination (writing the book) is more remote than the end of obligation (cultivating the musical taste). How does it happen, then, that the latter appeals as the command of an external power, the former as the fulfilment of the agent's own nature? The answer to this question reveals the fact that in last analysis the difference between obligation and inclination hinges, not upon the distinction of future from present, or of social from selfish, ends, but in a difference in the relation of the end to the human will itself. In the example used, the one end— of writing the book—although its attainment might be postponed to the far future, was already adopted, had been for a time pursued, and was thus in a measure identified with the will of the individual. The other end, on the contrary, was entirely new and untried. It represented new territory to him, a field unexplored. Hence its appeal, in contrast to that of the end already tried and so far found satisfactory, is that of an external authority which commands the agent "against his will." And so in a sense it does; for his will, finding satisfaction in the pursuit of an object already chosen, is disinclined at first to relinquish it in order to seek another object whose nature is not well known and whose capacity to yield satisfaction is untried.

5. **Significance of the Feeling of Moral Obligation.**— The feeling of obligation proves, therefore, to be a necessary accompaniment of all activity of volition. The human will, in order to gain the satisfaction it seeks, must go forward from achievement to achievement. It cannot afford to remain content with any end already attained, but must ever press on to the attainment of larger and more adequate ends, until its own possibilities for achievement and satisfaction are exhausted. When the pursuit of such new and untried ends requires the sacrifice of objects able to yield present satisfaction, the feeling of obligation arises. In its essence this feeling is unique, unanalyzable, irreducible —an original and necessary factor in the process of volition. It is the call which the human will makes upon itself

to venture into new and unknown fields, at the expense of satisfactions already achieved. It is the imperious command which intelligent volition lays upon its own nature to seek a larger and more comprehensive good. And like the appeal of the trackless ocean to the adventurous explorer, this feeling contains something of fascination in the alluring prospects of achievement held forth, something of fear in the hardships and perils suggested, and something of pain in the thought of the comfortable home left behind.

6. **Kant's View of Moral Obligation.**—Among moralists Immanuel Kant has given the most illuminating interpretation of the facts of moral obligation. We are now in a position to understand his famous theory—both to appreciate the profundity of his thought and to detect some of the errors which it contains.

In Kant's view the Good always presents itself in the form of Duty. Duty is the obligation to act *from reverence to law*.[2] That is, good action is action whose end is obedience to the Moral Law. But the Moral Law as an end appeals to the human will through the feeling of reverence which it awakens. In good conduct, therefore, the will is determined objectively by the Moral Law itself and subjectively by pure reverence for the law as a principle of action. Now since conduct is good only when prompted by pure reverence for the Moral Law it follows that action done from natural inclination can have no moral value. This Kant explicitly maintains. Even in the case of an action which is *in accordance with* duty—such as for instance safeguarding one's life—if it is not done *for the sake of* duty, but from natural inclination, it has no moral worth whatever. Duty is a principle which is not dependent upon natural inclination, but overmasters it, or

[2] The abstract of Kant's thought given in this paragraph is based upon the *Metaphysic of Morality*, Sec. 1. Translation by Watson.

at least allows it to have no influence whatever in determining the course of action.

The sense of obligation thus signifies the constraint exercised by the Moral Law over the human will in opposition to, or regardless of, inclination.[3] This constraint appears to thought as a command, a command which, when expressed in words, takes the form of an *imperative*.[4] Hence it follows that the duties of morality come to us as imperatives. " Now all imperatives command either *hypothetically* or *categorically*. A hypothetical imperative states that a thing must be done if something else which is willed or at least might be willed, is to be attained. The categorical imperative declares that an act is in itself or objectively necessary, without any reference to another end."[5] All men by a natural necessity seek happiness. Certain actions are generally recognized by human intelligence to be productive of happiness. To these actions, then, when chosen as a means to happiness, a hypothetical imperative attaches. They are valued for the sake of the happiness they are expected to bring. But " there is an imperative which directly commands an action, without presupposing as its condition that some other end is to be attained by means of that action. It has to do, not with the matter of an action and the result expected to follow from it, but simply with the form and principle from which the action itself proceeds. The action is essentially good if the motive of the agent is good, let the consequences be what they may. This imperative may be called the imperative of *morality*."[6] Here we have before us Kant's celebrated doctrine of duty as the Categorical

---

[3] *Critique of Practical Reason*, Bk. I, Chap. III (Abbott's trans., p. 165).
[4] This account of Kant's doctrine of the Categorical Imperative is drawn from the *Metaphysic of Morality*, Sec. 2.
[5] *Ibid.*
[6] *Ibid.*

Imperative. This imperative, which bids us obey without any regard for consequences, attaches to the Moral Law. Every duty as a categorical imperative is an end sufficient in itself and never a means to anything else.

## 7. Goodness Not Always Different from Inclination.—

Kant is certainly in error in believing that acts done from inclination never possess moral value. It is indeed little less than absurd to hold that the conduct of a person who, gladly and from a sympathetic inclination, helps another in distress, possesses no moral value, while the conduct of one who renders the same assistance reluctantly and from a hard sense of duty deserves to be called good. To be sure there are acts done from thoughtless impulse which, although productive of good, possess a minimum of moral value, as when a man from kindly impulse tosses a coin to a beggar who importunes him, without a thought as to whether the recipient is deserving or undeserving, or whether the money will go for food or intoxicant. But, on the other hand, there are actions which, once performed with a feeling of obligation and contrary to inclination, have through long habit become a " second nature," and are now done gladly and from desire, as in the case of a public-spirited citizen who in earlier years becomes so used to subordinating private interest to public concern that in later life he turns from the pursuit of his own ambition to the service of his country gladly, and with no sense of hardship. Such conduct, while it involves no conflict with desire and hence is accompanied by no feeling of obligation, is superior in moral value to that which is prompted by the constraint of duty, because it represents a higher level of attainment. The saint, from the standpoint of morality, is the person who having, through long years of painful self-denial and heroic struggle, subdued the flesh and overcome the world, finds the pursuit of goodness his only desire.

Nevertheless, the facts of the moral life justify in a large measure the view of Kant. Obligation, not inclination, is the characteristic form in which the Good appeals to the human will. Moral obligation is temporary in the sense just explained that the regular performance of duty creates a new disposition which in time makes the practice easy and natural. But when this new interest is thus incorporated in the character of the agent, still further ends arise which forbid him to remain satisfied with what he has already achieved. Hence again the constraint of duty and the suppression of inclination. As long as possibilities of attainment open before man's will which require the sacrifice of present satisfaction, the pressure of obligation will be felt by the human individual. And such possibilities will be exhausted only when the Good itself is attained and the goal of moral development reached.

8. **The Duties of Morality Command Not as Categorical but as Teleological Imperatives.**—It is also a mistake to maintain that duty as we usually understand it has the authority of a categorical imperative. The recognized duties of morality, as important as they are, are not ends in themselves. If they were, why then, to be sure, we should tell the truth '' if the heavens fall '' or (what is more likely) we needlessly wound the feelings of our acquaintances and create continual irritation and discord; we should be honest even if the food and clothing which we will not take, without the owner's permission would restore self and relieve suffering comrades; we should be brave even if in entering the burning building injuries were to be received that cause suffering and expense to self and family far outweighing the value of the articles we were able to save. But in truth these duties possess value only as means to higher ends, to human happiness and well-being—ultimately to the full satisfaction of the human will. They have no authority in their own right, but derive what they

possess from the *summum bonum,* the supreme and only authority in the field of conduct. Only in conventional morality does obedience to these approved modes of action appear as an end in itself; reflection discovers it to be instrumental to the attainment of further ends. The imperative of duty is therefore not a categorical, but a teleological, imperative.

9. **The Summum Bonum Alone Has the Authority of a Categorical Imperative.**—When we turn to the *summum bonum* itself, to the realization of which the duties of conventional morality are but instruments, we find that which in truth is an end in itself and a means to nothing else. The value of the *summum bonum* does not depend upon its ability to lead us to some further end, but resides in its direct appeal to the human will itself—its own compelling attraction. The *summum bonum,* therefore, and that alone, possesses absolute authority over human conduct. And since the *summum bonum* must always be construed in terms of the conduct required to realize it, the absolute authority denied to the several duties in their independence is extended to them so far as they prove necessary to the attainment of the Good. In this way, the whole of the moral life is invested with the dignity and sublimity which aroused such noble enthusiasm in Kant.

"Duty! Thou sublime and mighty name that dost embrace nothing charming or insinuating, but requirest submission, and yet seekest not to move the will by threatening aught that would arouse natural aversion or terror, but merely holdest forth a law which of itself finds entrance into the mind, and yet gains reluctant reverence (though not always obedience), a law before which all inclinations are dumb, even though they secretly counterwork it; what origin is there worthy of thee, and where is to be found the root of thy noble descent which proudly rejects all kindred with the inclinations; a root to be derived from which is the indispensable condition of the only worth which men can give themselves." [7]

The Good is indeed worthy of all the reverence which Kant claimed for it—as an ideal it has drawn men upward with promise of a larger life and a deeper satisfaction, as an authority it has exacted obedience and sacrifice, as possessed in part it has yielded the most perfect happiness which man has experienced.

### REFERENCES

KANT, *Metaphysics of Morality* (Abbott's trans.).
PAULSEN, *System of Ethics*, Book II, Chap. V.
MACKENZIE, *Manual of Ethics*, Book II, Chap. III.
SPENCER, *Data of Ethics*, Chap. VII.
THILLY, *Introduction to Ethics*, Chap. V.
MUIRHEAD, *Elements of Ethics*, Book II, Chap. II.
GREEN, *Prolegomena to Ethics*, Book III, Chap. II.
MILL, *Utilitarianism*, Chap. III.

[7] KANT: *Critique of Practical Reason*, Bk. I, Chap. III (Abbott's trans., p. 180).

# CHAPTER VI

## THE MOTIVE OF GOOD CONDUCT

1. The Appeal of the *Summum Bonum* as the Motive of Good Conduct.—2. Possible Discrepancy Between the Intention and the Consequences of Conduct.—3. Good Intentions When Accompanied by Adequate Knowledge Are Usually Productive of Good Consequences.—4. Good Consequences in Most Cases Indicate Corresponding Degree of Goodness in Intention.—5. But Good Motive Does Not Absolutely Insure Good Consequences Because of Inability of Reason to Foresee Future Developments.

**1. The Appeal of the Summum Bonum as the Motive of Good Conduct.**—Motive, psychologically speaking, is the conscious condition of action. The motive of voluntary action—with which alone Ethics is directly concerned—is the desire of an object as end. We may now go a step further and return answer to the question: What is the motive of good conduct? The motive of good conduct is the idea of the Highest Good in its appeal to the will of an intelligent being. In this motive we have distinguished and considered separately two aspects, an intellectual and an emotional. On the one hand there is the conception of the object to be sought, the inducement of action; on the other are the feelings of interest or obligation aroused by thought of this object, the incentive to act. Both of these factors are necessary as constituents of the motive; only through their coöperation is it able to discharge its office in the determination of conduct. The motive of good conduct is then composed of thought and feeling joined in an effective unity—it is the idea of the Good become dynamic, converted into a living force for the creating of conduct, the constructing of character.

The statement that all good conduct has for its motive the attainment of the *summum bonum* does not imply that every act which is truly good, results from conscious thought of, and has explicit reference to, the *summum bonum*. This need only from time to time be so attentively studied and clearly understood by the agent that he is constantly aware of the general principles which its progressive attainment imposes on his daily conduct, and that its appeal to him shall be so strong that a feeling of compelling obligation is communicated to these principles of conduct. When this is the case and such principles determine human conduct, either operating consciously as motives, or having done so in the past and now governing through habit, the conception of the *summum bonum* is in verity discharging its proper function as the motive of good conduct.

2. **Possible Discrepancy Between Intention and Consequences of Conduct.**—Thus far we have assumed that an action which aims at the Highest Good will, within the limits of its own field, result in its attainment. No account has been taken of a possible discrepancy between intention and performance, motive and consequences. The possibility of such disagreement has impressed many writers on Ethics as so real and important that it has affected their whole conception of goodness. They have felt obliged to choose either intention or consequences, the one to the exclusion of the other, as determining the moral value of an act. Either it is only the intention that counts in morality and the consequences do not matter, or it is the actual consequences which make an act good or bad, without regard for the motive of the agent. Kant is the leading representative of the former extreme. He held that " Nothing in the whole world, or even outside of the world, can possibly be regarded as good without limitation except a *good will*. . . . A man's will is good, not because the consequences which flow from it are good, nor because it is

capable of attaining the end which it seeks, but it is good in itself, or because it wills the good."[1]   J. S. Mill and others of the Utilitarian school take the opposite view, believing that the consequences of an act, in increasing or diminishing the sum total of human happiness, make it right or wrong.[2]  Thus Mill says: " Utilitarian moralists have gone beyond almost all others in affirming that the motive has nothing to do with the morality of an action, though much with the worth of the agent.  He who saves a fellow-creature from drowning does what is morally right, whether his motive be duty or the hope of being paid for his trouble: he who betrays the friend that trusts him is guilty of a crime, even if his object be to serve another friend to whom he is under greater obligations."[3]

Everyday human experience gives ample warrant, one may think, for thus contrasting the intention with the consequences of action.  It is proverbial that good intentions often go with poor performance.  Persons who mean well, but do ill are easily found in every community.  We are all acquainted with men and women who, although working with best intention for others' welfare, nevertheless do harm and mischief among them through ignorance of their needs, their abilities, and the conditions under which they live.  Such well-intentioned altruists are frequently condemned as meddlesome busy-bodies.  Conversely human life and history can show us many cases of good consequences issuing from intentions either bad or indifferent.  Excellent laws—laws that do much to advance human welfare—are sometimes enacted through the influence of political leaders who seek only party success

---

[1] KANT: *Metaphysic of Morality*, Sec. 1.
[2] MILL: *Utilitarianism*, Chap. II.
[3] The distinction made by Mill and other Utilitarians between intention and motive is ignored here as tending to produce needless perplexity in the mind of the student.  Intention is here contrasted, according to popular usage, with actual results,—consequences.

and personal preferment.  Many a war undertaken from love of conquest and plunder has in its outcome increased human liberty and happiness.

3. **Good Intentions When Accompanied by Adequate Knowledge Are Usually Productive of Good Consequences.**—Does the logic of our view compel us to hold that any act whose motive is the attainment of the Highest Good is itself good, no matter what its consequences may be?  Before giving a final answer to this question let us consider whether the possibility of a real discrepancy between the intention and the outcome of action is as great as it has been made out to be—whether it is possible for the inner and outer aspects of conduct to enter into such sharp conflict.[4]  In the first place, good intentions which result in evil do so usually because the agent is ignorant of the conditions in which he acts, of the true character of the situation.  The ultimate end conceived, the final object aimed at, is good, but there is almost complete ignorance of the means which must be employed in its attainment.  In such circumstances can the intention be said to be *altogether* good?  Scarcely.  Conduct is good in intention when it intends the attainment of the *summum bonum*.  But the *summum bonum* is an object of action, to be realized in conduct.  Hence, if the agent is truly to understand the Highest Good, he must see it in its bearing upon his own situation, as the outcome of his own conduct, the expression of his own will.  In other words, for the Good fully to determine an action as motive, it must be known, not abstractly as the faraway goal of endeavor, but concretely in terms of the conduct required to attain it.  To make an intention good, then, it does not suffice that it have goodness for its final end, that it aim at human

---

[4] For further light upon the subjects discussed in the remainder of this chapter, *cf.* Professor Dewey's able discussion (DEWEY AND TUFTS: *Ethics*, pp. 246-54).

happiness or social welfare,—it must also include a knowledge of the means necessary for its realization. On the other hand, when these conditions are fulfilled, and an action has for its motive the realization of the Good, accompanied by a knowledge of the means requisite to this end, we may reasonably expect that its consequences will be good also. Thus far, at least, do good motives guarantee good consequences.

The objection must arise at this point that, in many cases, a person is not responsible for his ignorance of means and methods whereby to realize his ideals. Where it has not been possible for the agent to gain the needed knowledge, should his lack of it affect the moral value of his intention? Certainly, in judging of moral values, care should be exercised to distinguish between cases where opportunities for acquiring the information in question have been neglected and those in which no opportunity has apparently existed, and to make due allowance in cases of the latter sort. Yet it is difficult to see how a motive can be regarded as *altogether* good when not accompanied by as much knowledge as human experience can furnish as to the ways and means by which the ends of Goodness are realized. Certainly intelligent public opinion is growing more unwilling to accept " good intentions " in the ordinary sense as an excuse for ignorance of actual conditions that brings disastrous consequences. We tend more and more to hold the engineer responsible for his ignorance of the conditions of his air-brakes which, failing to work, caused the accident —the physician responsible for his ignorance of the injurious after-effects of the medicine he prescribes—the orator or publicist responsible for ignorance of the misleading and inflammatory character of certain doctrines when accepted by unenlightened and prejudiced minds.

### 4. Good Consequences in Most Cases Indicate a Corresponding Degree of Goodness in Intention.

—Much less frequently than is popularly supposed—we find upon examination—is there any wide difference in moral value between the intention and the consequences of action. Given a good intention, accompanied by all available information as to how it may be carried out, i.e. given an intention that *is* altogether good, and good consequences may be expected to follow. Moreover, when we move in the reverse direction, from consequence back to intention, we find agreement, not discrepancy, the rule. In the vast majority of cases good consequences indicate good intentions. In order properly to understand the situation here one must make an allowance for a natural tendency to exaggerate the goodness of those results which do seem in any degree good, when the intention behind them is believed to be bad. Our surprise is so great to find goodness produced in this way by an evil motive that we incline almost irresistibly to heighten the contrast and thus exaggerate the amount of resulting good. We tend, for instance, to overestimate the amount of good resulting to Europe from Napoleon's campaigns of conquest, when once our attention is caught by the fact that good did result. Now when we do make this allowance and reduce the consequent good to its true proportions, we usually discover that the intention is good in a corresponding degree. The scheming politician secures the passage of good laws, say you, in order that his party may remain in public favor and he may retain office and influence? Yes, but since he is clear-headed enough to understand that fame and fortune will come to him only as he proves a loyal servant of his party, and that his party can retain its power only so long as it obeys the popular will and secures the general welfare, is his motive altogether selfish? He seeks his own interest, to be sure, but is shrewd enough to see that it is inseparably bound up with the success of party and the welfare of country; hence he seeks these also. The conduct of the man who gives to charity in order to advertise his business is probably as good in intention as it is in result. That also springs from an insight into the connection of private interest with public welfare, which possesses moral value in degree probably equal to the amount of actual good which is likely to result from such forms of charity.

5. **But Goodness of Motive Cannot Absolutely Insure Good Consequences Because of Inability of Reason to Foresee All Future Developments.**—Returning now to the question whether the moral value of conduct is not determined wholly by the motive, and not at all by consequences, we see that its difficulties have been largely removed. There is no possibility of such radical discrepancy between intention and consequences as would compel us to choose one and ignore the other in evaluating conduct. The two are inseparably joined in the unitary process of volition, where they reciprocally determine one another. When the motive is good, therefore, it is entirely probable that the consequences will be also.

Can we not go still farther and assert without reservation that where the motive is good the consequences *must* be good? Suppose the motive were good in that complete sense suggested above—an excellence of motive not often attained, it must be confessed. Imagine an individual seeking the *summum bonum* with all the knowledge that human experience has been able to gather as to means and methods of pursuit, concerning conditions to be met, and contingencies apt to arise. Would such a motive necessarily and without the possibility of exception produce consequences of the same degree of goodness? Or might fate or accident still intervene to frustrate expectation, set plans at naught, and bring evil out of good? The whole problem turns upon the ability of human knowledge, when as complete as possible, to anticipate the future.  Is a knowledge even theoretically possible that will enable one to foresee every contingency that may arise in prospective action? It is true that knowledge enables us in an astonishing manner to foresee and to predict.  But this very knowledge, now the possession and advantage of the race, was gained through experiments of which no one knew the outcome until it occurred.  Action has not, then, followed a program prescribed by thought; thought has rather recorded and systematized the results of action.  Volition is the primary, the original, capacity; intellect is secondary and derived.  Hence it is impossible that knowledge should ever foresee in detail all the possibilities of achievement, or anticipate every emergency which a voluntary agent may have to meet.  Entirely novel situations arise; the totally unexpected happens.  New discoveries are made, fresh developments occur, which upset every human calculation.  The best of motives may, through such a novel turn of events, have results in action which are not wholly good.  In such case the agent is only responsible for his motive—for aiming at the Good with the fullest information human experience can furnish.  For the consequences, so far as they are determined, not by his will, but by the new and unexpected course of events, he is not responsible except in future actions, when the new facts which at first surprised him and upset all calculation can be foreseen and provided for.

## REFERENCES

MACKENZIE, *Manual of Ethics*, Book I, Chap. II.
DEWEY AND TUFTS, *Ethics*, Chap. XII, §§ 1, 2.
MILL, *Utilitarianism*, Chap. II.
LESLIE STEPHEN, *Science of Ethics*, Chap. II.
ALEXANDER, *Moral Order and Progress*, Book I, Chap. II, §§ 1, 2, 3.

PART TWO

THE NATURE OF THE GOOD

# CHAPTER I

## THE NATURE OF THE GOOD—CONDUCT OR CHARACTER

1. The Supreme Importance of the Subject.—2. The Good as Determined by Custom.—3. The Good as Discovered by Reflection.—4. Socrates' View of the Good.—5. Merits of the Socratic Conception of the Good.—6. Defects of the Socratic Conception of the Good.—7. The Good as Action or the End of Action.—8. The Good as Conduct or Character.—9. The Good as Duty or Virtue.

1. **The Supreme Importance of the Subject.**—What is the Good? This is the question which must now engage our attention; for we have seen that all other questions of Ethics lead up to this one, and upon its successful solution depends the possibility of a rational morality. By the *Good* is meant that form of life which is required to satisfy completely the human will. When the Good is thus understood it is easy to see why the question of its nature—fundamental to all ethical inquiry—is the supremely important problem of human thought. Placed beside it, all questions of business profit and loss, of social order and adjustment sink into insignificance. Such questions as these latter may in themselves be important enough, touching thousands of lives in a vital and essential manner. But, after all, they concern only single departments of human life, while the problem of the Good concerns the whole nature of man as an active being. Hence a question of economics or politics, of education or of art, interests only a comparatively small number of persons, while the moral problem has interest for all human beings in virtue of their common humanity. And for this reason

—because fundamental in character and universal in interest—the question of the Good is of greatest practical moment, and its solution of highest practical value. Before an individual can practise an art or profession he must learn its principles and be drilled in its methods. If he is properly to determine his conduct as a free agent, must he not then learn the principles of human nature and the methods of obtaining satisfaction for it? And if it is worth while to spend four years in studying the principles and methods of a profession, is it not more worth while to spend a little time in studying the nature and requirements of human life itself? Ethics is the science of human life and human conduct, and, as such, underlies all the practical sciences. Compared with that of the highest human good, all other concerns have small value indeed. '' For what shall it profit a man,'' said our greatest moral and religious teacher, '' if he shall gain the whole world and lose his own soul?'' [1]

2. **The Good as Determined by Custom.**—So important a problem is this of the highest good that in the earlier stages of moral development its solution is not left to the reason of the individual. Instead it is settled for him by the customs of his race.[2] These customs are rules of conduct which prescribe what a man must do if his conduct is to meet with approval among his fellows. In general they serve to impose such restraint upon the instincts and appetites of the individual as is required to make group-life possible and, as conditions of social ex-

---

[1] Mark viii, 36 (A. V.).

[2] The superiority of custom to reason as an agency for securing actions demanded by social welfare is remarked upon by Lafcadio Hearn in his letters bearing on Japanese life. He alludes to practices required for hygienic purposes or necessary to an orderly community life which have been easily enforced by tradition and superstition, but which would be very difficult to enforce on grounds of reason except among the most highly civilized peoples. ('' Japanese Letters of Lafcadio Hearn,'' I, *Atlantic Monthly*, December, 1909, p. 727.)

istence, are handed down from generation to generation in the form of a race tradition. All custom in the field of morality has two aspects; a *subjective*, in the belief that actions of a certain kind are good, and, an *objective*, in the practices which flow from this belief. Thus the customs of a people lay down the conditions which the individual must fulfil if he is to deserve the title of " good man "—that, for instance, he must be a brave warrior, a successful hunter, the father of several sons, a worshiper of the tribal deities, etc.

The system of customs which constitutes the morality of primitive man is not the result of his reflection upon the question of the highest human good; these customs owe their origin and perpetuation largely to forces and agencies purely natural. No doubt chance or " luck " plays a large part in the origin of custom. Some action happens to precede or accompany a piece of great good fortune to the tribe, such as unparalleled success in the hunt or complete victory in warfare. This action is therefore regarded as lucky and is perpetuated as a custom long after the original circumstances have been forgotten.[3] With the continued existence of customs the law of natural selection, acting between societies, has much to do. Those tribes whose customs are such as to make them more efficient in hunting and warfare, survive in the struggle for life and their customs are continued, while tribes whose customs tend in the opposite direction—towards disintegration and inefficiency—are exterminated.

But while primitive morality owes its existence so largely to causes that are non-rational, its customs are by no means on a level with the set of instincts by which life is organized in an animal society, such as a community of ants or of

[3] For a brief statement of the factors which enter into the origin or custom, and of the means whereby customs are enforced, consult DEWEY AND TUFTS: *Ethics*, Chap. IV.

bees. The operation of custom in the most primitive human society calls for the exercise of intelligence and volition on the part of the individuals concerned.[4] A man must possess the power of thinking in general terms—of conceptual thought—before he can understand the requirements of a custom. He must be able to conceive of general modes of acting—of marrying within or without the clan, for instance—if the custom concerns marriage. Then the *obligation* that is felt to obey the custom implies the power of choice and selection. The individual must be able to represent to himself a certain form of conduct— say, marrying without the clan—as a possibility of action, and to contrast it with other modes of action. Thus only can he feel an *obligation* to pursue one alternative in action, an obligation which is neither the desire of a particular object on the one hand, nor the sense of external compulsion on the other. Nor can we doubt that the intelligence and volition required for the understanding and obeying of customs have in an increasing degree influenced their origination and continuance. The necessity of teaching the traditional customs of the race to the rising generation would set men to thinking of their meaning and value. Thus thoughts of possible changes and innovations would naturally arise. In result a new feature would be occasionally introduced into the tribal customs through the influence of some powerful individual. These changes, though slight enough in any one generation, would have cumulative effect and, as moral evolution proceeded, serve more and more to rationalize the existing morality.

3. **The Good as Discovered by Reflection.**—But the time comes in the history of the race, as of the individual, when man is no longer willing to have the nature

---

[4] A full and illuminating account of the psychological factors involved in custom is contained in WUNDT'S *Ethics*, Eng. trans., Vol. I, " The Facts of the Moral Life," pp. 127-34.

of his good determined for him by the customs of his race. He insists upon applying his own reason to the solution of the problem. The resulting reflection may seem at first productive of evil rather than good; for while general enlightenment follows upon the exercise of thought by individuals, it is generally accompanied also by *skepticism* or doubt of the existence of any universal standards of truth or goodness, and *individualism* or the further conclusion that the good for every individual is identical with his own advantage.

The most notable instance in history of such an overthrow of customary morality occurred in Greece in the fifth century B.C. This revolt against the morality of custom and tradition among the Greeks is especially important because, in the systematic reflection which grew out of it, we have the beginnings of ethical science among European peoples.—Victory in the Persian wars had increased the wealth and the commerce of the Greek states. Thus their citizens were given more leisure for study and reflection, and an increasing acquaintance with the beliefs and customs of other peoples. The rise of democracy gave greater importance and scope to action and initiative on the part of the individual, and the frequent changes in government tended to weaken his respect for established law and institution. When we add to these influences the fact that philosophic speculation during the century previous had practically destroyed the old mythology and undermined the foundations of the national religion, it is not surprising to find the moral customs and traditions of the Greek people losing their authority and falling into disrespect.[5] This spirit of revolt against authority in all departments of life finds expression in the teachings of

[5] For a description of the influences that coöperated to bring about the Greek enlightenment, and an explanation of the main tenets in the teachings of the Sophists, *cf.* WINDELBAND: *History of Philosophy*, Eng. trans. by TUFTS, pp. 66-70.

the Sophists. The Sophists came into prominence at this time as itinerant teachers, first of rhetoric and public speaking, and then, extending the scope of their instruction, of the whole conduct of life.[6] The effect of their teaching was to encourage the individual to disregard all accepted standards and established authority in the pursuit of his own interest. They denied that there were any absolute standards of truth and goodness which could claim authority over all men. Hence they maintained that the individual's opinion was truth for him, and that his advantage was his good. The Sophists were therefore skeptics— in the field of thought defenders of subjectivism, and in the sphere of conduct advocates of individualism.

4. **Socrates' View of the Good.**—The general acceptance of this individualistic doctrine meant the dissolution of all moral standards among the Greek people and the reduction of their social order to a chaos of contending desires and ambitions. To prevent this disastrous result there was need for a man to appear with a mind keen enough to see more deeply into the problem than did the Sophists, and a personality sufficiently vigorous to impress his views upon the thought of his age. Such a man was Socrates, who is justly esteemed as one of the great ethical teachers and moral heroes of history.[7] Socrates sought to reëstablish the authority of the old standards of justice and courage and temperance,—not

[6] First and most prominent among the Sophists was Protagoras of Abdera, born about 480 B.C. He taught for forty years throughout Greece, and with great success. He is the leading figure in the celebrated dialogue of Plato's bearing his name. Other Sophists were Gorgias, Prodicus, and Hippias.

[7] Socrates was born in 470 B.C. His father was Sophroniscus, a sculptor. He was trained in his father's profession. This he abandoned in response to what he regarded as a divine call to his peculiar mission. His mission he understood as the moral instruction of the Greek people. As a moral teacher he followed the indirect method of question and answer. By skilful questioning he

by appealing to the authority of tradition and the past, however, but by carrying still further that reflection on ethical subjects begun by the Sophists. He maintained that if men would not be content with mere feeling and opinion, but would take the trouble to think systematically on the subject of human conduct, they would discover what is man's true good and see that its attainment imposes on all men certain fundamental obligations. He declared, in fact, that virtue or goodness *is* knowledge. For by a necessity of his nature every man seeks his own interest. If he does wrong, this shows that he is ignorant of what his true interest is. Conversely, if he gains knowledge of his true interest he cannot help pursuing it, and hence must do right. This knowledge, which for man is identical with virtue, is primarily a knowledge of *himself,* of the needs and capacities of his human nature. It is also a knowledge of the conditions under which the individual can find self-satisfaction in human life and society. Such knowledge, leading the individual to consider the future as well as the present, and revealing the community of interest among fellow-citizens, will convince him of the necessity of discharging the commonly recognized duties as conditions of his own happiness. Thus that true knowledge which is identical with virtue is shown to be a means to happiness. Socrates is able, therefore, by a change of emphasis to define virtue as happiness—the true happiness attained through the control of action by reason.

forced his hearers into confusion and self-contradiction. Thus they were made to convict themselves of ignorance, and the way was opened for Socrates to suggest the truth. In his own life and conduct Socrates was a pattern of piety, patriotism, and justice. His frankness in exposing hypocrisy, his devotion to truth with an utter disregard of popular opinion, made him many enemies. As a result of a conspiracy of these he was tried, sentenced to death, and forced to drink the hemlock in the year 399 B.C.

For an interesting character-study of Socrates, *cf.* C. M. BAKE-WELL: "The Unique Case of Socrates," *International Journal of Ethics*, October, 1909.

**5. Merits of the Socratic Conception of the Good.**— The value of Socrates' contribution to the science of Ethics can scarcely be over-estimated. He was the first to offer a positive solution for the ethical problem; since he was the first to find ground in human nature for a Good which was the same for all men and would consequently unite them in the bonds of a common moral obligation. Although designed to refute the individualism of the Sophists, Socrates' view has not the one-sidedness which usually condemns a doctrine developed in the heat of controversy. While it upholds the authority of duty it provides for the satisfaction of the individual. In fact, Socrates' conception of the Good is a synthesis of two elements which often appear in open conflict. It contains, first, the rationalistic principle that sense-impulse and present desire should be subjected to the conceptions and purposes of reason. But we find, in the second place, the hedonistic doctrine that the exercise of reason should in its turn be a means to the satisfaction and happiness of the individual. Virtue is knowledge, but knowledge is happiness.

**6. Defects of the Socratic Conception of the Good.** —Just this synthetic character, which is the strength of Socrates' view of the Good, is also the source of its weakness. For it is a synthesis too easily achieved. If knowledge of one's true interest necessarily involved action in accordance with it, we should have here a final solution of the moral problem. But such is not the case. "For the good that I would, I do not; but the evil which I would not, that I do," says Paul,[8] and the facts of our moral experience are in accord with the statement of the Christian apostle rather than the view of the Athenian sage. Socrates' error seems to have arisen from an imperfect understanding of the working of the human will. In the

[8] Romans vii, 19 (A. V.).

process of volition the idea which reason connects with one's true interest does not automatically and inevitably translate itself into action and accomplishment. I may be thoroughly convinced that two hours' exercise in the open air every afternoon is required for my own best welfare, yet sit quiet in my office or study during every afternoon of the week. Besides the thought of the object and the feeling of satisfaction in its attainment, a third factor enters into volition whose significance Socrates did not appreciate. This is the *effort*, the *activity*, with which volition proper is often identified. This effort is mental— that activity of attention required to keep an idea steadily in mind despite distracting influences, while the steps necessary to its realization are duly taken. Now the amount of attention which any idea is able to command is not determined by rational considerations solely. (The most reasonable alternative is not always the most attractive one.) Rather is it in a large measure the result of the individual's tendencies and habits—tendencies which are innate and habits which have been developed through past action and experience. In the development of such habits the " training " of the will consists. And in order that an individual shall pursue his true interest it is necessary, not only that his intellect be enlightened as to its character, but also that his will be trained in its performance. Not only moral instruction, therefore, but also moral training is required if a man is to act for his own good. For the habituation in a course of action, which results from training in its performance, makes the idea of it attractive, and powerful over the attention. These considerations lead to a position the very opposite of that taken by Socrates— and one that sounds paradoxical enough when first stated— that one can know an idea *fully* only after he has acted upon it. Without attempting at this point to clear up the perplexities involved, we may acknowledge that this last statement contains sufficient truth to disprove the Socratic doctrine that virtue is knowledge. It is undoubtedly true that in many cases one can learn that an object is a part of his own good only by seeking and attaining it. He must have sufficient courage to make the trial, and then he will be convinced by the results of his action that the object which he sought is part of his own good. Thus it is only by pursuing another's good at the expense of our own that we learn the extent of our own interest—that it includes the welfare of others.

7. **The Good as Action or the End of Action.**—The difficulties in the Socratic conception show clearly that no theory of the Good can be accepted as final which neglects the conditions under which it is realized in action. The reason for this is plain. By definition the Good is that which completely satisfies intelligent volition. Volition is action in pursuit of a chosen end. Thus whatever else it may or may not be the Good must certainly be some form, or end, of action. Mr. Alexander states this fact with emphasis in his *Moral Order and Progress:* "Hence the object of morality cannot be a passive state like pleasure or the possession of knowledge. When these are the objects of will, what is willed is not the feeling or the state by themselves, but their production. It would be infinitely tedious to be obliged always to say so, but the condition is always implied." [9] To admit the truth of this is not by any means to decide the question of the Good in favor of some form of voluntarism.[10] The Good may still be a passive state—a condition of agreeable feeling or of complete knowledge. Or it may be the extinction of all individual activity —as in the Buddhist Nirvana. But these conditions of being or non-being will nevertheless be objects which are

[9] *Moral Order and Progress*, ed. of 1889, p. 165.
[10] The theory, that is, that the Good is found in the process or activity of willing itself rather than in any object or end attained by will.

actively pursued. The happiness must be sought after, the knowledge must be obtained, and even the Nirvana of the Buddhist must be achieved by long and persistent effort. In short the Good must be some form of conduct; for only in conduct can the will find expression.

8. **The Good as Conduct or Character.**—Thus to conceive of the Good as a form of conduct is not to identify it with outward and visible action in contrast with inner and essential nature. Such an antithesis of conduct and character is possible only on a false view of the human self. According to this view—held by a Psychology now antiquated—the self or soul is an entity or " thing " which possesses a nature permanent and in a large degree independent of outward act and condition. This view permitted of a sharp distinction being made between *character* as pertaining to this inner and unchanging principle of human selfhood and *conduct* as belonging to the outward world of visible and changing events. Modern Psychology, however, is dynamic, not static; it understands the self as a sum total, or better, an organized unity of conscious activities. From this standpoint it is impossible to make any hard and fast distinction between conduct and character. For conduct does not consist of a series of unrelated acts; these acts are acts of will, and represent so many choices. A series of such choices tends to produce a habit, and out of these habits are formed those dispositions and capacities which constitute the character of a person. Character in its turn does not consist of passive qualities which exist apart from the sphere of action. Rather it is made up of the dispositions and attitudes of the individual—dispositions to act and attitudes towards objects of action. But it is in just these modes of activity that the individual's conduct consists. Thus conduct and character resolve themselves into two sides, outer and inner, of a unitary subject, the active self or

personality.[11]   What a man *is* is manifest in what he *does*, and what he *does* is an expression of what he *is*.   If it is legitimate to define the Good as a form of conduct, it is equally legitimate to describe it as a species of character.

9. **The Good as Duty or Virtue.**—The relation is identical when we consider whether the Good consists in the performance of duty or the acquisition of virtue. By *duty* we understand a mode of action which is morally approved.   A virtue, on the other hand, is an attribute or disposition of character which is judged good. Now the moral ideal may be formulated in terms of either of these two conceptions.   The Greeks preferred the latter—explaining goodness as the acquisition of certain virtues.   Thus the greatest Greek moralists, Plato and Aristotle, discuss at length those virtues which are requisite to goodness, the so-called cardinal virtues of temperance, courage, justice, etc.   Christian Ethics has in the main adopted the former conception, understanding right living to consist in the performance of certain duties. Hence Christian moralists have laid greatest stress upon a code of duties which are conceived as laws prescribing the conduct of the good man.   The Ten Commandments are often cited by these moralists as constituting the fundamental code of duty, proceeding directly from God, the source of the moral law.   These two conceptions of goodness as duty and as virtue have been frequently contrasted as if they were in essential opposition and exclusive of one another.[12]   The Greek view of the Good as virtue has been charged with making morality self-centered, while the Christian conception of goodness as duty has been accused of making it external and formal.   Such a contrast is made possible only by that abstract and false

[11] This point is briefly but clearly put by SETH: *Ethical Principles*, ed, of 1908, p. 5.

[12] Sidgwick emphasizes this point of difference between Greek and Christian Ethics in his *Outline of the History of Ethics*, Chap. III.

separation of conduct and character which has just been condemned. As conduct and character are two sides, outer and inner, of one unitary personality, so duty and virtue are two aspects, outer and inner, of the expression of this personality. Whether we conceive of goodness in terms of one or of the other is altogether a matter of emphasis; for one cannot exist without the other. A man can acquire or possess no quality of soul which does not manifest itself in action, nor can he perform any intelligent action without affecting and modifying his essential nature. The Good may therefore be conceived, equally well, as the performance of duty or as the acquisition of virtue.

## REFERENCES

ALEXANDER, *Moral Order and Progress*, Book I, Chap. II, §§ 4, 5.

DEWEY AND TUFTS, *Ethics*, Chaps. IV and XIII, §§ 3, 4.

MACKENZIE, *Manual of Ethics*, Book I, Chap. III, and Book II, Chap. I.

WUNDT, *Ethics*, Vol. I, Chap. III.

WINDELBAND, *History of Philosophy* (Eng. trans.), Part I, Chap. II, § 7.

BAKEWELL, *Source-book in Ancient Philosophy*, Chaps. VIII, IX, X.

# CHAPTER II

## THEORIES OF THE GOOD—HEDONISM

1. Pleasure as the Good.—2. Cyrenaicism.—3. Element of Truth in Cyrenaicism.—4. The Inadequacy of Cyrenaicism.—5. Epicureanism.—6. Value of the Epicurean Theory of the Good.—7. Arguments in Support of Hedonism.—8. Error of Psychological Hedonism.—9. Criticism of Ethical Hedonism.—10. Transition to Rationalism.

1. **Pleasure as the Good.**—There is reason to believe that all actions whose results are beneficial to animal life are accompanied by pleasure, while harmful actions are attended by pain. As human beings, we know that actions which tend to conserve health and physical well-being are, generally speaking, pleasurable, while actions whose effect is to diminish health and lessen bodily vigor are usually painful.[1] Advancing from the biological to the psychological sphere, we find it true that the uninterrupted and successful exercise of our mental faculties is accompanied by a pleasant, affective glow, as in observation, thought, and imagination. Here, too, the reverse condition of frustrated thought and interrupted imagination is essentially unpleasant, as in doubt, perplexity, and confusion. In fact, psychologists tell us that

[1] " From the biological point of view, then, we see that the connections between pleasure and beneficial action and between pain and detrimental action, which arose when sentient existence began, and have continued among animate creatures up to man, are generally displayed in him also throughout the lower and more completely organized part of his nature; and must be more and more fully displayed throughout the higher part of his nature, as fast as his adaptation to the conditions of social life increases."— SPENCER: *Data of Ethics,* Chap. VI, § 35.

success in attaining the end of action always brings pleasure in result, and failure causes pain.[2]   In view of these facts, it is not surprising that in the sphere of morals the theory of Hedonism,—the view that *the Good is Pleasure,*—has appealed strongly to men's minds.  For is not pleasure the unfailing index of our success in attaining those objects which we as voluntary agents strive after?  If we pursue pleasure do we not therefore seek that satisfaction which our natures demand, and, if we obtain the greatest possible pleasure, do we not obtain the maximum of satisfaction for that faculty of will which is the source of all our action?

2.  **Cyrenaicism.**—Early in the history of ethical reflection Hedonism was proposed as a theory of the Good.  It was first definitely enunciated by Aristippus, who had been a disciple of Socrates and professed to derive this view from the teachings of his master.  Socrates' conception of the Good had, it will be remembered, two sides. According to the one, the Good was happiness, and reason was but a means to the highest human happiness.  Aristippus was deeply impressed with this aspect of Socrates' teachings and developed it to an extreme, neglecting the rationalistic element which offset it in his master's conception, and thus destroying the balance and unity of the latter.  He taught that the Good is pleasure and, since the past is gone and the future is uncertain, the pleasure of the present moment.  Thus man achieves his Good when, with skill and care, he extracts the greatest possible enjoyment from each passing moment.  This theory, that the Good consists in the enjoyment of present pleasure,—called Cyrenaicism [3]—is, of course, not merely a feature of the history of Ethics.  It is the view of all those in every age who consciously prefer the enjoyment of present pleasure because they regard the future as at best incalculable

---

[2] STOUT: *Manual of Psychology*, Bk. III, Div. I, Chap. III, § 3.
[3] From *Cyrene,* the birthplace and home of Aristippus.

and uncertain—believing it wise to " eat, drink, and be merry, for—to-morrow—we die."

3. **Element of Truth in Cyrenaicism.**—Cyrenaicism is so obviously impossible as a final solution of the ethical problem that it is easy to overlook the element of indubitable truth which it contains. Even the animals go beyond this standpoint, it may be said; since they forego present pleasure to provide for future need—as when food is hoarded for the coming winter. It must not be forgotten, however, that animals are prompted to such action by instinct—an inherited nervous modification that makes it pleasanter for the individual so to act in the present as to conserve future welfare. Man himself possesses an instinct of self-preservation which causes him to take present precautions to avoid future pain,—and the possession of this instinct renders it easy and natural for him to resist the pressure of momentary feeling. But, it may be asked, has not man an overwhelming advantage in the possession of his reason, which enables him to foresee the future clearly, and plan for it? This is of course true, yet it is also true that this very faculty reveals to man a fact of which the animals are not cognizant—that the future of any living being is essentially uncertain and incalculable. Or, to express the same truth in other words, reason has decided limitations in its ability to foresee the future. In an important sense reason is limited to the familiar, is compelled to interpret the future in the light of past experience. Life, on the contrary, presents what is essentially new, is ever revealing novel and unexpected aspects. In comparison, therefore, with a future which must remain to a large degree uncertain, the present has *actuality,* and this actuality gives it a genuine importance and rightful claim for consideration. It is in this emphasis upon the rights of the present moment as alone actual that the truth of Cyrenaicism consists. After all, life is constituted of

a succession of present moments, and always to sacrifice the now present to the future is to rob it of attainment and satisfaction all along its course.[4] American life has been justly criticised because, intent upon the pursuit of wealth or the fulfilment of ambition, it fails to find any true joy or satisfaction along the way, and hence becomes hard and barren and mechanical.

4. The Inadequacy of Cyrenaicism.—While we thus do justice to the truth in Cyrenaicism, its inadequacy as a theory of the Good can be made clear in a very few words. To assert that the human will finds satisfaction in the enjoyment of present pleasure only, is to admit that it has no scope beyond the confines of the present, no extension beyond the limits of the single moment, and is, in effect, to deny that human life has any real unity or is more than a succession of unrelated moments. It is, to be sure, a fact—a deplorable fact—that many human lives fail to attain any unitary meaning or significance; they remain but a succession of impulses which yield pleasure or pain, according as they succeed or fail of gratification. We think however that such lives miss the dignity of the truly human, and resemble in character the animal existence. In many cases this enslavement to present desire is due to mental deficiency—the individual being unable to imagine the future or think of its connection with the present with sufficient clearness and coherence to make it a determining factor in present action. An extreme instance of such deficiency is seen in the case of those constant offenders who fall repeatedly into the clutches of the law because they seem unable to represent to themselves the consequences of their actions. Yet, as we have seen, knowledge of the future does not insure adequate provision for it in the present. Moreover, reason, although

---

[4] Höffding brings out the point—of the right of the present moment to have its claims duly considered—in his *Ethik*.

it may forecast the future cannot guarantee it. To adjust present action to the needs of the future requires, therefore, the exercise of a faculty which transcends even reason—that is, *faith*—faith in one's future and faith in one's self. It calls for the exercise of *will*, the will to be a self, which includes many present moments and joins them in a significant unity. That the will has this power to transcend the limits of the present can only be learned by the exercise of it: yet its exercise is absolutely necessary if the will is to find adequate expression in human life and conduct.

5. **Epicureanism.**—When it is thus seen that in order to derive the greatest pleasure from life we must take into account the future as well as the present we adopt a second form of Hedonism, *Epicureanism.* Of this version of Hedonism the author is Epicurus, a Greek philosopher, who lived and taught in Athens a century after the time of Aristippus. He gathered about him a company of devoted disciples who perpetuated his teachings after his death in a school which continued for six centuries, and always held the name and writings of its founder in greatest reverence. Epicurus remained true to the fundamental tenet of Hedonism, that pleasure is the only absolute good in human life. Differing from the Cyrenaics, however, he held that it was not present enjoyment, but the happiness of a life-time which is the *summum bonum*. Now if man is to gain the greatest pleasure from his life as a whole it is clear that he must often forego a present pleasure in order to secure a greater pleasure in the future or to avoid a pain which will more than outweigh the present enjoyment. Epicurus saw the necessity for this and urged his followers to exercise strict self-control in all their enjoyments. He preached temperance particularly in the case of the bodily pleasures and, always, a prudent regard for the future. He even went so far as

to recommend that intellectual pleasures be preferred to those arising from the gratification of physical appetites—and did so, on the strictly hedonistic ground, that the intellectual enjoyments, although less intense, were more permanent and less exhausting. Epicurus also dwelt upon the pleasures of friendship, and of friendly intercourse with a circle of congenial acquaintances. In his own practice he sought a life of quiet contentment, having few desires, and satisfying these with strict temperance, and finding solace chiefly in the intellectual enjoyment of philosophic contemplation and friendly intercourse.

6. **Value of the Epicurean Theory of the Good.**—As a theory of the Good, Epicureanism cannot be dismissed as easily as was Cyrenaicism.[5] No justification can be found in its doctrine for a debauched or licentious life, for an idle dallying with present pleasure at the cost of future well-being. He who would obtain the maximum of pleasure in life must vigilantly guard his health, and this alone, the careful conservation of health and bodily vigor, requires the strictest temperance. Nor does Epicureanism excuse such absorption in the pleasures of sense as will exclude the higher satisfactions which come from the exercise of our spiritual capacities. Rather it enjoins us not to look solely at the present intensity of a pleasure, but also at the length of its endurance and its possibilities as a source of future enjoyment. Such reckoning, if honestly made, will usually lead the consistent Epicurean to seek such " intellectual " pleasures as those given by reading, music, or conversation, rather than the " physical " enjoyments of eating, drinking, etc. Nor, again, does Epicureanism recommend that the individual pursue his own selfish pleasure with a ruthless disregard of others' rights

[5] The good points in Hedonism are well stated by President Hyde in his *Five Great Philosophies of Life,* Chap. II, " The Epicurean Price of Happiness."

and happiness. On the contrary, a survey of human life and the conditions of its maintenance teaches the individual how largely his own happiness is dependent upon his relations to his fellows and their good-will towards him. Moreover, one of the purest and most lasting pleasures of human existence is that arising from friendly intercourse and companionship. Hence the true follower of Epicurus will sedulously cultivate a circle of congenial friends, and take pains to preserve a good reputation among a larger number of pleasant acquaintances. When consistently carried out, therefore, Epicureanism as a theory of the Good is by no means to be despised. It produces an orderly life and one yielding much genuine satisfaction. It develops a type of character dignified by many virtues. The true Epicurean will be temperate and law-abiding, industrious, saving, and prudent, a man quite content with simple pleasures, the enjoyment of which is enhanced by being shared with congenial friends.

7. **Arguments in Support of Hedonism.**—When we come to criticise Epicureanism the larger question of the truth in Hedonism is naturally suggested; for Epicureanism may be taken as the standard form of Hedonism.[6] Considering the matter in this more general way we find that arguments advanced in support of Hedonism fall into two main classes. The first is psychological and consists in the assertion that all men do pursue pleasure always, whether aware of it or not. The nature of the human will

---

[6] In modern times another form of Hedonism has arisen called Utilitarianism, which contends that the Good is not the happiness of the individual but the happiness of society, the "greatest happiness of the greatest number." This extension of pleasure as the Good, beyond the individual to society, is possible, as Sidgwick has shown, only through an appeal to reason. Thus the Hedonistic doctrine is complicated and obscured. Indeed, it is doubtful if Utilitarianism is a true species of Hedonism, since Hedonism finds the Good in a state of feeling, and feeling is essentially subjective and individual, while the introduction of reason in Utilitarianism gives it a predominantly objective and social reference.

is such that man can seek but one object and this his own pleasure. In fact, to " desire " and to seek pleasure are identical. In the words of J. S. Mill we have a classic statement of this view:

" It results from the preceding considerations that there is in reality nothing desired except happiness. Whatever is desired otherwise than as a means to some end beyond itself and ultimately to happiness, is desired as itself a part of happiness, and is not desired for itself until it has become so. Those who desire virtue for its own sake desire it either because the consciousness of it is a pleasure or because the consciousness of being without it is a pain or for both reasons united: as in truth the pleasure and pain seldom exist separately, but almost always together, the same person feeling pleasure in the degree of virtue attained and pain in not having attained more. If one of these gave him no pleasure and the other no pain, he would not love or desire virtue, or would desire it only for the other benefits which it might produce to himself or to persons whom he cared for. We have now, then, an answer to the question of what sort of proof the principle of utility is susceptible. If the opinion which I have now stated is psychologically true— if human nature is so constituted as to desire nothing which is not either a part of happiness or a means to happiness— we can have no other proof, and we require no other, that these are the only things desirable. If so, happiness is the sole end of human action, and the promotion of it the test by which to judge of all human conduct; from whence it necessarily follows that it must be the criterion of morality, since a part is included in the whole." [7]

If it is true that all men do pursue pleasure, and if, moreover, they do so because they must from a compulsion of their nature, why of course the whole question is settled and further debate concerning the *summum bonum* is unnecessary and futile. The Good is pleasure; for, since the human will can seek nothing else, in this it must find satisfaction. There remains for Ethics only the task of

[7] MILL: *Utilitarianism*, Chap. VI.

determining what forms of conduct yield the most pleasure.

The second type of argument in support of Hedonism while not claiming that the psychology of volition proves Hedonism by making all other theories impossible, maintains its position on strictly ethical grounds. Without holding that all men *do* pursue pleasure he may assert for given reasons that all men *ought* to pursue pleasure. Various reasons are given why happiness is the only end whose attainment completely satisfies human nature. Perhaps the most convincing are those suggested in the opening paragraph of this chapter. Since pleasure results from all successful endeavor, it signifies the satisfaction of the will which initiated the action. The ultimate end of human conduct cannot be objective in the sense of being external to the conscious life of man. It must rather be subjective, a state of human consciousness. Now the only state of consciousness desirable for its own sake is that which is *pleasant,* or *pleasure*. Therefore pleasure is the highest human good.

8. **Error of Psychological Hedonism.**—Whether or not pleasure is the sole and necessary end of all intelligent action is a question of fact which psychology must decide. Psychology has given its decision and this is adverse to the claims of Hedonism. Pleasure, the psychologist tells us, is by no means the sole and only aim of voluntary action.[8] To be sure, we frequently seek pleasure—the idea of the pleasure to be enjoyed being unmistakably the end of our action. But we do not always do so. In fact, it is not usual for us to act with any subjective state, pleasurable or painful, in mind as the end we seek to attain. Rather do we ordinarily pursue objects. Of course, in any case, the end of an action is an idea, but—the point is—not usually the idea of a subjective state which we wish to produce, but of an object which we seek to attain.

[8] JAMES: *Psychology,* Vol. II, Chap. XXVI, pp. 556-57.

Intelligent action normally has this objective reference—a reference beyond subjective states and individual feelings.[9] Thus the hungry man desires, not the pleasure of satiety, but a beefsteak or some other article of food. Even the man having a holiday is not intent upon producing the feeling of zest or invigoration which comes from this or that exercise or sport, but upon catching fish, or shooting ducks, or playing golf. Indeed, so obvious do the facts appear that one wonders why a view that contravenes them could gain so wide an acceptance. This question may be answered by a brief reference to one most important consideration which explains why psychological Hedonism has won the assent of so many minds.

The plausibility of the doctrine that pleasure is always the end of action depends upon an ambiguity in the terms which are usually employed in discussing the subject. Is it true or false that *man always seeks that which most pleases him?* It depends entirely upon what is meant by these words. If one means that man always chooses and pursues the object or action whose idea is pleasantest to him—most strongly suffused or colored by pleasant feeling —it is true. In this sense, the person about to have a tooth extracted, the mother going to nurse a child sick with some very dangerous and communicable disease, the martyr going to the stake, are all of them doing what pleases them most. But this tells nothing about the end, the motive, of their action. To say that man in his conduct always follows the pleasantest course is merely to recognize that the end chosen and pursued is the end most interesting, most attractive, to the agent who chooses and acts. In this first sense, therefore, the statement that man

[9] HÖFFDING: *Outlines of Psychology*, p. 323:—" Because the end or object of the impulse is something that excites or seems to excite pleasure, it need not necessarily be the feeling of pleasure itself. The impulse is essentially determined by an idea, is a striving after the content of this idea."

always seeks the object which most pleases him is true, but
is entirely irrelevant to the question at issue, which concerns only the end of action.  If, in the second place, this
statement is understood to mean that man always seeks
the object which promises to yield him the most pleasure,
it is quite false.  The mother does not undertake to nurse
the sick child because she expects to derive pleasure from it,
but because the idea of the child in pain and danger fills
her mind, and then the further idea of relieving his pain
and preserving his life appeals to her with overwhelming
force.  The martyr does not go to the stake moved by
the thought of the pleasure he expects to enjoy during
the experience or, later, in Heaven, but in order to uphold
the principles to which he has devoted himself, to defend
the cause to which he has consecrated his life.  To maintain
in these cases that men act, not in order to realize objects
—to save a stricken child or to defend an honored cause,
but to produce certain subjective states in themselves—
is to do violence to the plainest facts of human experience.
Thus we see that the dictum on which the Hedonist relies
to prove his case is capable of two interpretations.  According to the one, it is true, but irrelevant to the question;
according to the other, it is relevant, but untrue.  Undoubtedly many have been convinced by the arguments of
Hedonism because they thought that such a statement in
the same sense in which it was true was also relevant.

9. **Criticism of Ethical Hedonism.**—The argument that
all men ought to pursue pleasure is not as easy to disprove.
Many objections have been brought against it in the long
controversy over Hedonism; but not all of these objections
have weight.  For instance, the fact alluded to that the
will normally directs itself upon objects and objective conditions rather than subjective states may be urged as an
objection to making any state of feeling the Good.  While
it is true that single acts of will have normally this ob-

jective reference it must be remembered, however, that the Good is an end sought in no single act, but in all the voluntary activity of the individual. In order that the *summum bonum* may be thus universal and include all particular goods, it may be helpful to conceive of it—in contradistinction to them—as a subjective state. Thus we secure a common denominator to which to reduce them all, measuring their value and importance by the amount of pleasure they yield. Again Hedonism is charged with being impracticable because it involves the idea of a sum-total of pleasure. Pleasures cannot be thus added, it is said, nor the effect of doing or refraining from a certain act, in increasing or lessening the sum-total of pleasure, be calculated with strict mathematical precision. This is true, but the Hedonist may answer that he is compelled to make no such exact mathematical calculation. No theory of the Good can furnish a standard whereby the worth of each particular object or act may be determined with absolute quantitative exactitude. On the other hand, to endeavor to increase the sum-total of pleasure in life is as practicable as a guiding principle in our conduct as to endeavor to increase the amount of intellectual activity or æsthetic appreciation.

Nor does the fault of Hedonism lie in anything positive which it leads the individual to do or accomplish. We have seen that, so far from recommending a life of excess or profligacy, it enforces the very opposite. The man who obtains the most pleasure from life must maintain himself in health, comfort, and security. To do this he must accumulate property, win reputation, and provide exercise for his natural impulses in family and social life. Thus Hedonism secures for man many objects that are required to satisfy his will and are thus good. But the fatal objection to the theory is that it is limited to just these objects and hence prevents the complete satisfaction of human volition through the attainment of larger ends. The consistent Hedonist is limited in his choice to those objects which his experience, past or present, assures him will add to his life's enjoyment. Hence Hedonism can furnish no justification for real heroism or true self-sacrifice; since heroism and self-sacrifice consist essentially in surrendering objects known by the individual to promote his happiness for the sake of other larger objects which promise to make no equal return to him in comfort or pleasure. But the moral experience of man demonstrates that such sacrifice and heroism are necessary if those more comprehensive objects, ideal and social, are to be attained which are required to satisfy completely intelligent volition. The fatal defect of Hedonism lies, therefore, in the limitation which it imposes on man's will—limiting him to a circle of objects which his experience proves will add to his comfort and happiness, and shutting him away forever from those larger ends and loftier ideals whose pleasure yielding capacity must remain uncertain until the individual by effort and sacrifice has achieved them.[10] The Hedonist may be industrious and frugal, saving his pennies for a rainy day, but he can never sell all his goods and feed the poor, even in order to save his soul. The Hedonist may be honest and good-tempered, checking his ambition and bridling his tongue, in order to preserve a good reputation among his fellows, yet he could never invite death by entering a plague-stricken locality, even to relieve suffering or perchance discover some saving remedy. The Hedonist may be obliging and companionable, going to much trouble to retain a friendship, yet he could never lay down his life, even for the sake of a friend.

[10] Rogers makes the same criticism of Hedonism when, in discussing Epicureanism in his *Student's History of Philosophy*, Chap. I, § 14, 3, he describes it as essentially commonplace and unheroic.

10. **Transition to Rationalism.**—If the human will is to obtain complete satisfaction, therefore, man must transcend the standpoint of Hedonism, subordinating the life of sense and feeling to the ideals of reason and the imagination. It may seem inconsistent with statements already made thus to base the distinction between Hedonism and the more adequate theory upon an opposition of feeling to thought. For, on the one hand, have we not seen that thought plays an important part in all Hedonistic theories that go beyond momentary feeling and consider the happiness of a lifetime? And, on the other hand, was it not shown that reason alone is incapable of justifying absolutely the surrender of present pleasure for the sake of future happiness, not to mention the greater sacrifice of individual well-being to ideal or social purposes? Certain it is, most assuredly, that the man who seeks as his good the greatest pleasure in life must exercise his reason in considering the exigencies of the future and in forming those general purposes whose realization in the course of a lifetime produces the maximum of agreeable feeling. Yet such an exercise of thought is limited in range and need not extend far beyond the field of sense perception. The Cyrenaic, of course, considers only the objects of present perception and seeks to find in them gratification for the impulse momentarily uppermost. He seeks now an article of food, now a form of exercise, now a mode of companionship, etc., etc. The Epicurean is not limited thus to particular objects and actions. He generalizes upon his experiences, substituting for particular wishes and impulses general desires and purposes. He seeks, not specific objects, like an article of food or clothing, but more general and comprehensive ones, such as food, better health, or more property. Now these general purposes are the work of thought, and as such are not limited to the present, but extend into the future, and their successful realization in

the course of time requires the denial of present desire. But while such ideas as health, wealth, etc., standing for the natural goods of man, are concepts of thought they nevertheless represent only classes of sense-objects. Hence they do not rise far above the sphere of sense-perception and leave as the distinguishing feature of Hedonism its emphasis upon the natural feelings of the individual. Now turning to the second difficulty, it is admittedly true that in cases where individual happiness is sacrificed to larger ends reason cannot demonstrate in advance of the act of sacrifice that the result will be a larger and fuller satisfaction. Such satisfaction can come only after the character of the individual has been transformed by the voluntary sacrifice, and cannot be imagined previously, just because the transformation has not taken place. If reason could assure the individual of a larger satisfaction, of course there would be no real sacrifice, no genuine heroism. The fact that the human will has capacity for a fuller satisfaction than that found in individual comfort and happiness can only be proved by *exercising* this will in resisting the claims of present desire and the appeal of purposes whose realization past experience shows to be productive of pleasure, and turning to larger objects whose significance extends beyond the natural pleasure and well-being of any individual. But —and this is the point to be noticed—such objects, objects which promise fuller and more adequate expression to man's capacity of volition, are products of thought and imagination. They result, not from a mere generalizing upon the facts of experience, but from the exercise of free-ranging thought and constructive imagination, which take the materials of past experience and combine them in new and highly significant forms. Thus ideals of spiritual achievement and social betterment come into existence. Think of the case of a man who sacrifices his reputation and standing in the community in order to prepare the way for some social reform which he sees coming in the distant future. The objects which he sacrifices are such as appeal to his senses and arouse his feelings—the smiles and compliments of acquaintances, social opportunities and diversions, increase of wealth, etc. The object which he seeks to further is, on the contrary, nowhere visible and tangible—it is a social arrangement which as yet exists only in the imagination of its advocates, and can be brought to pass only in the far future. When we thus come to see the necessity for sacrificing the demands of sense and feeling to the principles and conceptions of reason and the imagination, we advance to the position of Rationalism.

## REFERENCES

SETH, *Ethical Principles*, Part I, Chap. I.
HICKS, *Stoic and Epicurean*, Chaps. V, VI, VII.
ZELLER, *Stoics, Epicureans and Sceptics* (Eng. trans.), Part III.
WARNER FITE, *Introductory Study of Ethics*, Part I.
THILLY, *Introduction to Ethics*, Chaps. VI, VIII.
MACKENZIE, *Manual of Ethics*, Book II, Chap. IV.
SPENCER, *Data of Ethics*, Chap. III.
SIDGWICK, *Methods of Ethics*, Book II.
HYDE, *Five Great Philosophies of Life*, Chap. I.

# CHAPTER III

## THEORIES OF THE GOOD—RATIONALISM

**1. The Standpoint of Rationalism.**—Rationalism finds the Good in the exercise and development of Reason. As an ethical theory it appears as the opponent of Hedonism and its view of the Good as rational activity is defined and accentuated by contrast with the Hedonistic view of the Good as pleasant feeling. In fact, the two theories are the great antagonists in the ethical field, and the history of Ethics is largely a record of the controversy between them. Affiliated, the one with the real and the other with the ideal, the one with the natural and the other with the spiritual, Hedonism and Rationalism are two poles between which ethical speculation swings and with an inclination almost irresistible towards one or the other. But while they are thus contrary, and appear as mutually exclusive alternatives, the relation between Hedonism and Rationalism is not merely that of opposition. Rather does Rationalism represent a further stage in the development of ethical theory in which the standpoint of Hedonism is transcended and its limitations overcome. It is a step onward towards the final solution of the problem of Ethics.

**2. Extreme and Moderate Rationalism.**—Just because Rationalism is an attempt to surpass and supersede Hedonism, it must retain as essential to its own position an attitude of protest against the Hedonistic doctrine. When the Rationalist recommends the life of reason as the highest human good he inevitably thinks of this intellectual activity as superior to feeling and sensation. He is bound to insist, therefore, that the demands of feeling and sense be strictly subordinated to the requirements of reason. The extent of this antagonism to the emotional side of man's nature varies with the different types of Rationalism and affords a convenient basis for classifying them. Theories of Rationalism may be called *extreme* when holding that a free exercise of reason, in which the highest human good consists, requires the complete suppression of all those desires and impulses through which man naturally seeks pleasure. Such theories demand the practical annihilation of the feeling and emotional life of man. In *moderate* Rationalism, on the other hand, the Good is found, not in the complete suppression, but in the regulation and control, of sense and feeling by reason. Thus feelings and emotions are permitted to enter the good life, but only in a subordinate rôle.

**3. Cynicism.**—The theory of Rationalism, like that of Hedonism, was originally derived from the teachings of Socrates. Indeed, its relation to the spirit of Socrates' doctrine is much closer than that of its rival. Of the two sides of Socrates' teaching the rationalistic was certainly the more prominent. He proposed that individual impulse and opinion be submitted to the rule of reason, because reason is the one faculty in human nature whose dictates are authoritative for all individuals. Soon after Socrates' death this element in his teaching was appropriated by a school of thinkers called Cynics and was developed by them into an extreme form of Rationalism. The founder of the Cynic school, Antisthenes, was particularly impressed by

Socrates' independence of character, his courage in time of danger, and his self-possession in every emergency. These qualities constituting, in the opinion of Antisthenes, the very highest type of virtue, are developed, he believed, only when a man suppresses his natural desires and appetites entirely and devotes himself to intellectual pursuits. For our natural desires and appetites require objects to gratify them, such as food, drink, clothing, houses, furniture, etc. He who seeks pleasure in such gratifications is dependent upon the possession of these objects and hence becomes a slave of external conditions—of every circumstance that may threaten his possessions or destroy them altogether, leaving him destitute and miserable. The exercise of reason, on the contrary, is in no such way dependent upon external conditions and influences. The man who finds satisfaction in intellectual activity has resources within himself and he is freed entirely from control by such circumstances as unpopularity, poverty, sickness, slavery. These are evils only if we allow them to be such. If we root out the desires for wealth, health, reputation, and the like, we shall no longer suffer from the lack of their objects. In such freedom is the highest type of virtue and the dignity of a life truly human. The Cynics carried their hostility to the life of feeling and the pursuit of pleasure to the farthest extreme, Antisthenes declaring that he would rather be mad than pleased. They attacked, not merely the enervating luxury and extravagance of their time, but all conventions and institutions of civilization as useless paraphernalia which encumbered man and hindered him from attaining the freedom of a rational being.

4. **Stoicism.**—Rationalism was amplified and developed in ancient times by a second school, the Stoic, which was contemporary with the Epicurean.[1] Stoicism may be re-

[1] The founder of Stoicism was Zeno, born about 342 B.C. in a Greek city of Cyprus having a considerable Phœnician population

garded as the typical Rationalism and, as such, it confronts
the typical Hedonism of Epicurus. In Stoicism, as with
the Cynics, the Good is found in the exercise of reason,
or knowledge. The Stoics—especially in the beginning—
relaxed little of the rigor and severity of the earlier school
in their attitude towards the life of sense and feeling. They
condemned all feeling and emotion as producing intellectual
confusion and leading to a slavish dependence on external
conditions. Such unselfish emotions as sympathy and pity
were included in this condemnation, and the destruction
of all feeling was therefore urged. The ideal state was
declared to be that of apathy or *non*-feeling, the state most
favorable to the exercise of reason. Now while the Stoics
thus agreed with the Cynics in identifying the Good with
the exercise of reason and the suppression of feeling, they
were able to give a new interpretation to the " life according to reason," which in its turn communicated a new and
more positive meaning to their conception of freedom, and
finally served to soften and humanize their whole doctrine.
According to this new insight, man's reason is merely an
expression of the Universal Reason, that rational principle
which pervades the universe and determines the meaning
and purpose of everything within it. In obeying his
reason man is but conforming to the rational order of
the world: he is playing his part in the universal scheme
of things. Life according to reason thus means life according to nature. The freedom that man gains through the
exercise of reason is not merely negative, a relief from
domination by external objects and forces, it is positive
freedom, the freedom of self-expression and self-development. For as much reality as a man possesses he derives

Zeno had Phœnician blood, which is thought by some historians to
account partially for the ascetic tendency in his philosophy. He went
to Athens at the age of twenty-two and became a pupil of the Cynic,
Crates. Later on he founded a school of his own, which, because
of its meeting-place, the Stoa Pœcile, was called the Stoic School.

from the universe. Hence in the degree to which the human individual discharges the part assigned to him in the Universal Purpose he achieves reality himself and furthers his own development. Thus the Stoics were led to believe that every person has a duty to perform in the world, and this belief tended to counteract the self-centered and exclusive character of their intellectualism. Moreover, if all men are expressions of the Universal Reason they are in an important sense equal in worth and dignity. This was recognized particularly in later Stoicism, where we have the principle of human brotherhood, if not explicitly realized, at least clearly suggested, in the lofty conception of a city of God which should unite all humanity in the bonds of a common citizenship. This increasing humanitarianism served to soften the earlier harshness and severity of the school, developing a sense of justice and toleration, and producing in its later development such upright and noble characters as Epictetus and Marcus Aurelius. While often the Stoic's " city of humanity " was to him but a vision, to be realized—if ever—only in some world to come, yet this vision did not fail to influence his conduct in the present world. Hence Stoicism was the most potent force working for moral and social improvement in the Roman Empire, and it aided in effecting many important reforms, particularly in ameliorating the condition of classes that were oppressed, such as slaves and subject-peoples.

5. **The Truth of Rationalism: Reason (a) As a Distinctively Human Faculty.**—The question now arises concerning the truth in Rationalism; for as a theory of the Good it must be subjected to the same critical scrutiny as was Hedonism. Such a critical study will justify the conclusion that Rationalism, if not the whole truth regarding the *summum bonum,* is at least a large part of it. In the first place, it creates a presumption in favor of Rationalism that it finds man's good in the exercise and

development of a faculty distinctively human. The animals possess the same senses that man does and they have, we believe, similar sensations. The animals also experience the fundamental feelings and emotions, seeking to prolong those which are pleasant and to avoid the painful. But man alone among living species possesses the faculty of reason, the power of self-conscious intelligence, with the ability to judge and to generalize, to imagine and to infer. The possession of this rational faculty has been rightly regarded as a distinguishing mark of the human species. Is it not reasonable then to conclude that the Good which must completely satisfy human nature will consist primarily of the exercise and development of this faculty? Certainly the argument of Aristotle on this point has lost none of its force. Man's Good, he maintains, must reside in the exercise of his proper function as man. What is the proper function of man? It cannot be mere life, involving the processes of nutrition and reproduction; since these activities are shared by plants as well as animals, and man's proper function must be peculiar to himself. Neither can it lie in sensation; for the life of sense and feeling is shared with the animal. It must therefore reside in the exercise of that capacity which man alone possesses, his Reason. " The function of man then is an activity of soul in accordance with reason," [2] and his Good is a life that is virtuous because controlled by reason.

Aristotle's reasoning here is wholly sound and a sufficient refutation of views at present widespread which find in the fact of evolution a justification for Naturalism and Hedonism in Ethics. Because man is the result of a long evolution from the lower forms of life and has the same origin as they—so the argument runs—the part of his nature which he shares in common with the other animal

---

[2] *Nicomachean Ethics of Aristotle*, trans. by Welldon, Bk. I, Chap. VI, p. 16.

species is the essential part. His Good will then consist in the satisfaction of these primary instincts which express his fundamental organic needs, for food, drink, shelter, clothing, offspring, etc. This reasoning is fallacious from the standpoint of evolution itself. For how does a species evolve—through the accentuation of what is common to it and other lower species from which it has sprung, or of what is peculiar to it and serves to distinguish it from these lower forms? Certainly the latter; and as it is in evolution universally, so it is with man. If he is to continue his evolution, to progress still farther on the upward road that has already elevated him above all living species, it must be by the exercise and development of those powers of intellect and will peculiar to himself. In this connection it is curious to observe persons interested in the doctrine of socialism attempting to find a scientific basis for the ideal of human brotherhood in the biological fact that all men are the outcome of the same evolutionary process and have in common the same fundamental instincts and impulses. Such thinkers seem to forget that as a creature of instinct man, like the other natural species, is subject to the law of natural selection, and his evolution is accomplished through ruthless competition and the survival of the fittest. Furthermore, it is only through the increasing power and efficacy of his reason that man is able to substitute for the blind action of natural selection with its tremendous waste the intelligent action of social selection which has for its conscious aim the highest human welfare. Human evolution, both social and moral, demands that we

> " Arise and fly
> The reeling faun, the sensual feast,
> Move upward, working out the beast
> And let the ape and tiger die." [3]

[3] TENNYSON: *In Memoriam*, CXVIII.

**6. (b) As Extending the View of Man to Include a World of Objects and Events.**—Reason is thus important in human life because it extends the view of man beyond the present, to embrace both past and future within a unified experience. While the animal is, we suppose, confined almost exclusively to the sensation of the moment, man may survey his life as a whole, seeing the present as the outcome of the past, and the future as the result of them both. We may therefore count it as the second point in favor of Rationalism that it is man's intellect which introduces him into a new and larger world of permanent objects in fixed and necessary relationships. For man's view is extended to past and future only through his capacity to revive by-gone events and experiences in the form of ideas, seeing these in their connection with each other and with the present situation. Our thought is not content, moreover, to accept every connection of events as it happens to be given, but seeks to discover what connections are fixed and necessary. Thus we gain an insight into the causes of things which holds for the future as well as for the past and present, enabling us to predict with much certainty what the future has in store, and to act accordingly. Through the work of thought the conscious life of man gains a totally new significance. His present experience and surroundings are seen as part of an orderly world of objects and events, of persons and forces, which are interacting and interdependent. To the animal a famine means only certain present sensations, such as hunger and weakness. But man through his power of thought sees it in the light of past experience and previous knowledge as an event in a complex system, the result of drouth, perhaps, whose more frequent occurrence is due to the denudation of watersheds, which in its turn is a result of careless or corrupt administration—and so on through a net-work of causes which has no end, but which if followed far enough would include all the forces and factors in the universe.

Now it cannot be doubted that if we as voluntary agents are to gain any true satisfaction from life, we must cultivate and develop that power of intelligence within us which shows us our position as permanent individuals in an orderly universe, and our relations to other individuals and objects included within the system. Thus only can we hope to achieve our aims, choosing those objects as means which are bound in the nature of things to produce the ends we desire. Spencer, himself a Hedonist of the evolutionary school, shows appreciation of the importance of reason in this capacity of guide to action when he says that the evolution of conduct has been throughout accompanied by an increasing control of " presentative " by " representative " feelings. " Throughout the ascent from low creatures up to man, and from the lowest types of man up to the highest, self-preservation has been increased by the subordination of simple excitations to compound excitations—the subjection of immediate sensations to the ideas of sensations to come—the overruling of presentative feelings by representative feelings, and of representative by re-representative feelings. As life has advanced the accompanying sentiency has become increasingly ideal; and among feelings produced by the compounding of ideas, the highest, and those which have evolved latest, are the re-compounded or doubly ideal. Hence it follows that as guides the feelings have authorities proportionate to the degrees in which they are removed by their complexity and their ideality from simple sensations and appetites."[4]

But reason, in its work of organizing human experience, is not limited to tracing the necessary sequence of events, and thus to the discovery of causes and effects. It also

[4] SPENCER: *Data of Ethics*, Chap. VII, § 42.

takes cognizance of the likenesses and differences of things, and classifies them on this basis. This work of cataloguing objects on ground of their qualitative similarity is in general of great importance to conduct; for thereby we systematize our world and are able to deal effectively with the endless diversity of things which it contains. One of its applications has, however, a peculiar and far-reaching significance for Ethics. In this case, man himself becomes the subject of classification. Through his own thought man sees himself as a member of the class of human beings, as one human individual among many. Thus he is enabled to view himself objectively, impartially. When he passes judgment on himself so considered, as merely a human person, an individual man, this judgment will apply equally to all other human beings, it will be *valid universally*. Now if we are to make the most of our given human capacities in a world of fixed conditions and definite facts, clearly we must often take the impartial and objective attitude towards ourselves, and reach conclusions concerning our conduct which are universally true. But such objectivity and universality can only be attained if we substitute for the warmth of feeling and the color of sense the " dry, white light of reason "—if we quiet the clamor of impulse, while we seek in the clarity of thought to view our case " steadily and view it whole." It was this fact, that only through reason do we reach precepts and principles that are valid universally, which profoundly impressed Immanuel Kant, the leading Rationalist of modern times. Inclination and desire he regarded as essentially subjective, since their objects are sought as means to individual happiness. The Good, on the contrary, consists in the conformity of the human will to the law of reason which, in contrast to inclination, is valid universally and is always an end in itself, never a means to anything else.

### 7. (c) As Enlarging the Experience of Man to Embrace the Lives and Personalities of Others.—Reason

performs another valuable service which deserves mention as a third consideration in favor of the theory which finds man's chief good in intellectual activity. Reason enables the individual to interpret the action and expression of others, and thus to gain an insight into their personal characteristics—theirs aims, motives, and abilities. We often overlook the part played by reason and imagination in all altruistic action. The sole requisite for such action —we are apt to think—is the proper state of " will " and feeling, the willingness to lend a helping hand, and the feeling of sympathy and fellowship. As for the needs and abilities of others, can we not observe them clearly and easily? Yet this is precisely what we cannot do. We cannot observe directly the conscious life or personality of another human being besides ourselves. The actions, words, and facial expressions of others may be thus observed, but not their motives, ambitions, or sentiments. The individual must interpret what he sees others do, and hears them say, in terms of his own conscious experience, and thus arrive at an understanding of their personal attributes and abilities. This work of interpreting the inner and unseen from its outward and visible manifestation can be done only by reason and imagination. Such interpretation is necessary, however, if there is to be any genuine coöperation or real helpfulness among men in society. For how is one man to serve another unless he knows his needs, and how coöperate with him unless he understands his nature?

Failure to recognize this necessity—that of understanding the thoughts and feelings of others—has caused many a well-meant act of kindness to go astray and do harm rather than good. Persons whose intentions are of the best are often condemned as meddlesome and officious because, having no knowledge of others' desires and sentiments, they ride rough-shod over them. If one is to do as he would be done by, he must make the intellectual effort to put himself in another's place. This requires *thought*—to understand the *alter's* conditions and surroundings—and *imagination*, to represent what his thoughts and feelings are in these circumstances. And not only is it necessary that we in this way project ourselves into others' lives, interpreting them in terms of our own conscious experience, but it is equally necessary that we make due allowance for differences between ourselves and them. This puts a still greater tax upon our powers of intelligence. Sufficient regard must be paid to the essential identity between self and others as fellow-workers or fellow-citizens, or even like human beings, and at the same time recognition must be made of differences of race, age, sex, and finally, most critical of all, of individuality. The non-observance of these differences of personal character and standpoint is a frequent source of misunderstanding and discord in social relations. This is particularly noticeable in domestic relations, where the husband, notwithstanding kindness of intention and genuine affection, offends and alienates the wife through failure to recognize that her sex gives her a standpoint fundamentally different from his own, and the parent becomes estranged from the child because of a failure to remember that youth has its own thoughts and desires, its own code of honor and attitude toward the world. Merely to understand one's friends and acquaintances with their varying characteristics sets a severe task for the rational and imaginative faculty. But only reason can accomplish it, and hence should be trained for the task. A recent writer urges that such training be made a part of the moral instruction of youth. He says: "It is of highest importance to recognize the place filled by imagination in moral development. Although no doubt this power may be used as an instrument of self-interest, it is in its nature antagonistic to egoism. We cannot easily look forward without letting our vision stray on one side or the other of the track of our own immediate personality. While selfish desires may be pursued with a minimum of prevision, even the rudiments of sympathetic feelings are impossible without a considerable measure of representative activity. The first task of the moral instructor, then, is clearly to feed the springs of imaginative sympathy to enable the child to put himself in the place of all those whom his actions may affect." [5]

8. **The Faults of Rationalism: (a) It Encourages Injurious Asceticism.**—Since reason is the faculty which raises man above the lower orders by revealing to him his place as a conscious individual in a world of inter-related objects and events, and by giving him an insight into the lives and characters of his fellow-men, it is not surprising that many moralists have found the *summum bonum* in its exercise and development. Just because so much may be said in favor of Rationalism, however, our criticism must be particularly searching and severe that its many merits may not blind us to its possible shortcomings.

We have already seen that in the logic of ethical development Rationalism arises as a protest against the continued domination of feeling and sense over human conduct. Hence the Rationalist thinks of intellectual activity as essentially opposed to the life of pleasure and sensuous gratification. Now no one can deny that the suppression of unruly passion and the regulation of wayward impulse is the indispensable condition of all moral attainment. Natural appetites and animal desire are strong within us, and there is no hope for the development of spiritual capacities unless these are curbed and controlled. Moral development is achieved through struggle, and he has but

---

[5] JAMES OLIPHANT: "Moral Instruction," *International Journal of Ethics*, July, 1906, p. 408.

a superficial understanding of its nature who would min-
imize the importance in it of self-development and self-
denial. The strictest control or even complete suppression
of natural impulse is justified if required to give intelligence a hearing. Even when there is no such special need
it may be wise to practise self-denial and to discipline our
natural appetites so that our control over them may be
greater in case of emergency. In this sense of spiritual
exercise, of moral athletics, *asceticism* is to be highly com-
mended. Thus Professor James, in an oft-quoted passage,
advises us to keep the faculty effort alive in us by a
little gratuitous exercise every day.[6]

But when an ethical theory makes such opposition to
man's natural desires and appetites its absorbing interest,
and treats the suppression of feeling, not as a means, but
as an end, the situation alters. Rationalism has shown a
constant tendency to go to this length—to condemn all the
pleasures of sense and to concentrate itself upon the destruction of natural feeling and emotion. Thus, in spite
of its many merits which one should not fail to recognize, it
has been primarily *negative,* not positive, in its attitude,
being characterized, not by what it enjoined men to *do,* but
to *refrain from doing.* Now, no theory whose recommendations are mainly negative can be accepted as the final solution of the ethical problem. It is necessarily limited by its
negation—being driven by its opposition, to a view nearly as
extreme and untenable as that of its opponent. It is not
unfair to say that there is inherent in Rationalism the tendency toward such an extreme—an extreme of asceticism
which condemns all the natural desires and gratifications
of human life as unworthy and evil, and which, when fully
developed—as in the Middle Ages—is as false in theory
and as injurious in practice as any form of Hedonism
could be. It is this kind of asceticism which Spencer

---

[6] JAMES: *Principles of Psychology,* Vol. I, p. 126.

attacks, calling it a product of devil-worship—of the worship of deities who are thought to take pleasure in human privation and suffering.[7]

The fact that such injurious asceticism is recommended by Rationalism of the extreme type and encouraged by its moderate forms must count as a serious charge against the theory. The mind of the present rightfully disapproves of the hostility to nature, the contempt for the flesh, that is implied in this asceticism. An attitude of this kind can be justified only by a philosophy which holds matter and the material to be essentially evil. But such a view is impossible to the thought of to-day which has accepted the evolutionary interpretation of the universe. From this standpoint all of human nature is the product of the evolutionary process. Some of man's faculties he received already developed from animal progenitors: others existed only in germ in the lower forms, their development being peculiar to man. But this fact furnishes no ground for making an absolute separation between the two, condemning the former as material and exalting the latter as spiritual. Instead we must regard all as alike natural and their difference one of degree only. Now as natural, man's sensuous impulses and " fleshly " desires may rightfully claim a share of his attention and a measure of gratification. The desire for food and drink and play, the impulse of sex and parenthood—all these are part of normal human nature. Hence the attainment of their objects is a necessary part of the satisfaction of man's will; and without it human volition will go unsatisfied. Moreover, certain of these sensuous impulses constitute the roots from which spring some of the most esteemed " spiritual " gifts. Thus the instincts of sex and sympathy are the source of altruistic qualities that distinguish the finest character. The instinct of combat is the source of those tendencies to rivalry

[7] SPENCER: *Data of Ethics*, §§14, 38.

and emulation which in their higher forms make the most effective spurs to personal achievement. One who, in mistaken moral zeal, exterminates any of these impulses does a double wrong to his human nature—he mutilates it by depriving it of one of its natural means of expression, and also stunts its future growth by destroying forces germinal to further development. Finally it is worth noting that such asceticism usually fails of its aim to remove from the mind all sensuous desire. The very effort to " crucify the body," to " mortify the flesh," results in over-attention to the pleasures of sense—not the normal and wholesome desire that is present at times and then gives place to other interests—but a morbid and unwholesome lingering of the mind upon the details of joys at once repugnant and fascinating. One of the most unpleasant chapters in the literature of monasticism is that telling of the visions of carnal pleasure and sensuous delight which were constantly tantalizing monk and hermit when alone in the cell to which they had fled to secure relief from the distractions of the world and opportunity for uninterrupted prayer and meditation.

9. (b) It Justifies Extreme Intellectualism.—Rationalism maintains that man finds his highest good in withdrawing his attention from those objects of sense that give him present pleasure and directing it upon the principles and conceptions of reason. Now these ideals of reason and imagination pertain to the future and the larger world of persons and principles. Hence they are different from the objects of sense and feeling which are confined to the present state or past experience of the individual. The Rationalist accentuates this difference by opposing the freedom and range of thought to the strict limitations of feeling. But the objects of sense and feeling, if limited in their scope, at least possess actuality. And here also the contrast which the Rationalist makes between feeling and

thought holds in all its severity. The principles and conceptions of thought, although their range may be as wide as the universe, do not possess this actuality. They may represent a condition better and more satisfactory than the actual but, as thoughts and ideas, they merely represent it, they do not realize it. Thought and imagination soar free from the limitations of the present and the actual, but the penalty they pay is that the world they inhabit is unactual and, in a sense, unreal. Thus the man who finds his Good simply in thinking about the ideal, in reasoning out plans for his own betterment, is justly criticised as a *mere* idealist, or even condemned as a visionary. He is dwelling in a world of his own thought and imagination and failing to give his nature the satisfaction it demands in *actual experience*. Moreover, when this absorption in intellectual activity is carried beyond a certain point it seems definitely hostile to any actual attainment; for it seeks, as the condition most favorable to its own existence, seclusion from the world of practical affairs and human intercourse. Thus the individual finds his Good in the life of secluded contemplation. That Rationalism encourages absorption in thought at the expense of actual attainment must be reckoned a grave fault. And there can be no question but that the logic of the theory leads towards such a barren intellectualism. The historical development of Rationalism in ancient and mediæval times abundantly proves it. Plato, with his artist's soul and dislike of extremes, despite a feeling for the beauty of a harmonious and symmetrical development of human nature, was impelled by his rationalistic premises to praise most highly the life of the philosopher who, removed from the distractions of the world, pursues without interruption his philosophic meditations. The same premise, that man's Good lies in the supremacy of reason in his life, leads Aristotle, notwithstanding his notable good sense and sagacity in dealing with all matters of practical morality, to esteem most worthy the speculative life. The greatest defect in Stoicism was that it encouraged aloofness from the world and self-absorption. The monasticism of the Middle Ages found justification in a rationalistic philosophy which condemned the material world and the desires of the flesh as evil and sought salvation in meditation and prayer, rather than in the teachings of Jesus. It is this tendency of Rationalism—the tendency to oppose to the doctrine which finds the Good in the pleasure of present attainment, another doctrine equally abstract and one-sided which asserts that the Good lies in thinking about larger ends and aims to be achieved in the future,—which Hegel roundly condemns in his Logic. The larger ends and ideals of reason constitute "that ought-to-be on the strength of which reflection is vain enough to treat the actual present with scorn and to point to a scene beyond—a scene which is assumed to have place and being only in the understanding of those who talk of it."[8] The Rationalistic position is a striking example of the false infinite which exists as merely the negative of the finite, and hence is always limited by it. Rationalism is limited by its opposition to Empiricism or Hedonism. Against it the latter may always maintain "the great principle that whatever is true must be in the actual world and present to sensation." "Yet what may be called the laziness of thought, when dealing with this Supreme Idea, finds a too easy mode of evasion in the ought-to-be; instead of the actual realization of the ultimate end it clings hard to the disjunction of the notion from reality."[9]

10. (c) It Is Individualistic in Tendency.—Rationalism, as has been seen, recommends an asceticism which cuts the individual off from social relationships and human intercourse. It also encourages an intellectualism which

[8] HEGEL: *Shorter Logic*, § 38 (Wallace's trans., pp. 77-78).
[9] *Op. cit.*, § 55, p. 112.

causes him to seek the seclusion favorable to continued thought and study. The result of these two tendencies is to encourage a self-centered life which feels no social responsibility and discharges no political obligation. Thus Rationalism is as individualistic—as selfish, if you please—in its final implications as is Hedonism. We are all familiar with a certain type of intellectual culture which shrinks from the ordinary human relationships as if fearing contamination, and avoids the performance of social duty, lest its own refinement should be diminished thereby. Such a type of character is the legitimate offspring of Rationalism; for when we make intellectual activity man's chief good, then it becomes right for him to seek the most favorable conditions for its exercise. These conditions will not lie in the busy walks of life, in the adjustments and readjustments of the family relation, in the wear and tear of social intercourse, but in the quiet of some secluded and comfortable retreat from which the world may be viewed as a passing show.

Thus in conclusion it is interesting to behold the theories of Hedonism and Rationalism, extreme opposites though they are, brought by their equal one-sidedness into a kind of identity. Hedonism recommends a well-planned and prudent life in which mainly intellectual pleasures are sought because they endure the longer and have less pain in after-effect. Rationalism advises the exercise of reason in a life freed from the pressure of social obligations in order to afford the most favorable conditions for intellectual activity and culture. The Rationalist will be more austere and less sympathetic, the Hedonist more amiable but less resolute, while the lives of both will incline to be equally narrow and self-centered.

### REFERENCES

SETH, *Ethical Principles*, Part I, Chap. II.
HICKS, *Stoic and Epicurean*, Chaps. I, II, III, IV.

ZELLER, *Stoics, Epicureans and Sceptics*, Part II.
FITE, *Introductory Study of Ethics*, Part II.
SIDGWICK, *History of Ethics*, Chap. II, §§ 13-20.
BAKEWELL, *Source-book in Ancient Philosophy*, Chaps. XVII, XX, XXI.
SIDGWICK, *Methods of Ethics*, Book III.
HYDE, *Five Great Philosophies of Life*, Chap. II.

# CHAPTER IV

## VOLITION AS AN ORGANIZING AGENCY

1. Volition as an Organizing Agency.—2. Volition as the Synthetic Activity Comprehensive of Feeling and Thought.—3. Development of Volition: Involuntary Action,—4. Voluntary Action: (*a*) From Desire,—5. (*b*) From Purpose,—6. (*c*) From Ideal. —7. Volition as Creative of Self-conscious Personality.—8. Volition Does Not Always Effect Complete Organization,—9. But to That Extent Is Not Fully Developed.

1. **Volition as an Organizing Agency.**—The leading ethical theories, Hedonism and Rationalism, have now been reviewed and the problem of the Good is still unsolved. Neither theory when followed out provides for the complete satisfaction of the human will. Only one way is open to us, therefore,—that of approaching our problem directly, seeking first to discover the essential character of volition and then to infer from its character as thus disclosed what is required for its complete satisfaction.[1]

When we approach the problem in this way our study of Hedonism and Rationalism proves to have been far from fruitless. Both of these theories throw light upon the character of volition, for both reflect essential aspects of this activity. Hedonism expresses its demand for success in present attainment, but would secure such success at the cost of limiting strictly the objects which it seeks to attain. Rationalism voices its demand for a larger range of objects to pursue, but at the expense of making these objects mere thoughts and leaving them unrealized. How can these two demands be met without the corresponding disadvantages? How can the will be assured of enjoying

[1] Compare Part I, Chap. II, § 3.

the success of present achievement without restricting itself
to objects which present perception or past experience
guarantee will furnish such satisfaction? And how can
the will overcome this restriction and direct itself upon the
larger objects of thought and imagination without abandoning the actual world for the realm of the ideal and
merely possible? Clearly, only when it takes a third step
and endeavors to convert the ideal into actuality. This
is accomplished by making the present act a means to the
realization of the principles and conceptions of reason. The
realization may be distant and the present act contribute
but little toward it, yet the two, actual present and ideal
future, are joined in a close and vital connection. This,
the third aspect of voluntary activity, is therefore a synthesis of the other two, which transcends and at the same
time unites them. Present achievement is rendered more
satisfactory because it is no longer restricted in its range
as to object, but extends to the most inclusive and far-
reaching ends. On the other hand, our knowledge of these
larger aims and ideals is increased and made more definite
by our experience in progressively realizing them. The
two aspects of will which at first appeared to conflict, its
demand for present attainment, and its demand for the
greatest range of choice among objects, now prove to be
complementary and inter-dependent. All this is evidence
that we now behold volition with its nature fully expressed.
As thus viewed, it reveals itself as an activity of adjustment, by which the various activities of the individual
are adjusted, or correlated, with one another—or, better, an *organizing agency*, whereby the successive acts
of the self are related as means to deliberately chosen
ends.

2. **Volition as the Synthetic Activity Comprehensive
of Feeling and Thought.**—Let us consider a little further
this organizing activity of will, with particular reference

to the part played in it by feeling and thought. An ordinary instance of volition will illustrate clearly how its organizing work is carried on. Suppose that a young man is intending to devote an evening to amusement in such company as he knows will furnish good-fellowship and pleasure. He happens to think, however, of a leading purpose of life, to prepare himself for a certain profession in which he hopes to win distinction, and, as he thinks, he begins to wonder uneasily if he is making his evenings contribute as they might to the realization of his purpose. In this connection there occurs to his mind the notice he has seen of a lecture to be given this very evening upon a subject relating to his proposed profession. He recognizes that attendance upon this lecture would further his life-purpose, and hence, contrary to inclination, he gives his attention wholly to the idea of it, goes, and remains an interested listener. The consequence of his thus acting in accordance with his larger purpose is that he gains new knowledge which makes this purpose clearer and more effective in his life, besides the encouragement which results from having taken a step in its actual realization. We see, then, that the young man—and the case is of course typical of all volition—through the exercise of will takes his evening's action out of its isolation and makes it a means to the attainment of a larger end which he has chosen to pursue. To adjust actions as means to larger ends, in this way, is to organize conduct. The particular act is given meaning through its subordination to the ruling purpose, while the purpose is made real through the instrumentality of the particular act.

When volition is thus conceived as an organizing agency, it appears as the all-comprehensive activity of intelligent life, including within its unity both feeling and thought, and assigning to each its proper place. Feeling is subjective and expresses the actual state of the self, a state of

pleasure when in possession of sought-for objects.[2]  Thought
is objective and represents the ideal conditions of a larger
life in the conception of objects as yet unattained.  These
two factors come into conflict and opposition.  Thought, by
representing new and greater possibilities of achievement,
destroys the unity and equilibrium signified by pleasant
feeling.  Then, through action, the new objects thought of
are attained and the unity of the self is felt to be restored
and increased by the possession of a greater variety of
objects.  Volition is the synthetic activity which includes
within its scope all these lesser activities of feeling, thought,
and action.  These minor factors exist only in so far as
they contribute to the main work of organization.  Hence
we see that it is absurd to regard volition as subordinate
either to feeling or to thought.  Volition is not the servant
of feeling, limited to seeking those objects whose possession
is sure to increase *pleasure*.  For the circle of such objects
is small, and, to obtain satisfaction, volition must go beyond
it in pursuit of objects whose pleasure-yielding capacity is
doubtful and uncertain.  Neither is volition the servant of
thought, limited to the *idea* of larger achievement, or to
the mechanical reproduction of a program of action previously thought out in every detail.  For thought, as
thought, does not communicate actuality to its objects, nor
can it anticipate with exactness the actual future.  But
volition demands actual achievement and must therefore
advance on its own initiative to grapple with a future
uncertain both as to feeling and fact.  Volition is essentially
a *venture*—a venture into the unknown.  To a degree reason

[2] " Hence in the case of happiness the subject takes the first place,
in the case of truth the object; there we have a vigorous concentration, here an unlimited expansion, there an expression, here
a repression of vital emotion.  From the point of view of the desire
for happiness the struggle for truth may easily appear cold and life-
less, while from the point of view of the latter the former may appear
narrow and selfish."—EUCKEN: *Philosophy of Spirit*, Eng. trans.,
1909, p. 276.

may direct, and feeling impel, but never to the extent of absolutely pre-determining what shall come to pass. The individual must surrender objects which assure him satisfaction in order to seek other more remote and far-reaching ends. It is true that these ends when achieved may afford a fuller satisfaction than those sacrificed to them, but this can be ascertained only by making the sacrifice—by taking the venture. An element of uncertainty is bound to remain, and from this fact it follows that, not pure reason, but rational faith, an effort of will guided by intelligence but transcending the limits of proof or demonstrable certainty, is the primary requisite of intelligent life and action. Every act of will brings an experience that is entirely fresh and unique and yields some results that possess absolute novelty. The occurrence of what is absolutely new, and hence cannot be anticipated is a distinguishing characteristic of all life. From it springs the necessity for faith in one's self and the courage to venture, and upon it rests the possibility of real spiritual growth and achievement through such exercise of volition.

3. **Development of Volition—Involuntary Action, Instinctive and Impulsive.**—If further evidence is needed to prove that volition is essentially an organizing agency, it is furnished by a survey of the different forms which this activity takes in the course of human development.

The earliest actions of the human individual are not voluntary if we understand action to be voluntary which is directed towards a consciously chosen end.[3] They have not even a conscious motive. Man is born with certain *instincts*—modifications of his nervous system which cause him to react in a definite manner to specific stimuli. Some

[3] For the account given of the development of volition in this and the following sections the writer is indebted to the standard psychologies of James, Titchener, and Stout, but is under special obligations to Höffding: *Outline of Psychology*, and Baldwin: *Social and Ethical Interpretations in Mental Development*.

object or influence of the outer world is usually the stimulus to which the instinct is keyed, and the action by which the organism responds to such stimulation is called *instinctive*. When a pencil or the handle of a rattle is laid in the hand of a very young infant, and the tiny fingers move and close around the object, we have an example of such instinctive action. The infant does not perceive the pencil or rattle, much less act with the intention of grasping it. Instinctive action is then originally without conscious motive. But with its repetition—and as the result of it—comes a growing consciousness of the object. The numerous pressures and strains that accompany the instinctive movement, and the pleasure or pain which is consequent upon it, associate themselves with the group of sensations set up by the original stimulus, cause them to be distinguished from the confused contents of consciousness, and finally to be given *meaning* as a definite object. Thus the babe comes to perceive the rattle or colored pencil and, when he puts out his hand for it, his movement is prompted by an idea of the object. His action now has a conscious impulse.

Action which is thus initiated by the perception or image of an object may be called *impulsive*. The number of objects which are thus perceived and may become motives of action rapidly increases in the early period of mental development. Each of the instincts dominant at this time leads to the perception of a class of articles constituting its objective stimuli. Thus the different kinds of food, a variety of playthings, etc., are consciously recognized and induce action. Then besides these instincts which are directed upon objects of a specific nature, there is the instinct of imitation, whose stimulus is any movement of any object, but particularly the movements of other individuals. Through the operation of this instinct the child learns to distinguish different people by their characteristic behavior which he has imitated, and from this imitation comes also to know something of his own strength and capacity. Moreover, in addition to an increasing knowledge of the nature of objects, we find at this period—as Baldwin points out—an increasing sense of their *worth*. The pleasure or pain which results from seeking an object attaches to the idea of this object and determines its power as an incentive to action. Objects are sought in the degree to which their suggestions are pleasurable, and avoided to the extent in which they have painful associations.

While impulsive action has a conscious motive, it is nevertheless not truly voluntary. It is action in pursuit of a consciously-perceived object. But it is not action in pursuit of a *consciously chosen end*. In true volition the object is not merely known, but known as the end of action. This is not the case with impulsive action. The impulse is only the instinct raised to clear consciousness, and is still dominated by the object. As Baldwin remarks concerning this type of action in the child,[4] " The object before him fills up his consciousness; he thinks nothing about it, he simply thinks it. His action goes out in channels of inherited tendency, directly upon the object."[5] In order that an object be a " chosen end," as in voluntary action, it must, in contrast to this, first be distinguished as ideal and future from what is actual and present, and, second, be distinguished from other ideal possibilities as the one required to satisfy the self.[6] Green says, speaking of desire, to him the typical form of volition, " The common characteristic of every such desire is its direction to an object consciously presented as not yet real and of which the realization would satisfy, i.e. extinguish the desire."[7]

[4] BALDWIN: *Mental Development: Social and Ethical Interpretations*, p. 369.
[5] *Op. cit.*, p. 366.
[6] HÖFFDING: *Outline of Psychology*, Eng. trans., p. 322.
[7] GREEN: *Prolegomena to Ethics*, § 131.

Before volition can arise, therefore, there must be ability to distinguish between the present and actual, on the one hand, and the ideal and merely possible, on the other. In contrast to the world of actual objects present to perception with nature and relations fixed, there must exist an ideal order, a world of free ideas in which the thought of the individual can range at will. This world of ideas, as it develops, represents the experience, abilities, and interests of the individual himself as distinguished from all objective conditions. Its development means the growth of self-consciousness and selfhood. With its appearance comes the possibility of acting to realize an end—an ideal chosen from among other ideal possibilities because the most satisfactory to the self—and thus of rising to the dignity of a voluntary agent.

The distinction between ideal and actual is, like all mental achievements, the result of a gradual process of growth. Ideal elements enter very soon into the experience of the individual in the form of memory-images. These images may constitute impulses to action just as do perceptions. Thus the clinking of spoon and glass calls up an image of the nursing bottle to the infant consciousness and prompts the same actions that the actual sight of the bottle would. If the prompting of an idea inwardly aroused (in distinction from a perception) sufficed to make an act voluntary, we should have volition very early in mental development. Animals are frequently moved to action by images rather than by perceptions, as when the dog which has been fed two mornings from the step behind the house begins to leap and bark when he sees the door opened on the third morning. But it is requisite to volition that the idea be recognized as in its ideality different from the perception, and at first this does not occur; the images simply fuse with the perceptions. As development proceeds, however, this fusion becomes less close

and complete—at least in the experience of the human individual.[8] The image when revived brings with it numerous associated images which, continuing for an interval of
time, serve to interrupt and dislocate the regular order
and sequence of perceptions from the outer world. Thus
the two series, inner and outer, ideal and actual, each having its own order and relation, tend to break apart and
run separately. But, as Höffding believes, probably the distinction between idea and actuality is first consciously made
as the result of the unpleasant experience of finding that
an idea, when acted upon as always in the past, does not
have the same result in the present, owing to change in
actual conditions. Thus the child seeing the whiteness of
the snow has an image of sugar called up, and, acting upon
it, fills his mouth with the cold substance. Such experiences, with their unpleasantness, teach him effectually the
distinction between ideas or memories and actual objects
and conditions. Thus " the first basis is laid of the contrast between possibility and actuality. Then only the free
ideas enter into a relation of definite contrast to sensation
and percept." [9]

With this distinction once made the individual becomes
capable of voluntary action, i.e. action in pursuit of a
consciously chosen end. When the implications of volition
are thus drawn out and stated, it may seem to be an involved and complicated activity. Yet in its actual exercise
it is direct and simple enough. The three-year-old, who
leaves his play out of doors, enters the house, and, disre-
garding everything else, goes to his mother and says, " I
want an apple to eat," fulfils in his behavior all the requirements of true volition. The object of his action, the
apple, he distinguishes as ideal from all actual objects

---

[8] Höffding gives a full and illuminating account of the growth
of the distinction between ideal and actual in his *Outline of Psychology,* Eng. trans., pp. 122-33.

[9] HÖFFDING: *Op. cit.,* p. 133.

present to his perception, and he disregards them for it. He also distinguishes this idea and prefers it as an end to all other ideal possibilities—it is the apple he desires, not bread, or sweet-meats, or any other eatable. In the formation of this ideal order which the individual learns to distinguish from the actual world and to identify with himself, two factors deserve especial mention. The first is that of imitation. Through imitating others the individual acquires, in addition to his ideas of objects that give pleasure, conceptions of various activities which yield him satisfaction.[10] The second is language. The human individual is able in the manner indicated to construct an ideal order which has permanence and unity largely because of the faculty of language which he possesses. Through the use of words he gives body and definition to ideas which otherwise would be too tenuous to persist in memory and too shifting to enter into any permanent relationships.

4. **Voluntary Action: (a) From Desire.**—The first stage in the development of volition is that of *desire*. Action from desire has for its end the present attainment of some single object.[11] An idea of the object in question has been produced by past experience in the mind of the individual. That idea has acquired interest and value because in the past its object has given satisfaction to some need or capacity. That idea now becomes an end of action which the individual consciously seeks to realize. The object of desire, although single, may vary greatly in its meaning and importance. The apple sought by the child in the simple illustration just used and the rare book or picture sought by the art collector, the flower by the roadside, and the great mansion are, equally, in their way, objects of desire. Action from desire differs from instinctive

---

[10] BALDWIN: *Op. cit.*, p. 34.
[11] BALDWIN: *Op. cit.*, p. 372, and HÖFFDING: *Op. cit.*, p. 323.

or impulsive action not so much in the nature of the object as in the relation of the object to the self. Previous to the appearance of desire, the action of the individual is determined by the objects and forces of the environment, as they play upon his different instincts and impulses. Not the individual is acting, but the forces of nature are acting through him.[12] But in desire, the first form of voluntary action, all this is changed. The individual seeks an object thought of as an end to be realized, and, consequently set in sharp opposition to the world of objects, actually existing.[13] He resists the appeal of externally existent objects to his instincts in order to pursue this end, which, of all the ideal possibilities of the situation, appeals most to himself. Through effort he overcomes the opposition between ideal and actual, by making the ideal actual, by realizing his end.[14] Thus actual objects and conditions are determined by the self and not *vice versa*. The effect of desire is to release the actions of the human individual from their subservience to various external objects and to make them means to ends chosen by himself. Thus the different acts are all made instrumental to self-expression, and the first step is taken in the organization of conduct.

5. **(b) Action from Purpose.**—With the growth of intelligence single objects are grouped, according to their affinities, into more or less comprehensive classes; general ideas or concepts are formed which include a number of particular perceptions.[15] Volition, in the next stage of its

[12] GREEN: *Op. cit.*, § 91.    [13] *Ibid.*, § 131.

[14] Alexander in his account of desire emphasizes the conflict which it involves between ideal and actual, ideal end and actual conditions. He describes desire as consisting in "a feeling of tension which may be described as a sense of disparity between the ideal object and the actual state of the agent." (ALEXANDER: *Moral Order and Progress*, Bk. I, Chap. I, § 3, p. 22.)

[15] As Alexander says, while each desire is a single particular in mental history, in content it includes many qualities which as universals serve to connect it with the content of other desires. (*Op. cit.*, p. 65, also p. 100.)

development, has for its end the attainment of such classes of objects, the realization—that is—of these general ideas. For the sake of clearness in distinction, desire has been defined as action whose end is the attainment of a single object. As a matter of fact, however, no hard and fast distinction can be made between actions whose object is particular and those whose object is general. Since it is a case of development the difference is always one of degree. The child who desires " something to eat " or " something to play with " is well on his way to the formation of general purposes. Such purposes appear, clearly conceived, as soon as infancy is passed and childhood fairly entered. The resolves of the boy to stand well in school, to gather bird's-eggs or stamps, or to learn to throw curves with a ball, are examples of such purposes. The boy who adopts one, seeks not a particular object to be attained in the present, but a group or series of objects whose attainment is prolonged into the future. Indeed, the object of present desire, in its relation to such a comprehensive group or series, becomes but one of many particulars. Like all particulars it is reduced to a subordinate position within the inclusive whole. Thus the eventual attainment of the larger end may mean the denial or limitation of present desire. This influence of the general over the particulars is soon manifest—for instance, in the case of the purpose to avoid punishment which, when once taken, imposes a strict limit on the gratification of present desire.

The second stage in the development of volition we may thus call purposive action. It is action in pursuit of a group of objects to be realized in the course of future time, rather than in pursuit of a single object to be realized now. The object in purposive action is always general, but may vary greatly in the range of its generality, the extent of its inclusiveness. One purpose, such as to do one's morning's work well, may embrace a comparatively few acts and extend over a little time; another—such as to preserve one's health—may extend over the whole of a lifetime and include thousands of acts. The purpose to secure wealth is representative. Its end is a general idea standing for a large group of objects—money, land, houses, clothing, jewels, etc. Its attainment usually occupies a period of time—often a lifetime. It requires the individual to restrict many of his particular desires for food, drink, clothing, amusement, and the like,—the attainment of the general purpose necessitating the strict subordination of all the particular acts. What, then, is the procedure of volition in purposive action? It is first to check the action of present desire and to turn the attention of the individual from the particular object he now craves to the more general object he purposes in the future to attain. The bearing of this larger purpose upon the present action is next considered, and finally the original desire is allowed just that degree of gratification which is consistent with the realization of the ruling purpose. Thus, through purpose, the second form of volition, the successive acts of the individual are taken out of their isolation as expressive of a variety of particular desires, and are related as means to the attainment of several general purposes,—the second step being thereupon taken in the organization of human conduct.

6. (c) **Action from Ideal.**—But thought can go beyond the ideation that yields the object of desire and the generalization that furnishes the object of purpose. It can take the material of experience, analyze it into its elements, and then by synthesis construct from it a new and significant conception. It is this constructive activity of thought, more or less freely exercised, that produces the *Ideal*, which constitutes the object of the next and highest form of volition. Through free ranging thought and imagination an end is created more comprehensive than the

particular object of desire or the general object of purpose. This end extends in its scope beyond the limits of the individual's life, and involves the effort and coöperation of many individuals. It is a *cause* to which the individual devotes himself rather than an object which he desires or a purpose which he pursues. It serves to identify him with his fellows and to make his very existence itself a means to the realization of universal ends. The discovery of truth is an example of such a cause or ideal to which many men in modern times have devoted themselves. Naturally these ideals appear later in mental development than do desire and purpose; for while their growth may be encouraged by teaching, they can become effective as ends of action only after the individual is able to interpret them in terms of his own experience and apply them to his own life. Hence they are only anticipated in early years—perhaps in the boy's passing fancy of himself as doing some noble work as President or Premier. The subsequent period of youth and adolescence is the great flowering time of ideals, when the young man sees himself serving humanity as patriot or explorer, artist or inventor, physician, lawyer, or teacher.

Through the adoption of an ideal as the ultimate end of action, volition completes the organization of conduct. Since the ideal is all-comprehensive and includes the individual himself, it also embraces all his life-purposes. These purposes are adjusted as means to the realization of the supreme ideal, just as previously the various desires were made means to the attainment of these larger purposes. Indeed, such a supreme end is needed as the final court of appeal between the conflicting claims of different purposes. In the specific instance the attainment of one ruling purpose might require the denial of a desire, the attainment of another its gratification, and what is to decide between the two unless a still larger end exists to which the purposes themselves are subordinated? When this is done, and the particular act performed with a view not merely to the attainment of a life-purpose of the individual, but also to the realization of his supreme ideal, we have volition in its fullest development. Here choice is preceded by full deliberation in which the consequences of alternative lines of action are carefully traced out and thus their bearing upon leading purposes of the individual is ascertained. The relation of these ruling purposes to the supreme ideal is next considered; and finally, returning from the universal to the particular, that act is chosen which promises to further the purpose most in harmony with the ideal.

7. **Volition as Creative of Self-conscious Personality.**—Volition proves to be, then, the formative and sustaining activity of conscious selfhood, or personality. Thinkers of to-day are agreed that the *self* is not a spiritual substance or entity which has permanent existence apart from the succession of mental states. Rather it is just the unity of these conscious states, the inter-relation of our different experiences, which gives to them unity and coherence as a whole.[16] Now it is volition that originates this unity among the contents of consciousness and maintains it through the appropriation and assimilation of new objects. In the initial period of mental development the materials of personality are accumulated in the form of memory-images of objects and activities. But these memories do not constitute a self until they are distinguished as ideal from the actual world, and, through the exercise of will, are made actual possessions of the self; for it is only through the realizing of its different ideas that the self becomes real. Then these various objects of *desire* are connected and inter-connected as means to ends, being thus subordinated to more comprehensive *purposes*. Finally

16 BALDWIN: *Op. cit.*, pp. 8, 374.

all the contents of consciousness are woven into one organized system when these purposes are made themselves instrumental to the realization of a supreme and all-inclusive *ideal*.

Thus the process through which the self develops is that followed by all life in its growth—evolution. Like all genuine evolutions, this organization of personality by volition has two aspects, differentiation and integration. When an object is chosen as an end of action, difference is introduced into the life of the self. Inasmuch as the object is an end for the self it exists within the unity of self-consciousness; but in so far as it is unattained it is at the same time external and opposed to the self in actual existence. Hence tension arises in the self and even pain, the pain of unsatisfied desire. This tension is relieved and the pain changed into pleasure when, through action and effort, the object is attained. In integration, the coördinate aspect, the difference is overcome and the object is appropriated by the self. Thus the unity of the self is restored, but with a richer and more varied content. In this way the development of the self proceeds through the agency of volition—ever expanding its boundaries to receive new objects, and by this very process strengthening and perfecting its own unity.

**8. Volition Does Not Always Effect Complete Organization.**—To the statement that volition is essentially an organizing agency the objection may be made that it does not in all cases actually manifest itself as such. In the conduct of the majority of men, volition fails signally to effect complete organization. The action of many never passes the first stage of unregulated desire, while comparatively few ever reach the final stage, where all action is governed by a few controlling purposes which are themselves subordinated to a supreme ideal. If volition does not inevitably and of necessity pass through these successive stages, what right have we to assert that a law inherent in its nature causes it to follow this development, effecting a more and more complete organization of conduct? To this objection the reply may be made that there can be no doubt of the fact that in actual life volition often fails to organize action completely. The only question is: How serious a difficulty does this fact constitute for the view that volition is *in its essential nature* an organizing activity? The difficulty, such as it is, is really but a particular aspect of a more general problem upon which Paulsen [17] remarks, as confronting all theories which identify the Highest Good with the full expression of the human will. If the normal human will finds complete and natural expression in the thoughtful and well-regulated action which we usually call *good,* how does it happen that the actual will of man seems usually to rebel against such action? Can organization and adjustment be regarded as the truest manifestations of will when it appears most flourishing and vigorous in the demand for unlimited power and unrestricted gratification?

9. **But to That Extent Is Not Fully Developed.**—The difficulty is not great in the present case, however. If we are seeking to discover the essential nature of volition, surely we must base our conclusions upon its fully developed form, and not upon phases of incomplete development. For only in its completed development shall we find the true character of volition revealed. In earlier stages of growth this remains largely latent and concealed. Now such is just the case when, in the lives of men, conduct remains unorganized. In that degree their wills fail of their normal development. To that extent, in fact, volition is absent from their lives. Such individuals, we correctly say, fail to " exercise their wills." And not being exercised their wills fail to display the larger possibilities they

---

[17] *Cf. System of Ethics,* Bk. II, Chap. I.

possess. Such cases of arrested development are sometimes
due to external causes, but oftener to the individuals themselves. Volition is an activity self-initiated and self-controlled. Its exercise and development require effort, the
effort of close attention, studious thought, and discriminating selection. Whether or not this effort is made depends
for the most part on the self. Of course the individual's
capacity for such effort may itself be referred back to his
will, his " will-power." But not in such a way as to make
the lack of organization in his life fairly chargeable to the
inherent nature of his will and not to himself. For the
whole point of the matter is that the individual's capacity
for " effort," his " will-power," is not fixed, having its
amount pre-determined by his heredity or some other cause
outside his control. Rather is his exercise of the power
of volition, and the increase in this power which follows
upon its exercise, determined by himself alone. It is, in
fact, identical with the power-to-be-a-self which, once present in germ, can, like all vital principles, be maintained
and strengthened only from within. But upon the actual
effort put forth depends the development of volition into
the fullness of its capacity as an organizing agency, and
upon this hangs the moral destiny of the human individual.
As Professor James says in a celebrated passage: " Thus
not only our morality, but our religion, so far as the latter
is deliberate, depend upon the effort we can make. ' *Will
you or won't you have it so?* ' is the most probing question
we are ever asked; we are asked it every hour of the day,
and about the largest as well as the smallest, the most
theoretical as well as the most practical things. We answer
by *consents or non-consents* and not by words. What
wonder that these dumb responses should seem our deepest
organs of communication with the nature of things! What
wonder if the effort demanded by them be the measure
of our worth as men! What wonder if the amount we

# CHAPTER V

## THE GOOD AS SELF-REALIZATION OR FREEDOM

1. **The Good as Self-Realization.**—The nature of volition has been investigated with the hope that knowledge of this subject would furnish a key to the fundamental ethical problem of the Good; for insight into the true character of volition should enable us to answer the further question as to the form of conduct required for its complete satisfaction. Volition has upon investigation proved itself to be in essential nature an organizing agency. Can we not infer from this fact what is man's highest Good? This query receives at once an affirmative reply; for the truth lies open before us, as a moment's examination of what is implied in the idea of *organization*, will show.

What is the work of an organizing agency? What is meant by organization? Clearly, to organize is to establish a relation of inter-dependence and coöperation among the parts within any whole. This inter-dependence is the most thorough, this coöperation is the closest, that is possible. So thorough is the inter-dependence that every part has its nature altogether constituted by its connection with the other parts of the system, and ceases to exist in independence of it. So close is the coöperation that every part has

its life altogether determined by the office it discharges
within the system, and ceases to act independently. Organization means, therefore, such a relation within a system
that the whole finds expression in every part, and to organize is to establish this relation. Thus it is with the living
body which, because such a relation obtains among its
parts, is called an *organism*. The members are so related
that each has its nature wholly determined by its function
within the whole. This is what social organization means,
too,—such coöperation among the different individuals that
each finds expression for his own individuality in the discharge of his specific office in society. To organize a business or industry involves such a distribution and adjustment of its various activities that each department shall
work with maximum efficiency in the interest of the whole.
Nor is it otherwise in the organization of human conduct
through the instrumentality of volition,—to organize is to
relate the different activities of the individual so that each
may promote most effectively the exercise of all—and organization means that the sum-total of the individual's
tendencies and capacities shall find conscious expression
in each single act. Now the sum-total of the individual's
active tendencies and capacities, *expressed in their conscious
unity*, constitute, as we have seen, his selfhood or personality. Consequently, the complete organization of conduct, the goal which volition strives to attain, and which is
required to satisfy it fully, is identical with complete self-
expression—or, in the more familiar phrase, self-realization.
Self-realization is therefore the *summum bonum*, the highest
human good, which we have been seeking to discover. It
is that form of conduct wherein each single act is made
contributory to the welfare of the whole self and, conversely, the whole self is given expression in every
act.

**2. Self-Realization Through the Instrumentality of Volition: (a) The Present Self.**—The Good is Self-realization, because volition is an organizing agency, and complete self-organization is identical with complete self-realization. This is the conclusion to which the argument as thus far pursued has led us. Volition, whose demands for satisfaction are expressed in the Moral Ideal, now appears as the faculty through whose instrumentality the self is realized. How this result is accomplished through the exercise of will becomes clearer if we glance back at the successive stages in the development of volition and see what is the effect of each upon the existence and nature of the self.

A person or a self is, as Royce remarks, a life lived according to a plan.[1] Now such purposiveness or aim is introduced into human consciousness through the work of volition in its earliest and simplest form—that of desire. In action from desire a number of experiences are united as means to an end, the attainment of an object. The consciousness of the child who desires a toy, and hence goes in search of it, acquires a unity which it did not possess when he acted from instinct or impulse. In instinctive or impulsive action his successive experiences might be united by the fact that they were all adapted to produce a single result, but he would not be conscious of this unity, and it is in a consciousness of the unity of different experiences that selfhood or personality consists. Since through desire unity is first brought to the individual's consciousness from within, this first form of volition may be said to establish the existence of the self. Of course the unity introduced is not extensive or thorough-going. A desire does not embrace a class of objects and hence unite the experiences of the individual over any considerable span of time. Instead it is directed upon a single object and the measures which must be taken for its present attain-

[1] ROYCE: *Philosophy of Loyalty*, p. 168.

ment. Hence the self that is realized in desire is not the whole self, nor even a large part of the self—it is the self in form most limited and circumscribed, *the self of the present moment*.

This present self is realized, then, through the pursuit and attainment of the object of momentary desire. Its character, even at the moment of its inception, is, to be sure, largely the outcome of past experience. The idea of the object, now the end of conscious desire, has been produced by past experience, when the same object prompted to instinctive and impulsive action. Even when the desire is for an object of present perception it is not for the object merely as perceived, but for the perceived object thought of as an end of action, i.e. a means of self-satisfaction, and the perceived object could be thus regarded only as the result of previous experience with it. Thus it might be said that in desire, not the self of the present simply, but that of the past as well, is realized. While this is to an extent true, desire does not allow of any conscious reflecting or generalizing upon past experience with a view to determining present conduct. For such use of the past involves the subordination to it of the present as of a particular instance to a general class, and this is action from purpose and not from desire.

3. (b) The Natural Self.—Through action from purpose a more inclusive unity is established within the individual consciousness. Objects of like nature, desired and sought in many different moments, are now grouped together and pursued as a class. Such purposes show by their generality that they are not confined in their scope to the present. Including many particulars, they arise only out of the accumulated experiences of the past when these particular objects have been singly desired, and can be fulfilled only in the course of future time, when these same specific objects are serially attained as parts of an inclusive

end. Thus purposive action unites experiences past, present, and future, relating a succession of acts as means to the attainment of an end embracing them all. By its instrumentality the boundaries of the self are therefore extended beyond the limits of the present moment to include past and future. A larger self is realized—how large depending upon the scope of the purpose. Some purposes are restricted to a particular period, or place, or undertaking,—as the purposes of youth or of old age, or the purpose of a man starting upon a journey. But the typical purpose extends in its scope over the natural lifetime of the individual—the period of his physical existence. An instance would be the purpose to win favorable recognition from, to be " liked by," one's fellows. Formed as the result of many agreeable experiences of pleasing others, this purpose is pursued throughout the remainder of life and runs like a binding thread to the very end, tying together diverse actions which would otherwise appear isolated and discrepant. Since the typical purpose extends over the natural lifetime, we may call the self which is realized through purposive action the *natural* self. It is the self as natural individual whose existence covers a definite period of years and is cut short by death.

4. (c) **The Personal Self, Individual and Social.**—By the third and highest form of volition, action from ideal, a unity is produced which transcends even the limits of natural individuality and physical existence. The ends sought, the ideals of Truth and Honor, of Justice and Beauty, are such as involve the coöperation of many persons in a community of intelligence and endeavor. Hence they include the natural self with its purposes, reduced now to the rank of means to a more comprehensive end. The self which is realized through the attainment of these ideals is therefore not the natural self, the particular individual external to, and exclusive of, others, but rather

the self in its universal aspect, the *human person as such*. In this the culminating stage of self-realization the existence and action of the natural individual are made instrumental to the expression of the powers and capacities of human personality. This largest self may, therefore, be called the *personal* self. The development of the personal self through voluntary action follows two lines, which may be clearly distinguished, although they are in close and constant connection. It may be achieved through the pursuit of such ideals as the discovery of truth or the conquest of some department of nature—ideals which, while they implicate and refer to other persons, still concern primarily the *individual* person and his relation to objective reality. Or it may be achieved through the pursuit of such ideals as those of patriotism and humanitarianism, in which the welfare of other selves is sought directly and explicitly. In this way the *social* person is developed. The two modes of personal expression, individual and social, although distinguishable in direction, are really two aspects of a unitary development, and hence are complementary and inter-dependent.

5. **The Possibilities of Selfhood as Actualized by Volition.**—Through the exercise of volition in its successive stages, therefore, the self is created, developed, and brought to full realization. The effect of the organizing activity of will is to extend the limits of the self over a larger and larger field. In action from desire the unity of selfhood is manifested only in a grasp of the possibilities of the present situation. Through purposive action this unity is expanded to include events past and future and finally to include within its scope the whole of a natural lifetime. Action from ideal pushes the boundaries of personality out still farther until the lives of others and the whole of the real universe are brought within its unity. Thus voluntary action, when continued, discloses the pos-

sibilities of that selfhood which we all possess. Our self-hood or personality is an ideal unity, capable of infinite expansion, from a mere point in the present back into the past and out into the future until the period of natural existence is covered, and then in a wider sweep embracing the lives of fellow-men, the epochs of human history, and finally comprehending the vast process of universal evolution. Each self is capable of becoming an epitome of the universe—in truth, a microcosm. That these potencies shall be made actual, that the possibilities of selfhood shall be fulfilled, requires only that volition be exercised in the fullness of its powers. Absolutely correct, then, was the statement that the goal of volition as an organizing agency is full *self-realization*. Equally true is it, also, that only in such complete self-realization can volition find complete satisfaction, and that herein, consequently, lies the highest good for man.

6. **Self-Realization Identical with Self-Determination.**—The process of self-realization, which now becomes a subject of especial study, is equivalent to an increasing control by the self of its own action—in other words, to growing power of self-determination. The power of self-determination, the ability of the individual to direct and control his own conduct in accordance with his own wishes, is a faculty peculiar to man. It is not possessed in any degree by the lower animals, whose action results from the interplay of forces of the environment, with certain fixed instincts present in the individual as part of his race in-heritance—for example, the actions of birds in nest-building are due to the influence of external conditions connected with season, locality, etc., which stimulate a highly devel-oped and powerful instinct. The action of the animal can-not then be said to be in any true sense self-determining or spontaneous; the individual remains a part of the great system of nature, acting out its laws and expressing its

forces. With man, the first actions are, like those of the animals, instinctive; the actions of the individual are not directed by himself but, instead, only register the effect of external objects upon his nervous mechanism. With the entrance of volition all this is changed, however, and self-determination begins. Action from desire is not elicited by an external object which stimulates a fixed instinct; it is prompted by an ideal object which the individual takes for his own good. Such action may be properly regarded as an expression of the individual himself. But while the act expresses what the individual now desires— his present self, that is—its performance may serve to prevent the gratification of a desire equally strong in the future. In this case, the act does not express the future self, but goes counter to it. It is not determined by the entire self, therefore; it is not wholly self-controlled. How can the control of the self over such acts of desire be increased? Clearly not by the absolute denial of desire or cessation from action. Rather by relating the different objects of desire and comprehending them within more extensive ends which represent the good of the self in the future as well as the present. This work of relating single actions to larger aims and more general purposes is carried forward by volition in its higher stages until, finally, present conduct is made instrumental to the attainment of that ideal end expressing the good of the whole self, present and future, natural and personal, individual and social. Then, and then only, action becomes entirely self-determined—expressing the self, the whole nature of the self, and nothing else. Now this process of self-determination is of course the identical process of self-organization or self-realization that we have been discussing. But it is important to notice their identity; for self-determination is in its turn identical with true freedom. The correctness of this last statement will appear if we compare this conception of freedom with the opposing views which have long and vainly contended for supremacy in the field. We shall see that the progressive self-realization, which we have agreed is man's highest good, is equally the attainment of absolute freedom.

7. **Libertarianism.**—As one extreme among possible views of human freedom is Libertarianism. According to the Libertarian view man's will is free in the sense that it is *un*-determined, that it acts *without a cause*. Of course the Libertarian does not deny that our will is, in a way, influenced by our motives and tendencies. The field of choice is limited by the knowledge and experience of the individual and the possibilities of action that they suggest to him. But when it comes to actually choosing between courses of action open, the Libertarian believes that the human will is uncontrolled by any influence whatsoever. In this crisis no one motive is stronger in its influence upon the will than any other. All motives are reduced to a common level, in fact, since all are equally powerless to control the will. Hence, as far as the ability to choose is concerned, it is a matter of absolute indifference to the will which of the possible courses shall be taken. Any possibility may with equal readiness be chosen or rejected.

In the course of the long controversy upon the subject, many considerations have been advanced in favor of this and the opposing view. The leading arguments on both sides may perhaps be summarized under three heads. The Libertarian, with whose argument we are now concerned, claims that his view is supported by facts of the following classes. (1) *Psychological*. Men are generally conscious of freedom in the sense just explained. They are conscious before acting of the ability to choose with equal ease any one of the alternatives offered, and, after acting, of the fact that they might have chosen otherwise than they did. (2) *Ethical*. Only if men's wills are undetermined can we justly hold them responsible for their actions. For if the human will is strictly determined no man can prevent his conduct's being what it is. He should not be punished for what he cannot help. (3) *Metaphysical.* Only if man's will is thus uncaused is he freed from the chain of natural causation and given power and dignity as a spiritual being.

8. **Determinism.**—The other extreme in the free-will controversy is occupied by the Determinists. They hold that volition is strictly determined in its activity. Every choice is the result of a conflict of motives or tendencies in which the strongest always wins. Being thus the necessary resultant of certain fixed forces no choice could be other than it is. Hence the act of will—so far from being arbitrary or uncertain—is, like all other events, the inevitable effect of definite causes. In defense of his position the Determinist has on his side many arguments. The most important are the following, grouped under the three heads used above. (1) *Psychological.* Study of the psychology of choice shows us that the strongest motive does win. The idea is acted upon which succeeds better than all others in holding the attention. Now, in this struggle of ideas for command of the attention, the victory is bound to go to the one which is inherently most attractive, i.e. most pleasant to the individual with his character and disposition such as they are. (2) *Ethical.* Only if action is the necessary outcome of the character of the agent can we hold him responsible for it. If, in the final choice, the will acts in entire independence of all the motives and tendencies of the agent, the act cannot fairly be regarded as *his*, nor can he with justice be punished for it. (3) *Metaphysical.* Nowhere in the world of our experience do we find action without a cause. Science has proved that the uniformity of law and the necessary sequence of cause and effect, prevail throughout nature. To suppose that the human will acts without a cause is to introduce an arbitrary

and lawless factor into the system of nature and thus to contradict the fundamental principle of science.

9. **Freedom as Self-Determination.**—The conception of freedom as self-determination goes to neither of these extremes, but in a sense stands between them, and thus includes the truth in each. This conception makes freedom, as Paulsen says, a " real, positive property of human nature." [2] It is the ability to seek an object chosen by one's self; hence the power to direct one's own conduct. So understood, the animals do not possess freedom; for they act as they are compelled to act by instinct or impulse. Freedom is exhibited, however, by all men who act voluntarily, i.e. in pursuit of a consciously chosen end. In this sense, it is sometimes called *psychological freedom,* since it is a property of developed intelligence and is possessed by all men of normal mental faculties. It is sufficient for responsibility, moreover; because, even though the act proceed from momentary desire, it is nevertheless an expression of the self. But in action from momentary desire we have not an expression of the *whole* self, but only a part, a fractional part, the self of the present moment. Hence the act is not wholly self-determined. Neither is it entirely free. This fact is recognized when, for instance, we condemn a man for being a " slave to his desire," as in the case of the drunkard or the glutton. The drunkard is free, when he returns to the drink, inasmuch as his act expresses himself. But since he acts from momentary desire and in spite of good resolutions to the contrary, he is not free inasmuch as the strength of present appetite thwarts and prevents the expression of his permanent self. Action is entirely free, therefore, only when it is determined by the whole self. This requires such a complete organization of conduct that each single act shall be an expression of the total self. Freedom in this meaning, often termed *moral*

[2] PAULSEN: *System of Ethics,* p. 476.

freedom, is not a natural possession of man, but is a condition to be attained. Its attainment is equivalent to reaching the goal of moral development, full self-realization. For only he who realizes in his conduct all the possibilities of his nature is entirely free.

If we understand that the true meaning of freedom is self-determination we are able to perceive how far both Libertarianism and Determinism are right, and, at the same time, to detect the errors in each. Our consciousness of freedom, emphasized by the Libertarian, is no illusion. Man is free in the sense that he is subject to no external compulsion in his conduct, but can direct his own action. Moreover, since it is the individual himself who decides in any instance of choice, it may with truth be said that all the alternatives remain open until he himself makes up his mind. But this does not imply that in the final choice the will acts in equal independence of all the tendencies and characteristics of the individual that have been in play, or that, with the aspect of the self that was uppermost at the culminating moment, the decision could have been other than it was. Determinism is, therefore, right in maintaining that the strongest motive always wins. But it is wrong in treating the motives as if they were forces separate from the self and acting upon it from without. Instead they are all expressions of the self, and to say that the strongest wins is simply to say that the dominant aspect of the self determines the action. Again the Libertarian is right in asserting that the individual cannot be held responsible if his act is the necessary resultant of forces within him which he cannot control. But he is wrong in his further conclusion that responsibility attaches only to those choices in which the will acts in independence of disposition and character. Rather is the view of the Determinist correct—that a man is responsible only for those actions which are an expression of his character.

Only we must not think of character in this connection as a factor given, fixed, or ready-made, but rather as subject to constant direction and development at the initiative of the self. Finally, we agree with the Libertarian that man can claim the dignity of independent personality only in so far as he is relieved from the constraint of mechanical necessity and left to be master of his own destiny. But this does not require us to exalt to the supreme place in his nature a perfectly arbitrary and lawless will. It only requires that the laws by which this will acts should be grounded deep in the nature of the self.[3]

10. **Objections to This View.**—It is not supposed that the foregoing paragraphs remove every difficulty connected with the vexed problem of free-will; but only that they indicate the general direction in which present thought is moving toward a solution of this problem. Many difficulties remain. For instance, the Libertarian may object that the view just advanced provides for no genuine freedom. Action is said to be always the necessary expression of character, while character is admitted to be, at the time of action, fixed, itself the necessary result of past actions and influences. Why speak as if the individual had any real freedom of choice when, in every case, the very bent of his will—i.e. its power and direction—is fixed and determinate as a part of his character? In answer to this objection two things should be said. In the first place, it is a mistake to think of a man's character as something distinct from himself which acts upon him from without, and, as an external force, constrains him to behave thus and so. This is a false abstraction. Rather is his character just himself, and, when *it* determines his action, *he* is determining it. In the second place, it is wrong to conceive of the character of the individual as if it were once for all fixed and defined by agencies quite beyond

[3] GREEN: *Op. cit.*, §§ 98, 105.

his control. The fact is that his character, and particularly his tendencies and dispositions of will, are subject to constant modification and development. And this modification and development is largely under the control of the individual himself, so that he is responsible for the present state of his character. The amount of " will-power " which he possesses in the present emergency is in a great measure the result of efforts which he has made to exercise his will in the past. Man may thus, if he chooses, train and form his own will, building up such habits as he judges will be beneficial, taking thought to avoid situations that will serve to awaken a desire that is excessive, or reducing the strength of such a desire by more drastic measures of repression and denial.

But, it may be urged, this is merely to push the difficulty a little further back and not to remove it. For is not the individual's ability thus to develop his own character, to train his own will, the necessary resultant of causes which lie altogether beyond his own choice or control—of his heredity, that is, and the influences of his environment? Race, sex, and family stock all combine to produce in the individual through heredity certain definite characteristics and capacities. Age, country, and local habitation have an inevitable effect upon his nature. One man inherits a taste for liquor, another is endowed with marked inventive ability. The spirit of one age leads men in great numbers to enter upon religious crusades, that of another makes the pursuit of art equally popular. Is not, then, the individual's ability to form and develop that character, which in any particular case determines his action, itself the result of forces outside his own will? In the last analysis, therefore, is not the human will determined by external influences?

At this point it will be necessary to inquire how these influences, particularly heredity and environment, operate in determining the will. Obviously, what they do is to determine the comparative attractiveness of different objects to different individuals. Thus from hereditary tendency one man is attracted to wealth, pursues it, and becomes a millionaire; another man is attracted to machinery, studies it, and becomes a great engineer. But in what lies the attractiveness given to these objects by heredity and surroundings? Is it that in consequence of hereditary constitution more pleasure results from the pursuit and attainment of these objects than any others? In this case human freedom is not destroyed; for we have seen that the will is not determined by a necessity of its nature always to seek the greatest pleasure. Does not the influence of heredity and environment consist rather in determining for the individual how *pleasant,* how *interesting* certain objects shall be when they are represented as ends of action? Now there is no doubt that these factors do wield a momentous influence over the will in just this way; since the pleasantness of any object is the measure of its command over the attention, and hence its power over the will. The fact that a certain desire is by heredity especially strong in a man means that its object is much pleasanter to him than to most other men, and that, consequently, an unusually strong purpose will be required to overrule it and reduce it to proper submission. The idea of being a prosperous and useful citizen must be especially attractive and appealing if it is to hold the attention and be pursued as a purpose by a man with an inherited craving for liquor. We must admit, therefore, that heredity, and environment too, do influence the will in its expression and development, by determining the natural or inherent attractiveness of different objects for it. And if the will were merely a faculty whereby particular objects are sought and obtained, its acts would simply reflect the varying attractiveness of these different objects and thus be determined exclusively by the two factors above mentioned. But will is more than this: it has a positive nature of its own.[4] In essential character will is an organizing agency, and this fact means that whenever it is exercised and to the extent in which it is exercised, the pleasantness of the larger and more inclusive object is increased. Hence it is always possible for man by an effort of will to overcome the strength of hereditary tendency and environmental influence and act in accordance with his own larger good. And this exertion of the will is dependent on nothing but the will itself. In the exercise of its own peculiar power, therefore, it is an independent and original source of spiritual energy. Thus while heredity and environment often influence the action of the will, in some cases setting practical limits to its expression by making some desire so strong that its subjection requires a disproportionate and exhausting effort, it is inconceivable that the will should be completely controlled by these external factors.

The Determinist may now, in his turn, accuse us of reinstating the idea of will as an '' uncaused cause,''[5] as the

[4] The ultimate question in this matter of human freedom appears to be this,—Is the individual an original source of spiritual power the amount of which is undetermined and hence may, by effort, be self-augmented? This question must receive an affirmative answer, it seems, if there is to be any genuine self-determination. Paulsen, in his *System of Ethics*, asserts that freedom as the power of self-determination is a positive property of human nature. The actions of the human individual are determined by his tendencies and predispositions, he holds, and these, constituting his character, are determined by the various influences, natural and social, that affect him (p. 457). But, he further maintains, man may, by the exercise of thought and the discipline of impulse, form his character, educate his will (p. 469). Yet he admits, still further, that he cannot do this unless the formative principle in sufficient strength is native within him (p. 470). And if this power exists in an amount fixed by hereditary endowment in the individual it is difficult to attach much positive meaning to his capacity for self-determination. Does not true freedom imply, as James suggests, the presence in human nature of a power not fixed in amount but an '' independent variable, among the fixed data of the case, our motives, character, etc.''?

[5] GREEN: *Op. cit.*, p. 100.

one faculty of man which acts in absolute independence of other tendencies in human nature and of the forces in the outer world. This conception of will, he may say, has been already discarded, as false to the facts of psychology, and without any ethical value. In answering this charge it is perhaps sufficient to say that the phrase, " uncaused cause," does not in the least apply to the self-determining will as it has been described in the previous paragraphs. This *will* is not conceived as the one member of a group of forces that is out of relation to all the rest, the single event in a causal series that is itself undetermined. We have seen that it is volition as an organizing agency which establishes the unity of human experience and assigns place to every object and interest therein. It is therefore the source of the self and all its acts—or, better, it *is* the self acting in its unity. Every act and every tendency of the self is an expression of will, for will is just the power of the self in all its acts. How is it possible, then, to suppose that will is determined and limited by one of these dispositions or tendencies which are but minor expressions of itself? As easily suppose that the power and potency of life is limited and defined by the various species which it has already produced. And the independence and initiative which we thus ascribe to will is only a fuller manifestation of that power to originate new forms and initiate new activities which is admitted to belong to all life and which is the condition of all development and evolution. The explanation of freedom is self-determination, the explanation of self-determination is development—the realization of the latent and often unknown possibilities of human nature.

## REFERENCES

Stout, *Manual of Psychology*, Book IV, Chap. VII.
Baldwin, *Social and Ethical Interpretations in Mental Development*, Chap. VII.

the student of Ethics cannot be content with a principle
that is merely formal. He must know the content of the
Good as well as its form. What are the activities that go
to make up a completely organized life? What are the
qualities and characteristics of the self whose nature is
completely realized? If mere organization is the Good, will
not every life in which the different acts are all strictly
subordinated to a ruling purpose—even though, as in the
case of the criminal, this purpose is a cruel and sinister
one—be morally approved? Suppose a boy is reared in the
belief that it is his chief duty to avenge the death of a
murdered father. As he grows to manhood such vengeance
becomes his ruling purpose,—perhaps connecting itself with
an ideal of personal honor. In finally gaining his revenge
he himself meets death. Is not his life completely organized? Does he not—or does he—fully realize himself?
Such an example shows the necessity of going beyond the
formal principle of organization and discovering what definite characteristics and capacities are displayed by all normal human beings in the course of their development.

2. **The Incidental and the Essential in Human Nature.**—The task now before us is to ascertain what are the
fundamental characteristics of the human self and to see
how these are expressed in the process of self-realization.
Now while the *form* of the Good was discovered by an investigation of the faculty of volition, which is the source
of all conduct, this, the *content*, can be determined only
by a study of the facts of human nature and human experience. The effects of such a study—especially a first
general survey—are discouraging. The facts are many
and complicated, and the variations of character between
men of different races and ages are apparently endless and
certainly bewildering. It seems that all men possess in
common only the bare faculties of thought and action, while
the many ideas and beliefs which spring from the one, and

the varied tendencies and dispositions which pertain to the other, are different in each individual case. What characteristics have the Norse viking, the mediæval recluse, and the modern man of business in common? To what extent will the course of self-realization for the Kaffir, the Esquimo, and the European be identical? Or even within a modern civilized state, how many activities are shared equally by street-sweeper, stock-broker, and charities-worker?

The activities involved in self-realization must necessarily differ with the time, race, sex, and occupation of the self. In fact, self-realization is bound to have a different meaning for each separate individual; since each possesses certain attributes and abilities peculiar to himself, which enter into his self-realization. Despite this infinite diversity among men there are, nevertheless, certain characteristics which are essential to human nature as such. They are consequently possessed by all normal human individuals, and serve to direct the course of self-realization in each. In fact, these essential characteristics determine the activities which all men must put forth as conditions of their self-realization. They may hence be said to prescribe the laws of self-realization, valid universally within the field of human conduct. Before we proceed to a consideration of those essential characteristics of human nature which constitute the universal and necessary conditions of self-realization in the life of man, a question must be answered which will naturally arise at this point. To what extent can such a process as self-realization which, as we have seen, is the expression of the free agency of volition, an original and spontaneous power, have its course predetermined by any influence whatever?

The mere idea that it is possible by reflection to discover conditions of moral development which hold for all men, and hence pre-determine the course of self-realization in human life, may seem in direct contradiction to the previous assertion that the future must always contain for the voluntary agent an element of uncertainty which reason can never eliminate, and that consequently human conduct must ever remain a venture in which the surprising and unexpected are constantly encountered. If this latter assertion be true,—it will be urged,—it is manifestly impossible that the course of self-realization should be predetermined or its successive stages prescribed. If the future course of moral development *is* thus determined, the power of human volition is limited, the will is not truly free. Conversely, if we are to have true freedom in human conduct and real evolution in human life, the possibilities of change and difference must be unlimited. Indeed, the logic of the situation may appear to require from us the admission that not even the *goal* of moral development is fixed, but that it is subject to indefinite change and variation in response to new and different conditions which may arise in the future. This view—that the logic of development forbids us to attribute to development any definite goal or ultimate end—is repugnant alike to reason and to common-sense; it warns us against the over-emphasis of one aspect of the truth, itself of great importance, to the exclusion of the other aspects which in real experience offset and balance it. Now the indubitable truth which finds expression in the view we are considering is that no genuine development realizes an end set for it by some external agency; it, so to speak, unfolds its result out of its own nature. The moral ideal of self-realization is rooted in the nature of volition itself. For development, to be development, must be the development of something, not of nothing. The thing in this case is *will,* and we learn from experiencing its activity that it is essentially an agency of adjustment and organization. It is inconceivable, therefore, that the goal of its development should be other than the completed organization, perfected adjustment. Further than this, reflection upon the achievements of volition in human life shows that it works under certain fundamental conditions, conditions fixed by the characteristics of human nature, or by the character of the real world. The existence of these conditions, revealed by the results of past action, makes it reasonable to conclude—as we shall presently see—that self-realization in the case of all men must involve an integration of impulses in the individual and an adjustment of interests in society. But in addition to these necessary implications, which are of a very general nature, the process of self-realization holds forth enough uncertainty to test the courage of the most adventuresome soul. The methods whereby self-organization can be achieved in the individual and social spheres can be ascertained only by trial and experiment. Guided of course by the results of previous experience, man must ever advance to meet new situations; in meeting these situations he must have the strength of will, the courage of conviction, sufficient to risk happiness already attained in putting to the test new and more promising solutions. All that ethical reflection can do is to make such generalizations from the moral experience of humanity as will afford us most effective guidance in solving the problems of future conduct.

What, then, are the essential characteristics of human nature which constitute the universal and necessary conditions of human self-realization?

3. **Man as a Natural Being.**—Man is primarily a natural being, a member of the highest of the animal species. He is the outcome of the same natural evolution that has produced the other living forms, and is, therefore, related to them by descent. His genealogy may be traced down through a succession of species to the earliest and simplest forms of life. As a result of this, his natural origin and

development, man possesses certain qualities which must be reckoned as fundamental to his character. Most important in their influence upon conduct are the instincts which all men thus possess. These instincts are a part of man's natural inheritance, and hence are shared in common with the lower animals. They are modifications of the nervous system originally developed in our animal ancestors by natural selection because giving an advantage in the struggle for existence. Originating in this way they have been transmitted by physical heredity and made a permanent part of man's physical structure.

4. **His Native Instincts.**—Hence the first of the characteristics fundamental to human nature is the possession by all men of a set of natural instincts. These instincts have an important bearing upon man's conduct, since they cause him at first to react involuntarily to certain kinds of objects and then consciously to desire and voluntarily to seek them. It is difficult, if not impossible, to enumerate and classify the various instincts of man. This is not because their existence is in the least doubtful; but in many cases the objects and movements involved in a group of instinctive reactions are so related that it seems an arbitrary matter whether we attribute the whole group to one instinct or divide it among several. Are the instincts, so-called, of defense, combat, and rivalry three separate instincts, or just varied manifestations of one instinct? Who shall decide? Still it is possible to make a rough catalogue of the more important human instincts, which will be sufficient to our needs; since, for ethical purposes, we do not require a complete classification of every variety of instinctive reaction in man. For purposes of the present discussion, then, man's instinctive reactions may be divided into three classes, in accordance with the nature of the object upon which they are directed, whether it be the individual himself, an inanimate object, or another

living individual.  Under the first head comes the instinct of self-preservation, which causes man to seek his own health and pleasure, and equally to avoid conditions of harm and pain.  Under the second head we may note the instincts of food, drink, shelter, and acquisition.  Thirdly, come the social instincts, among which are those of sex and parenthood, of speech and sympathy, of resentment and emulation.  We may add as another to these three classes, certain instincts whose object may be either an inanimate thing or another living individual—that is, the instincts of imitation, curiosity, beauty, and play.

Originating as conditions of survival with the lower forms of life, these instincts serve—through the actions they prompt—to maintain the existence of the human organism in the natural world.  Thus they relate man as individual to the objects of nature, giving value to material things according as these minister to human needs.  The world of the human individual is consequently not a world of objects that merely exist as facts, but a world of objects which appeal as possible ends of action because supplying food, shelter, clothing, amusement, etc.  In the same way man's native instincts relate him to other members of his own species.  Other individuals acquire interest for him because furnishing companionship, arousing resentment, or appealing to sexual or parental emotions.  Through his various natural instincts, therefore, man is set in certain definite relationships to objects of the material world and to other men as natural individuals.

5.  **Man as a Conscious Self.**—But man is more than a natural individual: he is a conscious self.  As a self or person, he is not a material thing with boundaries to separate it from other things in space, he is a spiritual being to whom no such limitations can be assigned.  Man's selfhood or personality resides in the conscious unity of his experience.  " To have a conception of one's own self,"

says Hobhouse, "one must be aware of a certain identity running through the mass of past experiences, and inferentially prolonged into the future."[1] Now man's consciousness of the unity of his experience, in which his self-hood consists, depends upon his ability to weave together the facts of his experience into a connected system. He must do more than associate experiences in the order of their occurrence; for this the animals do and yet have no selfhood or personality. He must be able to establish permanent relations among the objects of his consciousness "upon the basis of their affinities and the more remote connections that follow therefrom."[2] Now this work of the organization of experience, which is the condition of conscious selfhood, proceeds ultimately from volition, the spiritual force in man which builds out of the materials of animal life a self-conscious personality. We already know how volition in its first and simplest form begins this work. In discovering the means which must be used to attain the end of desire the individual is made aware of relationships among objects that are permanent and necessary. Imitation and language are, as we have noted, also important factors in the development of the self. The social character of selfhood is therefore marked from the first; since self-development in its earliest stages is dependent upon the influence of other selves and the possibility of communicating with them.

With the appearance of volition, then, in the third or fourth year of human life, the growth of the self begins and it continues through childhood. But full self-consciousness does not arise until the power of free thought and imagination is developed in the later period of adolescence. This power enables the individual to deal with his experience in its larger masses and more comprehensive relationships.

[1] HOBHOUSE: *Mind in Evolution,* p. 301.
[2] HOBHOUSE: *Op. cit.,* p. 300.

He may behold himself as a physical being, a denizen of a planet in a great solar system and an insignificant atom in a vast universe of suns and stars, or in his social nature as one among the many millions of souls now existing in the world. He may view his present in its connection with the past which is fading in memory, and with the long future which stretches out before, filled with unknown possibilities. In such consciousness of self the existence of other selves is necessarily implied. The very relationships by which the experience of the self is organized are assumed to hold for other selves as well. The real universe in which the self finds its home is assumed to exist for other selves also. In fact, consciousness of self-existence involves constant appeal to the existence of others. From his nature as such, the self-conscious person must identify himself with, and yet at the same time distinguish himself from, other persons. He must recognize that all have the same world, yet each occupies therein his own point of view.

6. **His Spiritual Capacities.**—As a conscious self man has certain spiritual capacities the possession of which may rank as the second of the fundamental characteristics of human nature. And as his natural instincts serve to sustain and strengthen his physical existence, so his spiritual capacities maintain and enrich his conscious personality. These capacities are all expressions of the basal activity of volition which, through its work of organization, builds up the unity of selfhood. But in the discharge of its office volition manifests itself in three highly specialized forms which it is permissible to distinguish as different capacities. These spiritual capacities in man are: first, the *Intellectual*, the power of thought, the ability to acquire knowledge; second, the *Technical*, the ability to contrive, to construct, to invent what is serviceable; third, the *Æsthetic*, the ability to perceive and enjoy what is beautiful. Now the effect of the operation of all three of these capacities is to extend and

to enrich the unity of the self. The *intellectual* capacity does this by introducing within the unity of self-consciousness the objects and fixed connections of the real universe. The scientist, with his telescope or microscope, is continually enriching human experience by bringing into it new facts. In a like manner also does every individual enlarge the content of his own personality, who by serious thought discovers a new factor or hidden cause within the ken of his own experience. The *technical* capacity of man extends the unity of his own selfhood by subjecting the agencies of the environment, natural and social, to the ends of intelligence. This the inventor does when he devises a machine by which the forces of nature are compelled to fulfil the purposes of man; the educator, too, when he devises a new method for communicating knowledge—for teaching spelling or arithmetic or grammar. The same ability is exercised by all individuals who, through skill and contrivance, adapt external surroundings to the uses of their own personal intelligence. The *æsthetic* capacity in its way also enriches the content of the unitary self; through exercise of the imagination and perceptive faculties such form and arrangement are given to experiences of color and sound as to create in them new suggestions of meaning, and thus to provide the agent with new sources of satisfaction. This ability is of course displayed primarily in the work of the artist; but in a less degree by all those who enjoy beauty in any of its forms.

Since these activities spring from the nature of the self and all contribute to its extension and development, we should expect that the objects which they seek to realize would be ideal or spiritual. Such is indeed the case; the objects of the three spiritual capacities mentioned are ideal in character and possess none of the limitations of material things. Of course any object which becomes an end of action is of necessity *ideal*. This is just as true of the material object which instinct causes us to desire as it is of the best considered purpose or most comprehensive ideal. But the material object which becomes an end of natural desire is particular in character and limited in time and place; hence it cannot be pursued by all men, but only by a few individuals. Through the power of intelligence, generalizing upon experiences of achievement by race and individual, however, objects of much greater range are furnished as ends for volition in its three-fold capacity— objects extending in their scope to all places and all times and being possible of pursuit by all individuals. In this way simple curiosity about a particular object becomes a wish to know about a whole class of objects, then a number of classes of objects, and at last develops into the craving for knowledge of all possible objects—i.e. for Truth. Interest in the steps which must be taken to secure a particular object grows into a desire to discover the best means or methods for attaining all objects of the same sort: agencies and methods are standardized, technique is developed, and finally Power or Efficiency is adopted as an end to be sought by all individuals. Liking for a special object which, when seen or heard, gives a peculiar kind of delight develops into an interest in all objects which produce æsthetic pleasure, in their relation to one another, and the conditions of their existence; out of this interest grows the yearning to produce in every sphere the conditions necessary to this species of enjoyment and thus realize Beauty universally.

Truth, Power, and Beauty, the three ideals sought by man as a spiritual being, are therefore ideal in the sense of being *universal,* and thus having a scope and comprehensiveness that natural objects do not possess. In proof of this, compare the ideal of Truth, the object sought in all intellectual activity, with the object of a natural instinct—say, food. Food is material, hence is perishable in character and strictly limited in amount, so that what one individual gains the rest must necessarily lose. Truth, on the contrary, being ideal, survives even the limits of man's natural lifetime, enduring and increasing as the successive generations of men are born and die. It is not restricted in quantity; it cannot be " cornered " by any individual. Rather does the individual, in the measure of his success in obtaining it, increase the possessions of all the rest; for truth requires for its pursuit and discovery the coöperation of many individuals in a community of intelligence. Nor is it otherwise with Power or Efficiency, the end sought in technical activity. The engineer who designs a new type of bridge, and the agricultural expert who devises an improved method of farming are not seeking material things with their narrow limits—combinations of stone and steel, bushels of grain, or tons of hay. Instead their object is ideal—the control of the forces of nature by the power of intelligence. The same may be said of efforts made in the social and political spheres to devise methods and instruments whereby the aims of intelligence may be attained in commerce and government. The purposes which direct these undertakings, because intelligent are universal, and hence the object of the inventor or engineer, the master of industry or the statesman, when attained, is of benefit to all humanity. Thus the originator of the suspension bridge and steam engine pursued and attained ideal objects which, as such, had permanence and universality; for the inventions survived the natural life of the inventor and became the common possession of humanity. Likewise Beauty, which we in our æsthetic capacity seek to create and enjoy, is identical with no block of chiseled marble or piece of painted canvas which can be bought and sold. It is ideal, consisting of the pleasant harmony of imaginative faculties induced by certain aspects of nature and works of art. In seeking it, then, we seek, not a particular object which can be possessed by but one individual, we seek an ideal quality which resides in this object for all persons of cultivated imagination, and thus may be seized on and enjoyed by them all.

Each of the three " spiritual " activities of man has its distinctive end. These three ends constitute the three ruling ideals of self-conscious personality, Truth, Power, and Beauty. In a sense they are coördinate and independent ideals, each having its own distinctive sphere and rightfully demanding supremacy within it. Sometimes, however, the ideal of Goodness is given equal standing with these three or with the first and last, Truth and Beauty. Herein a serious mistake is made; for the ideal of Goodness represents the demands of the agency of volition, of which intellectual, æsthetic, and technical activities are but subordinate expressions. Ultimately, then, the three ideals we have been discussing must all be measured in terms of goodness, and all are subject to the requirements which the complete satisfaction of the power of will imposes on human conduct. By true ideas we mean, in last analysis, ideas that can be realized as ends of action, by efficient agencies or methods the ones that will produce the desired results, and by beautiful presentations those in which the ends of intelligence are immediately apprehended. Thus do intellectual, technical, and æsthetic activities contribute to the satisfaction of volition in its work of organizing and enriching personal life.

7. **Necessary Stages in Self-Realization.**—Two characteristics, we find, must be regarded as fundamental to the human self. They are consequences of the fact that man is at once a natural being and a conscious self. The first is the possession by him of a number of natural instincts which relate him to the material objects of his environment and to other individuals of the human species. The second is the development in the human self of certain

spiritual capacities which serve to relate it both to other selves and to universal reality. These conditions, fundamental to human nature, determine the course of self-realization for all men. They prescribe what activities must have place in the conduct of every human individual who would realize himself. Hence we are now prepared to learn of the *content* of self-realization, as well as the *form*, to ask what course self-realization must take in human beings thus characterized.

It will be convenient to recognize in advance three leading aspects of self-realization in man, which are consequent upon the above-noted relations in which he stands, as natural being, and conscious self.

Full Self-realization, or the complete organization of human conduct, requires the realization of:

(1) **The Individual Self.**—Through such adjustment of the activities in man that all are made means to the promotion of individual interest.

(2) **The Social Self.**—Through such adjustment of the interest of the human individual to the interests of others that his activity is made a means to the furtherance of social welfare.

(3) **The Universal Self.**—Through the adjustment of human welfare to the Universal Purpose.

Thus an outline is furnished which may be regarded as provisional until it is filled in and verified in subsequent discussion. Let us now ascertain in further detail what activities are essential to self-realization under the conditions set by the nature of man. Or, since self-realization is achieved by voluntary action, through the pursuit of what succession of ends the self is fully realized.

8. **(a) The Individual Self.**—Self-realization within the individual sphere means that the total interest of the individual shall be realized by all of his acts. Now, as we know, the human individual possesses both natural in-

stincts and spiritual capacities. In virtue of these characteristics of his nature, certain objects appeal to him and prompt him to act. In order that his conduct shall express *himself*, it is first necessary that the objects of instinct become the ends of conscious desire. When this is accomplished, he seeks in each succeeding act for the thing which he at the moment desires—be it food, play, companionship, or what-not. But the total interest of the individual is not attained in this way; for these desires often conflict, and to satisfy one to-day may prevent the satisfaction of another to-morrow, or even for days to come. Self-organization, then, requires such adjustment and correlation of these varied and opposing desires that each may receive a measure of fulfilment consistent with the due and proportionate satisfaction of those remaining. This adjustment is not merely a compromise, however, in which all the desires are treated as independent units and thus admitted to have equal rights. Certain desires are given a preference, but—consistent with the principle of Self-realization—upon one ground only, that is, their *greater comprehensiveness*. The measure of fulfilment which self-realization permits to one of the particular desires or purposes of the self is determined entirely by the comprehensiveness of the object concerned, the degree to which it includes other objects sought-for, and hence is expressive of the whole self. As illustrative of difference in this regard, compare the objects of two natural instincts; for example those of food and of resentment or anger. The first is much more comprehensive than the second. Upon the obtainment of a sufficient quantity of the proper food depends the effective exercise of the most of the other activities of the human individual. The other desire has a very narrow range—since the attainment of its object, retaliation, in any but the most restricted form and unusual circumstances, acts as a hindrance to the attainment of other objects desired. Of all the objects which man seeks through natural instinct, the most comprehensive is *self-preservation*. This instinct leads the individual to desire those pleasant conscious states which are indicative of physical well-being, and equally to shun that consciousness of pain which signifies bodily disorder. Generalizing upon particular experiences of pleasure and pain, he is further led to form the purpose to secure in life the greatest enjoyment, or, in other words, gain the maximum of pleasure. Now pleasure, in the sense of agreeable consciousness, is the most comprehensive of the objects which man is led by instinct to pursue, and therefore the purpose to pursue it deserves to be made supreme over all other desires and purposes having a like source. For the greatest amount of pleasure in the case of the human individual is generally an accompaniment of the highest degree of health, security, and comfort in natural existence. And, since all other instincts which man possesses have been developed to maintain and promote his natural existence, the different objects which they cause him to desire—wealth, amusement, reputation, etc.—fall into subjection as means to the inclusive end of *Pleasure,* or natural well-being. Thus Pleasure emerges as the first of the ends which, in the process of self-realization, represent the whole self in contrast to any of its parts; and we make due recognition of the truth contained in the Hedonistic conception of the Good.

We have already seen, however, that the ideal objects of man's spiritual capacities—Truth, Power, and Beauty—are larger and more comprehensive, not merely than any particular thing which he naturally desires, but even than his natural existence and well-being itself. Self-organization in the individual life requires, therefore, that the end lately made supreme over all natural desires and purposes now be subordinated as a means to the realization of these spiritual capacities. The individual, that is, must make his natural well-being and pleasure a means to the exercise of his intellectual, technical, and æsthetic activities. The ends of these higher activities of the human self taken together may be expressed by the word *Culture*. Culture thus appears as the ideal which transcends all other ends in the conduct of the individual, because representing his largest interest and embracing all lesser goods. To its attainment, the natural existence and well-being of the individual must be made subordinate, including of course such lesser purposes as those to gain wealth, amusement, fame, etc. These have now to be realigned and made instrumental, not to the gaining of Pleasure, but to the attainment of Culture. In thus making Culture supreme among the ends pursued by the individual we provide for the truth in Rationalism, which finds man's Good in spiritual activity rather than natural pleasure. The ideal of Culture on which we dwell, as representing the highest interest of the self as individual, is practically identical with the Highest Good as conceived by Plato [3] and Aristotle.[4] According to Plato Justice, the supreme and all-inclusive virtue, consists in a strict division of labor and harmonious coöperation between the three principles in the nature of man—it being understood that it is the function of reason to control. Aristotle, in his doctrine of the Mean, would allow to each desire that measure of gratification consistent with the realization of the Supreme End which is the fulfilment of all man's capacities under the direction of reason.

9. **(b) The Social Self.**—Man is related as a natural being to other members of the human species, and, as a conscious self, to other selves in a community of intelligence. Self-realization requires that his interest as individual be adjusted to the interests of others in society.

The human individual becomes aware of the existence

---

[3] PLATO: *Republic*, 443, C.
[4] ARISTOTLE: *Nicomachean Ethics*, 1106, B.

of others as soon as he becomes conscious of existing himself. One of his leading instincts, moreover,—that of sympathy, —makes him desirous of increasing others' pleasure and lessening their pain. The formation of a general purpose to promote the happiness or well-being of others usually waits upon the development of a definite self-interest in the individual himself. At first the sympathetic impulse is correlated with other natural tendencies of the individual and made a means to the promotion of his own interest, and it is only after a comparatively clear consciousness of self and self-interest arises that there comes also a recognition of the interest of others. This conception of another's interest becomes fuller and more adequate as the development of self-interest proceeds, growing from the idea of another's comfort and happiness merely, to the cultivation of his higher personal capacities. The impulse of sympathy, attaching to such an idea of another's good, makes it attractive as an end of action. Thus a well-defined aim to seek the interests of other individuals appears and exists along with the ideal of self-interest. These varied interests often conflict, so that it seems possible to gain one's own ends as an individual only by thwarting the ambitions of others, and, conversely, others' good can often be realized only at the expense of one's private ambition. Self-organization makes necessary the adjustment of these warring interests. As always, it insists that the less inclusive shall be subordinated to the more inclusive end. Consequently the realization of the self requires the adoption of the ideal of Altruism on the part of the individual—the determination to seek the interests of others with whom he comes into contact as well as his own. This means that he shall surrender his own desire—or partial interest— when it is opposed to the total well-being of another. In cases where *ego* and *alter* seem to have equal interests at stake, Self-realization enforces the doctrine of self-sacrifice, since allowance must be made for the influence of a strong and persistent tendency to over-estimate the interest of self and under-estimate that of others, due to the fact that one's own interest is keenly felt, while that of others is only thought or imagined. There are limits, to be sure, to the extent of self-sacrifice which self-realization requires. It would not, for instance, require the individual to sacrifice his own well-being to the passing whim of another. For here the interest of the self is the more comprehensive end.

Self-realization in the social sphere is not completed when the individual adjusts his own interest to the interests of others of his acquaintance. For the selfhood of which man is conscious is a universal principle present in all human beings and uniting them in a community of intelligence and personality. For full self-realization, therefore, it is not sufficient that man pursue his own highest interest as an individual, or that of other individuals with whom he comes into contact; he must go further and seek the good of human personality, of conscious selfhood, whenever and wherever found. Thus a new end appears, more comprehensive than *Altruism,* which may be called *Humanitarianism.* It means the development of humanity—the full, free, harmonious exercise of all the capacities of human personality. To this ideal, Self-organization requires that the individual subordinate his own interest and the interests of all other particular individuals. The conflict at this point between culture and humanitarianism—between the interest of the individual or a privileged group or class of individuals and the welfare of humanity—while less obvious—may be as acute and persistent as that between egoism and altruism. It cannot be doubted, however, that the fullest expression of the self is found in pursuit of the more comprehensive end, and the highest culture can mean nothing less than the fullest self-development. The artist or the scientist may regard it as a hindrance to be obliged to recognize a social responsibility in their specialized activities. Yet the very capacities, intellectual and æsthetic, which they are exercising are implicitly universal, involving the union of many persons in a common knowledge and appreciation. Can one of these spiritual capacities of man be exercised most effectively, then, unless it contribute to the highest personal development of humanity?

10. (c) The Universal Self.—Finally, man is related through his spiritual capacities to Universal Reality. His thought discovers the necessary connections of things and shows how all natural objects are part of an inter-related system. Through constructive activity he learns how the objects and forces of nature are adapted as means to the purposes of intelligence. Through his æsthetic faculty he feels the order and harmony of nature. Self-realization in its third and culminating phase requires the adjustment of human interests to this all-comprehensive Reality. Now it is plain that the character of this adjustment will vary in accordance with the degree of development which self-interest has undergone—whether it is still mainly individual or has been broadened to include the welfare of humanity. But since in all cases of incomplete development the adjustment is only provisional we may safely neglect them and consider only the interest of the self when thoroughly socialized. The question is, therefore, that of the adjustment of human welfare to the Real Universe. It must not be thought, however, that here we go outside the boundaries of the self and inquire concerning its relation to an external reality. On the contrary, just because the real universe is a necessary factor in self-consciousness, it must be reckoned with in the process of self-realization. The problem of the relation of man to the universe is of course the problem of religion, and, as such, is an essential aspect of self-realization.

The difficulty of the adjustment in question is that the ultimate character of the All-encompassing Reality is unknown. It cannot be directly observed or logically demonstrated. Hence man can only speculate, and such adjustment as he is able to effect will rest upon an assumption. But speculation upon this subject need not be without rational grounds. In fact, it is man's own moral development that is most illuminating at this point. For, in the process of self-realization, natural objects are sacrificed to spiritual activities because the latter *prove to be more comprehensive.* Is it not reasonable to assume, therefore, that Universal Reality, which is by nature all-comprehensive, is spiritual—that it is the expression of a Universal Self within which all our human interests may be included and harmonized? Of course the existence of such a Universal or Divine self is in last analysis a matter of faith rather than knowledge; but we have seen that faith is called for along the whole course of moral development. The very existence of the self is rooted in an act of will, and each step forward in its realization is a venture, the abandonment of one good which, although restricted, is assured, for the sake of another which, although it promises a larger satisfaction, is uncertain and largely unknown. Religious belief is simply the last of these acts of faith, the final venture, in which man commits his welfare into the hands of the Universe, believing that since Spirit is Universal no natural agency, in life or in death, can lessen or destroy the reality which has been attained by a conscious self.

Man thus subordinates his interest to the Universal or Divine Purpose, adopting the latter, so far as it can be known, as his own good. To describe in detail the character and conditions of this adjustment is the task of religion rather than of Ethics. It involves, for the ordinary man, not a number of specific activities in addition to those prescribed by individual and social duty, but rather, a personal attitude—of resignation to the divine will, and trust in the divine wisdom. The end now pursued is of all the most comprehensive—the realization of the Universal Purpose, the Cause of Universal Progress.

----

Thus we see that with human nature characterized as it is, the process of self-realization for man is definite in its direction and specific in its requirements. In its three aspects it involves the attainment of a progression of ends, each of which includes and supersedes the one before, until the supreme and all-comprehensive ideal is reached.

In tabulation these ends appear in the following order:

### Self-Realization

*Agency*—Organizing Activity of Volition.
*Material*—Natural Instincts and Spiritual Capacities of Man.

| *Aspects* | *Ends* |
|---|---|
| Individual . . . . . . . . . | Pleasure / Culture |
| Social . . . . . . . . . | Altruism / Humanitarianism |
| Universal . . . . . . . . | Universal Progress |

### REFERENCES

BALDWIN, *Social and Ethical Interpretations in Mental Development*, Chaps. VI, IX, XII.
JAMES, *Psychology*, Chap. XXIV.
PILLSBURY, *Essentials of Psychology*, Chap. X.
GREEN, *Prolegomena to Ethics*, Book III, Chap. VI.
ALEXANDER, *Moral Order and Progress*, Book II, Chap. II.
DEWEY AND TUFTS, *Ethics*, Chap. XX.
MACKENZIE, *Manual of Ethics*, Book III, Chap. I.
LESLIE STEPHEN, *Science of Ethics*, Chap. III.

## PART THREE

# THE GOOD AS SELF-REALIZATION

# CHAPTER I

## THE CONCEPTION OF SELF-REALIZATION

1. The Relation of the Good to the Existing Human Individual.—
2. The Good as External to the Individual.—3. The Good as
Identical with the Interest of the Individual.—4. These Two
Aspects of Goodness Explained by the Principle of Self-Realization.—5. Arnold's Contrast of Hebraism with Hellenism.—6.
Hebraism.—7. Hellenism.—8. Relation of Christianity to Hebraism and Hellenism.

## 1. The Relation of the Good to the Existing Human Individual.

—In the preceding part the nature of the Good
was considered and the conclusion reached that the *summum
bonum* is Self-realization. Concerning the Good another
question may be asked which, although closely related to
that of its nature, is nevertheless distinct from it. This
question refers to the relation of the Good to the human
individual in actual life. How does the Good stand related to the normal man—is it connected intimately and
essentially with himself, expressing his own deepest desires
and highest hopes, or is it only partially an expression of
his nature, representing his social impulses only and at
variance with other tendencies, or does it present itself
altogether as an authority from without, a command of
God or a law of the universe to which he must conform or
perish? Upon this question two conflicting views have
arisen in the course of ethical reflection. The one holds
that the Good is identical with the interest of the individual
and stands for the complete fulfilment of all his desires.
The other regards the Good as external to the individual

and usually opposed to his actual inclinations.[1]    The line of
division between these two views does not correspond to,
or even parallel, that between Hedonism and Rationalism.
Rather it cuts across this, although obliquely.    Thus one
may hold the view first-named, that the Good is identical
with man's actual interest, and be either a Hedonist or
Rationalist, according as he finds this interest in the enjoyment of pleasure or the exercise of reason.   Doubtless, this
first view has closer relationship logically with Hedonism;
feeling is the subjective factor, expressing in its warmth and
immediacy the present state of the self.    Yet as a matter
of historic fact it has frequently appeared in union with
Rationalism, as in the case of Greek Ethics, which at once
identifies the Good with the nature of the individual and
believes it to consist in the supremacy of reason in his life.
On the other hand, the second view, that the Good is
external to the individual, may be maintained by one who
is either a Rationalist or a Hedonist.    But here the leaning
is still more marked toward one of these rival theories, in
this case that of Rationalism; since reason is the objective
factor in human nature and its requirements, possessing
universal validity, seem frequently to have the force of
external authority.    If the Good is pleasure and still external to the individual it must be the pleasure of other
men or of God.    But we already know that Hedonism as
a historic doctrine has relied chiefly on the psychological
argument that every man must, from a compulsion of his

---

[1] Such a view of the Good may appear to be a contradiction in
terms, since the Good has been defined as that form of conduct
which satisfies the human will completely.    The fact of the dependence of the Good upon the demands of human volition has frequently
been obscured, however, by the features of moral experience described
in the following section, and the whole subject has been complicated
by the belief, more or less prevalent, that man's will, although
originally directed upon the Good, has been perverted by the sins
of our first parents and thus turned altogether to the pursuit of
selfish pleasure.

nature, seek his own pleasure.  Hence a view which finds the good of the individual in the pleasure of some other person or persons does not appear as a true or consistent Hedonism.

2. **The Good as External to the Individual.**—Both of these views of the relation of the Good to the human individual are supported by facts whose importance cannot be gainsaid.  The view, second-named, of the externality of the Good, is in accord with the apparent facts of moral experience.  In the experience of the majority of persons the requirements of goodness are opposed, more frequently than not, to natural inclination and present desire.  Conformity to these requirements is possible, therefore, only when inclination is thwarted and desire is repressed.  The moral life is correctly described as a struggle—a struggle with rebellious tendencies and a recalcitrant nature.  We must be ever watchful, always on our guard, not against the principalities and powers of the outer world, but against our own wayward impulses, the frowardness of our own hearts.  Moral development is not the unconscious maturing, the spontaneous blossoming forth, of our nature.  Rather is moral progress a slow and painful ascent in which each step upward is hard-won and costs pain and privation.  We develop morally by subjecting ourselves to a law which our natures resist because of its apparent rigor and severity.  Hence even when we have come to recognize fully the authority of the Good over us and to acquiesce in its dictates, we never regard it with the affection and familiarity that we do our private plans and ambitions.  Fear and dislike of the Good may turn to admiration and reverence, but our attitude towards it never loses something of that awe which we feel in the presence of a power greatly superior to ourselves.  In spite, then, of moral development and an increasing conformity to the demands of the Ideal, duty always retains a suggestion of

that stern and inflexible authority expressed in the lines
of Wordsworth:

> " Stern Daughter of the Voice of God,
>    O Duty, if that name thou love
>    Who art a light to guide, a rod
>    To check the erring and reprove;
>    Thou, who art victory and law
>    When empty terrors overawe;
>    From vain temptations dost set free;
>    And calm'st the weary strife of frail humanity! "

3. **The Good as Identical with the Interest of the Individual.**—When the facts of the moral life are made the
subject of conscious reflection the identity of Goodness
with the nature and interest of the individual assumes
greater prominence than any semblance of opposition between them. It is true that the voice of duty never loses
the note of authority when it demands the subjection of
present desire or natural impulse. Yet it is not an authority external to the human individual constraining him
against his will. So far from this, the distinguishing characteristic of duty or moral obligation is its utter difference
from such external compulsion. When the individual
recognizes a moral obligation, he feels that he owes the
act in question, not to any person or power outside him,
but to himself. To his conscience, he may say it is, but his
conscience is an integral part of his own nature. The
authority of conscience is therefore an authority self-constituted, and the law of duty is a law which we impose
on ourselves. Neither can be understood except as an
expression of the will of the agent—a different will from
that which flames out in momentary desire, but as the very
contrast suggests, a steadier and larger will. There is no
disputing that the demands of goodness express the nature
of the individual and are identical with his true interest.
This identity of the Good with the highest interests of

man cannot be doubted even in the most extreme cases of opposition between the requirements of duty and the apparent interest of the individual. Duty may demand that he give up comfort and possessions, health, and even life, in the discharge of some service to the state whose importance is not recognized or appreciated. Is not the Good opposed to the interest of the individual in this case? No, the fact that he felt this political or social obligation shows that there was a side of his nature which could not be satisfied with wealth, comfort, or pleasure, but which required for its expression some positive contribution to social welfare. Even though the action is one which a fuller understanding of the matter will show to be actually at variance with the true interest of the individual or his fellow-men, the simple fact that the agent feels an obligation to perform it proves that for him in ignorance, for him with his limitations and prejudices,—it is a genuine expression of himself and hence represents at the time his highest interest. It has been truly said in the case often cited of the zealous Puritan, who was willing to be damned if it would increase God's glory, that for this particular man as he was, possessed of the peculiar theological conceptions and intense religious convictions of his sect, such a fate for himself, with the resulting augmentation of the divine glory, might represent the fullest satisfaction of his nature. Such discrepancies between the form and the content of goodness are fortunately rare and destined to become rarer as moral enlightenment proceeds. One of the greatest services of ethical reflection has been to make perfectly clear this dependence of the Good, or the Moral Ideal, upon the nature of man. A better understanding of this fact by people at large will make it less easy in the future than it has been in the past for politicians and ecclesiastics to work upon the consciences of men through the agencies of school and church, arousing in them a reverence for laws and institutions actually opposed to the highest human welfare, on the plea that they express the commands of Deity for mankind.

4. **These Two Aspects of Goodness Explained by the Principle of Self-Realization.**—These two aspects of the relation of the Good to the human individual, neither of which can be denied, yet which seem to contradict one another absolutely, are explained and adjusted when we view the Good as Self-realization. From this standpoint the Good is interpreted as the realization of the whole self. But the whole self, it must be remembered, is actual only at the end of the process. This, the goal of moral evolution, is seldom if ever reached in the present world, and exists— it must be confessed—rather as an ideal limit than as an actual state. In all stages of incomplete moral development, which is the condition of all human individuals, only a part and not the whole of the self is actual. Hence the Good, which is always identical with the demands of the larger total self, is partially external to, and may be sharply at variance with, the desires of the actual self. The existence of the larger self, as yet latent and unrealized, is demonstrated, however, by the obligation felt to transcend the narrow boundaries of the actual nature and enter a larger life. Thus a solution is reached of the chief antinomy of the moral life—that the Good is identical with the interest of human nature and at the same time opposed to it. The Good is identical with the interest of the whole self, which exists during the course of moral evolution only *in potentia,* and opposed to the interest of the part self, which is alone actual.

Of course, the character of the self is continually changing as moral development proceeds, and consequently the battle-ground between its actual nature and latent possibilities is constantly shifting. There are, however, certain points in the pathway of moral progress where the conflict between the actual and the ideal seems especially severe. These assume the proportions of crises in moral experience; for upon the issue of the battle here waged depends the further progress of the individual. Perhaps the most important of these conflicts are those between the sentient or " natural " self and the personal or " spiritual " self, and between the individual or egoistic and the social or altruistic self. In the first case we find that the regulation and adjustment of animal impulse, which is the first step in self-realization, has apparently increased rather than diminished the desire for sentient satisfaction. For such regulation is productive of fuller health and a higher degree of physical energy. Hence the craving for pleasure to be obtained from the due gratification of all sensuous desires becomes stronger and it is accompanied by an increasing consciousness of power to gain such gratification. To the demands for a larger spiritual attainment the nature of individuals, thus dominated by a desire for sentient satisfaction, interpose the most stubborn resistance. A striking instance of such conflict is afforded in the case of young men who, in the full tide of youthful vitality, are confronted by the necessity of submitting to a long period of preparatory discipline as the condition of successful achievement in some professional sphere. To oppose the insistent clamor of fully awakened senses for their appropriate satisfaction is indeed to battle against nature. Yet such a conquest of nature is the *sine qua non* of all further attainment and many a promising career has been ruined through failure to achieve it.

In an analogous way, the second conflict arises when as the result of the organization of all the desires and capacities of the individual into a unitary system, a well-defined self-interest appears. This self-interest, when it first emerges from the confusion of opposing tendencies, stands for the individual in his individuality as a single unit among many, and thus is of a markedly exclusive character. The individual is sharply conscious of himself as possessing plans and purposes—in short, an interest—which is entirely his own and quite different from the interest of every other human being. Hence one prominent part of his true good is external to the nature of the individual at this stage. The welfare of others, which constitutes an important element in the Good when completely realized, is largely absent from the interest of the self when this is first defined in moral evolution. The cost of increasing coherence is at first increasing narrowness of character; the immediate result of concentration may be accentuated selfishness. When a man, by the ordering of his various impulses, first awakens to the existence of his own individuality his attention is naturally centered upon himself and upon his hopes and plans as a separate individual. He finds that his ambition often conflicts with the purposes of others. The whole tendency of his awakened self-consciousness is to fulfil this ambition of his, to satisfy his own desire at any cost, regardless of the welfare of others and the suffering he may cause among his fellow-men. If, notwithstanding his natural inclinations, he feels obliged to promote another's interest at the expense of his own, he regards the Good which he realizes as entirely external to himself. Duty appears to him as a foreign authority coercing him against his will and compelling him to give up his own Good. Yet here also it is necessary for the individual to surrender his private plans and his actual ambitions if he is to participate in the fuller life of social interchange and community.

It must not be forgotten, when we dwell thus upon the conflict of the ideal with the actual nature of the individual, that the feeling of obligation, the recognition of a duty, to overcome the limitations of this narrow, actual self, proves clearly that a larger nature exists latent and undeveloped. No matter how reluctant the admission, no matter how grudging the assent, still the fact that the duty is admitted, the obligation assented to, shows that the larger self is there waiting to be developed. And the development follows, by the necessity of psychological law, when the obligation is met and the duty performed. Led by a sense of duty, and with great unwillingness, a man may engage in the politics of his own city. He may not at first feel the slightest interest in the matter—in fact, may have a strong repugnance for the associations and activities which it involves. But after repeatedly acting as civic duty demands in caucus and election, he begins to form new habits which make these activities easier and more natural. Direct participation in political affairs gives him first-hand knowledge and more intimate acquaintance with them. This in turn arouses interest, and before many years the newly-formed habits pass into a permanent disposition or trait of character which seeks expression and finds pleasure in the discharge of those offices which formerly were performed with dread and disgust. Thus the actual nature of an individual is extended and enlarged, with its boundaries approaching ever more nearly those of his total self,—the universal self, that is,—present implicitly in all human individuals. This larger self which is developed through effort and struggle is often called the " second nature " to contrast it with the first nature which is partially the result of heredity and early training. Speaking in the same fashion, Hegel says: " The harmoniousness of childhood is a gift from the hand of nature: the second harmony must spring from the labor and culture of the Spirit." [2] When the Good thus becomes a second nature it is no longer in any sense external to the self, but becomes the spontaneous expression of a character which has been so

[2] HEGEL: *Logic* (Wallace trans., p. 55).

broadened as to include the interests of others and so organized as to realize all of the capacities of intelligent personality.

5. **Arnold's Contrast of Hebraism with Hellenism.**— These two aspects of the Good which we have been considering are connected by Matthew Arnold, in his famous essay, *Hebraism and Hellenism,* with two great historic forces at work in human society. The final aim of these two spiritual forces, he asserts, is the same,—man's perfection or salvation; but they pursue their aim by very different courses. The one emphasizes action. Its leading idea is conduct and obedience—obedience to the divine law, in strict conformity to the demands of conscience. Only thus can man conquer the sinful tendency in his own nature and realize in himself the perfection of the divine. The emphasis of the other is upon intelligence. It seeks to know human life and the world of human experience as they are. And to such insight the Good appears as a reasonable and beautiful thing—the condition of human happiness, to be pursued spontaneously and joyously. "And these two forces we regard as in some sense rivals—rivals not by a necessity of their own nature, but as exhibited in man and his history. And to give these forces names from the two races of men who have supplied the most signal and splendid manifestations of them, we may call them, respectively, the forces of Hebraism and Hellenism. Hebraism and Hellenism—between these two points of influence moves our world. At one time it feels more powerfully the attraction of one of them, at another time of the other; and it ought to be, though it never is, evenly and happily balanced between them." Christianity, according to Arnold, is but a modification of Hebraism. "Christianity changed nothing in the essential bent of Hebraism to set doing above knowing. Self-conquest, self-devotion, the following, not our own individual will, but the will of God,

*obedience,* is the fundamental idea of this form, also, of the discipline to which we have attached the general name of Hebraism.'' Hellenism was re-born at the beginning of the modern era, in the Renaissance with its desire for knowledge of the material world and its appreciation of the beauty in nature and human art. It persists in the ideal of culture which aims at a perfection of man's natural qualities. It was met, however, by a new form of Hebraism, the product of the Reformation. Protestantism called upon men to find their chief good in obedience to the divine will as revealed in the Scriptures. This, the Puritan ideal, which makes duty or conscience supreme in human life, is still the strongest moral force in the world.—Neither of these two great spiritual disciplines which have for so long opposed one another and still offer to humanity sharply conflicting ideals is to be looked upon as furnishing the law of human development. '' They are, each of them, contributions to human development, august contributions, invaluable contributions; and each showing itself to us more august, more invaluable, more preponderant over the other, according to the moment in which we take them and the relation in which we stand to them.''

6. **Hebraism.**—It will be illuminating to dwell a little longer upon these two tendencies in the spiritual development of humanity which Arnold contrasts so effectively; for here, as in many other cases, history gives vitality and concreteness to a distinction which of itself might seem abstract and theoretical. Let us therefore compare the two conflicting doctrines upon important points, and then inquire if there has not arisen in history a third view which may be taken as a synthesis of the other two. We derive our knowledge of Hebraism chiefly from the literature of the Old Testament. There man's good is represented as existing, entirely outside his own nature, in the

will of God.[3]  Man is, in fact, believed to be entirely sinful and incapable of knowing his own good.  The primary and essential condition of goodness for him is obedience to the divine will.  The commands of God are not discovered by the exercise of human reason : they are revealed, in the form of a divine law, by inspired law-givers and prophets.  The revelation of this divine law to a particular people is based upon a covenant in which God as Law-giver agrees, in reward of their obedience to this law, to make of them a favored race and to continue them under His protection and guidance.  The result of obedience, if given, will not be goodness or perfection in man like to that of God.  But man will attain, through obedience unto righteousness, a state of conformity to the divine will.  The sphere in which this righteousness is exercised is to be not a political state, but a theocratic kingdom, a divinely established order to be set up in Israel.  The people of God's choice may live righteously, ruled by God Himself.  This ethico-religious system under which the Hebrew people lived had the great merit of holding before men a lofty ideal raised above the level of individual interest because believed to proceed from the Creator and Sovereign Power of all the world.  Thus the requirements of morality were given the dignity and majesty of a law with a superhuman source and supernatural sanctions.  But this very separation of the Good from the nature and interest of man had evil consequences which in time seemed to outweigh the merits of the system.  Since the Good found expression in a law imposed upon men from without, it was inevitable that they should pay more and more attention to outward conformity and less and less to inward motive and disposition.  Great care was expended in learning with literal exactness the requirements of the law and in practising with formal

[3] *Cf.* BRUCE: *Ethics of the Old Testament*, Chap. I, (2) " Fundamental Principles of Old Testament Ethics."

precision the observances which it required.  Thus Hebraism degenerated into that arid legalism and barren formalism which permitted an exact outward compliance with the law—a mere husk of righteousness—to exist along with injustice and cruelty and avarice,—a condition denounced by the later prophets and still more strongly reprobated by Jesus himself.

7. **Hellenism.**—In all essential points the Ethics of Hellenism is the antithesis of the Hebrew doctrine.  For the Greek thinker it was a truth self-evident that the Good was based upon the nature of man and identical with his true happiness.[4]  Not that all the Greek moralists were Hedonists, but it was an assumption common to all their theories that, whatever the Good was, it would be such as to bring man that happiness which results from the fulfilment of his nature.  Even the Cynics, who recommended the renunciation of all natural pleasure, did so because they believed that only through such asceticism could the human soul gain peace and the opportunity to exercise freely and uninterruptedly its own capacities.  With regard to the primary and essential factor in goodness, practically all the Greek moralists agree that this is the exercise of reason.  Wisdom, the distinctively human capacity, is the one sterling coin for which all the virtues may be exchanged,[5] and constitutes the foundation of every good life.  Reason when exercised gives man an insight into his own nature and into his relations with his fellow-men: it enables him to foresee the consequences of his conduct and to act with a view to his future happiness.  The effect of thus applying reason to the conduct of human life is to produce order and harmony.  The several activities of man's nature are so regulated and adjusted that their expression is harmonious and proportionate.  Such balance

---

[4] ARISTOTLE: *Nicomachean Ethics,* Bk. I, Chap. V.
[5] PLATO: *Phaedo,* 69.

and proportion in the play of its different activities are equivalent to the health of the soul, which is identical with virtue or goodness.[6] The sphere in which this rationally ordered life is attained is the body-politic, the city-state; since man is a social animal, and complete satisfaction is possible to his nature only when, through the discharge of his duties as citizen, he is brought into varied and intimate associations with his fellows. For its effort thus to connect the Good with man's nature Greek Ethics is deserving of highest praise. Represented as the perfection of human nature, the Ideal is made to appear in its demands both reasonable and beautiful. Morality, instead of being an unwilling obedience to a law exacting and inflexible, is the spontaneous expression of a soul enlightened by reason. But this identification of the Good with the culture and perfection of man's faculties had unfortunate results in Greek thought. For an imperfect understanding of human nature led to an inadequate conception of the Good. Reason was made supreme, and thus the Good limited to what could be reasonably expected to increase the satisfaction of the human individual. Hence no sufficient basis was provided, after all, for social obligation. It was possible to show that the citizens of a Greek city had mutual interests, and, for that reason, were bound in duty to assist and serve one another. But that such a community of interest extended to barbarians and slaves could not be demonstrated, and consequently no social obligation was admitted which extended beyond the limits of the Greek nation to humanity in general. And when the Greek states lost their independence and their citizens were brought into more direct contact with other nationalities and classes, this individualism in their ethical thought was further accentuated until, in the later theories, the chief function of reason in human conduct was to give the individual a

[6] PLATO: *Republic*, 443.

means of satisfaction within himself which should free him from the need of all social activities and relationships.

8. **Relation of Christianity to Hebraism and Hellenism.**—In the opinion of Arnold, as we have seen, Christianity is only a modification of Hebraism, sharing its one-sidedness and inadequacy. Such criticism may be justly applied to the interpretation of Christianity which regards it as a continuation of the Hebrew cult, in which an intellectual assent to the divinity of the Founder is offered as a substitute for that perfect conformity to the divine law which God demands and man is unable to achieve. But we find in the teachings of Jesus another and a higher view—in all important respects identical with that of " self-realization "—which raises Christianity far above the limitations of both Hebraism and Hellenism and makes of it a comprehensive synthesis of the profound and enduring truths contained in these two historic doctrines. Jesus based the Good neither upon a divine will external to man, nor upon the actual nature of the human individual. He always taught that goodness consisted in inward disposition and not in outward conformity : it must be rooted deep in the soul of man and develop as a true expression of his nature. " Have salt in yourselves " (Mark 9 : 50), he admonishes his disciples, and always sought to arouse and strengthen the better part of their natures. Of all the laws of the old Hebrew dispensation, none was more distinctive or held in greater reverence than that concerning Sabbath observance. Yet Jesus did not hesitate to break this law when human welfare could be benefited thereby, and to his critics he replied, " The Sabbath was made for man, and not man for the Sabbath." (Mark 2 : 27.)  Nor, on the other hand, did he identify the Good with the actual interest of man. Rather did he insist that its attainment was an arduous task, involving struggle and submission.

The individual must prepare to see his own nature thwarted and his own desires suppressed if he proposes to pursue the Ideal. The sacrifice of private aim and ambition was said to be the condition of achieving the higher good. He who would find his life must be willing first to lose it. As the death of the seed is the condition of the growth of the plant, so the death of the old self is the condition of the development of the new life of virtue and goodness. Not, then, in a law imposed upon man from without, nor in desires existing within him, does Jesus find the ground and source of goodness, but in a larger self latent in human nature. This larger self pertains neither to God nor man exclusively, but is common to both and testifies to the union of the human and the divine. It is, in fact, the divine principle in man, and in its realization man shares the divine life, while God is expressed in human nature. Through the submission of his actual nature the individual realizes his larger self, and this perfecting of his own nature brings him into harmony with his fellow-men and with God.

In further evidence of its synthetic character Christianity finds the prime condition of goodness neither in wisdom nor obedience, but in a union of thought and action—i.e. *faith*. It does not exalt as the essence of righteousness in man an unquestioning obedience to a will external to him and a law arbitrarily imposed upon his conduct. Instead Jesus based his injunctions upon a well-defined and consistent view of man and the universe. According to this, the Christian view of the world, man is not what he seems, a merely natural being whose Good lies in the satisfaction of his material wants. He is in his deepest nature spiritual and the child of the Divine Spirit, who is the source of all reality. Hence the larger life for man, the more real existence, is a spiritual life in which those ends are sought which have universal value. But in the teachings of Jesus no attempt is made to prove or demonstrate the truth of these views. Since they concern the possibilities of human development they lie beyond the region of direct proof or demonstration. The only proof which the individual can have of their truth comes from acting upon them. He must be willing to make the venture before he can experience the satisfaction of the larger life. This venture involves the surrender of objects known to have value for the sake of others which are untried, in actual experience unknown. Faith in the Christian conception is therefore an act of will—enlightened by reason, but not prescribed or pre-determined by reason. The will in this action only expresses the larger self, voicing the latent possibilities in the human individual of a more comprehensive and completely organized life.

The larger self, which is the basis of Christian Ethics, furnishes also a new social bond among human beings. Since all men possess this divine principle latent in their natures they are all united by ties of spiritual kinship. A recognition of this kinship awakens in the individual a love for his fellow-men. This love is different from a natural sympathy for a limited number of friends and acquaintances; it is an enthusiastic devotion to the ideal possibilities which are present in every human individual and give to each an infinite value. This love, when it is awakened, constitutes the only motive sufficient to impel men to unlimited social service. To such motive Christianity appeals, and arouses the individual to effort in behalf of all mankind. Its sphere is therefore not that of the political state, or an ecclesiastical organization, but of the whole human race, and its social ideal, that of the Kingdom of God, is a universal society in which the divine spirit of justice and benevolence prevails and each individual is given an opportunity for the fullest personal development.

# CHAPTER II

## SELF-REALIZATION AND THE STANDARD OF GOODNESS

1. **The Idea of the Good as Furnishing a Standard of Moral Judgment.**—One of the reasons why it is worth our while to inquire at length into the nature of the *summum bonum* is that the conception of the Good when attained should provide us with a satisfactory standard of moral judgment. Indeed it seems that this is the chief reason for such a study as we have undertaken; since the leading aim of Ethics is to rationalize human conduct, and this is accomplished only by substituting a rational basis for the authority of custom and tradition, in all judgments of moral value. Now, as previous discussion has shown, the idea of the Good ought to furnish just this rational basis for the deciding of all questions of good and evil, and hence for the practical guidance of life. We have a right to expect, therefore, that Self-realization, if a true view of the Good, will fully meet this requirement. To the question of whether the theory of Self-realization actually furnishes such a standard of moral judgment we now address ourselves.

**2. Self-Realization Criticised as Failing to Furnish Such a Standard.**—Unfortunately, difficulties are encountered at the very beginning in the form of charges recently made that Self-realization fails in just this matter of supplying an adequate criterion of right and wrong. It is asserted, in the first place, that Self-realization gives no ground for discriminating between different acts of the individual, since all are equally expressions of the self and hence good. Professor W. R. Sorley has thus criticised " self-realization " because it affords no standard for estimating the moral value of the different actions of the individual. " In every action whatever of a conscious being," he says, " self-realization may be said to be the end: some capacity is being developed, satisfaction is being sought for some desire. A man may develop his capacities, seek, and to some extent attain self-satisfaction,—in a manner realize himself—not only in devotion to a scientific or artistic ideal or in labors for a common good, but also in the selfish pursuit of power, or even in sensual enjoyment. So far as the word ' self-realization ' can be made to cover such different activities, it is void of moral content and cannot express the nature of the moral ideal." [1]

In the second place, it is charged that Self-realization does not permit us to make distinctions of moral worth, as between the conduct of different individuals. For are not all individuals equally *selves*, and in so far as the activities of each express his own nature, are not all upon the same plane of goodness? In this connection, Professor Boodin, for instance, criticises Self-realization and charges it with failure to furnish a standard for the evaluation of conduct. " There are many types of selves, and each type desires its own fulfilment. If self-realization is to be the criterion of life, what self is to be realized, the baboon self, the pig self, or what sort of self? If all but human

[1] W. R. SORLEY: *Recent Tendencies in Ethics*, p. 90.

selves are to be excluded, what sort of human self? Not the criminal or the insane self, surely? Only a normal self could be the standard. As Plato says, it must be a very wise man who is to be the measure. But what is normal?"[2]

These critics strike at a vital point in the Self-realization theory. The defect dwelt upon is not an unimportant or external feature which can be easily removed. Instead it appears to be inseparably connected with the fundamental principle of Self-realization. For it is the peculiar merit as well as the distinguishing characteristic of this view that it finds the Good not in the exercise of any one part or faculty of human nature, but in the harmonious development of the whole self. But does not this fact, which is the boast of the Self-realizationist—that his theory recognizes as equally legitimate and worthy all the tendencies and powers of conscious personality—prove a stumbling-block when the attempt is made to use the theory as a basis of moral judgment? For how discriminate between acts, approving some as good and condemning others as bad, when all are equally necessary expressions of the self? And how impose the same standard upon different selves, when they vary in character and ability, and the ideal demands that each should realize his own capacities?

Because they exalt one side of human nature at the expense of the rest, the time-honored doctrines of Hedonism and Rationalism have been discarded. But by virtue of this very quality—one-sidedness, we consider it—they succeed, where Self-realization seems to fail, in furnishing a definite standard of moral judgment. Take Hedonism, for instance; pleasant feeling is declared to be the Good. Hence all acts that bring pleasure now or in the future are morally good; all acts that bring pain are morally

[2] "The Ought and Reality," *International Journal of Ethics*, July, 1907, p. 457.

bad; all other acts are morally indifferent. The case is the same with Rationalism, if the exercise of reason be substituted for the feeling of pleasure. If we take either of these two doctrines as the rule of life, we can contrast acts which satisfy the chosen part of the self with acts that satisfy other parts, draw a sharp line of distinction between them, and judge the former actions to be good and the latter to be bad. Thus we gain a serviceable principle for the ordering of our lives, which is certainly better than no principle at all, and perhaps better than a principle which presents an attractive ideal but supplies no guidance for the conduct of daily life.

3. **The Ideal of Self-Realization as the Standard of Moral Judgment.**—Self-realization need rest under no such condemnation, however; since such criticisms as those just mentioned result from a misunderstanding of the theory. It is a mistake to think that because Self-realization identifies the Good with the expression of no one part of the self to the exclusion of the remainder, it therefore approves of all activities of the self as good. True it is, that our view finds the Good in the exercise of no one faculty of human nature, but this does not mean that it is consequently deprived of any criterion by which right action can be distinguished from wrong. On the contrary, it furnishes a very definite criterion. For, according to Self-realization, the Good lies in the realization of the *whole* self in distinction from any part or division of the self. From this ideal we secure a clear and decisive standard of moral judgment. The line of distinction is drawn between actions which contribute to the satisfaction of all the capacities of the human self and those which serve to gratify only single ones. The former are judged good: the latter are pronounced bad. So far from making only vague and ambiguous recommendation, Self-realization issues the most definite and peremptory commands. All

acts which hinder or frustrate the fulfilment of man's entire self it condemns as utterly wrong, and it demands their absolute suppression. Thus we gain a secure and adequate basis for all judgments of moral value.

The Ideal of Self-realization furnishes no infallible touchstone of good and evil, to be sure, deciding off-hand the moral value of every particular act. It is an ideal of a very general character. Its application to specific questions of right and wrong is often not apparent, and can be made out only by protracted and careful thought. This does not lessen the value of Self-realization as the Ideal, however; for, in order to fulfil this office, a conception must be sufficiently general to comprehend within its scope all practical considerations whatsoever, and to be universally applicable throughout the entire field of conduct. Hence while in the regulation of daily life we may find that principles, more definite in meaning and limited in range, are usually of greater assistance, still on critical occasions when these principles themselves are called into question such an ideal is indispensable as a final court of appeal. The Ideal may be likened to the polar star which, far removed from the affairs of our planet, gives to the surveyor of the earth's surface his ultimate direction of reference. He does not take it into consideration every time he measures a distance or computes an area. Yet since it furnishes the direction upon which all other directions are based, there is a tacit reference to it in every calculation of the surveyor, and, in all cases of serious doubt, it is the final court of appeal.

Whenever we are driven back to first premises we have need of such a standard as the Ideal of Self-realization supplies. This may occur in the case of acts that are comparatively unimportant. An action which in itself is trivial, like playing a game of cards or calling upon an acquaintance, may take on the significance of a test case and involve all the issues of morality. Ordinarily, however, we have recourse to an ultimate standard only when considering such broad and fundamental problems of human life and relationships as call in question otherwise accepted principles of conduct. This is the case when we are required to pass judgment upon existing political and social institutions. Then the value of such a standard as Self-realization is most clearly manifest. Suppose that it is a form of government which we are critically considering; for instance, democracy or aristocracy. Then it is illuminating and even necessary to know that the final aim of government is neither to promote the interest of a special class nor to register the will of a majority, but to further the development of human personality in all individuals, to express the '' general will.'' Or if it is a social institution, like monogamous marriage, of which we are seeking to ascertain the value—then we must recognize that the worth of such an institution depends, not upon the extent to which it fulfils a supposed divine command or continues a historic development, but rather upon the degree to which it contributes to the self-realization of the persons involved. Or, better stated perhaps, the pretensions of any social or political arrangement to be of divine origin or in the line of moral development may be rejected as false when this arrangement does not minister to the personal welfare of humanity.

4. **This Standard When Applied to Human Life Yields Further Principles of Moral Distinction.**—Still it must be admitted that if Self-realization were limited to enjoining every individual to realize his entire self, there would be sufficient justification for the second criticism noted above, that the theory provides no definite principles of conduct which are binding upon all individuals. For since individuals differ in character and in capacities the expression of the entire nature will involve quite different

forms of conduct for each one. Self-realization, as thus far considered, an ideal which recommends the realization of the whole as distinct from the part self, leaves undecided the question of what kind of a self is to be fully realized, normal or abnormal, primitive or civilized, masculine or feminine, intellectual, emotional, or practical. But this objection also disappears after further reflection. When the Ideal of Self-realization, which we have accepted as the standard of moral judgment, is applied to actual human nature, it yields certain definite principles of action which hold for all men equally and constitute in themselves an adequate answer to the objection. For while human nature varies almost without limit there are, as has been shown, fundamental characteristics which all men possess in common. In the first place, all men have the same natural instincts, which relate them to a world of objects and to other members of the human species. Secondly, men are all alike in the possession of certain spiritual capacities, which relate them to fellow-men in a community of intelligence and to the real universe as an orderly system. In consequence of this essential identity of human nature, the realization of the whole self requires from all of us the same modes of action. It is possible, therefore, to derive from the Ideal of Self-realization, when applied to the actual nature of man, a set of principles and maxims which enable us to distinguish between good and evil in our daily experience. Of course, the whole self is not realized in a single act or all at once. Rather is it gradually unfolded or developed in a number of spheres and through a succession of stages. What we wish to know is what form of conduct expresses the whole self and hence deserves to be called *good* in each important sphere and at every necessary stage.

The two most important spheres or aspects of the life of the self are the *individual* and the *social*. In the sphere first-named, the self is manifest as an individual, gaining expression through a system of objects. In the second, the self appears as united with other individuals in a social community. In the first sphere the whole self is represented by the total interest of the individual or the satisfaction of all his desires and capacities in their organized unity, in contrast to his partial interest or the satisfaction of one or more desires at the expense of the rest. In the second sphere the whole self is represented by the welfare of society or the social self, in contrast to the interest of any individual or limited number of individuals. When applied to both of these spheres the Ideal of Self-realization thus yields two principles of moral judgment, each of which may be briefly considered.

5. **The Principle of Individual Interest.**—The principle which Self-realization furnishes to guide moral judgment in the individual sphere is that *the total interest of the individual is to be preferred to any partial interest whatsoever.* And since this total interest is the result of the adjustment of various activities and tendencies of the individual into an organized system, its attainment will involve the proportionate expression of all these activities— and that in contrast to the gratification of any single desire or group of desires. Some moralists do not admit the existence of such an adjustment within the life of the individual in distinction from the adjustment of the individual to society. For example, Mr. Alexander, in his *Moral Order and Progress*,[3] tells us that Goodness may be understood either as (1) an adjustment of activities in the individual or as (2) an adjustment of individuals in society. These adjustments are identical in process and result. Hence the individual who gives harmonious expression to all his impulses at the same time discharges in full his obligation to society. The same writer endeavors

[3] ALEXANDER: *Moral Order and Progress,* Book II, Chap. II.

to show how all the virtues usually regarded as solely individual have also a social reference. Now it is assuredly true that the individual and the social spheres cannot be separated, and that they imply one another at every point. Such a virtue as temperance, ordinarily thought of as individual, has a decided social bearing. But nevertheless to deny the existence of a sphere at least relatively distinct from the social, in which the individual is concerned only with his own interest, is to overlook certain of the most salient features of morality. It is to neglect the importance of the development of individuality in the moral life, both in itself and as a condition of the further adjustment of the individual to society.

The need for recognizing a distinctly individual sphere of action is apparent when we think of the principles which should determine the individual's choice of a profession or occupation. While it is important for the individual to take account of social conditions and demands, it is still more important for him to consider his own abilities and limitations, and select that line of work in which the one shall receive the fullest expression and the other offer the least hindrance. For genuine ability in a man when honestly exercised may always be socially useful, while a work undertaken for social benefit will fail of its purpose if the individual is unfitted to perform it. When social influences or economic pressure interfere, therefore, to prevent the individual from consulting his own aptitudes and preferences in this matter of a life-work, the result is morally injurious. In European countries young men have been drawn in large numbers into the clergy and the army, not because of any particular fitness for these professions, but because social convention has set an artificial premium upon activity in these lines and thus put at a comparative disadvantage other professions. In America accepted social standards tend, in like manner, to infringe upon the liberty of the individual by setting a premium upon business and political success, and reflecting corresponding discredit upon scholarly and artistic achievement. As Professor Münsterberg says: " If we are sincere we ought not to overlook the fact that the scholar, as such, has no position in public opinion which corresponds to the true value of his achievement. The foreigner feels at once this difference between the Americans and the Europeans. . . . The finest men go into business and industry, into law and medicine; and those who turn to the graduate schools of the country are, in the majority, men without initiative and ambition, and without promise for the highest kind of work." [4]　And what is here said applies, not merely to professions and " callings," but to every trade and occupation which men pursue. The establishment of vocation bureaus in some of our large cities, through which individuals are relieved of economic pressure for a short time, during which they are assisted in finding the occupation for which their natures have fitted them, shows how far the rights of individuality in this respect have been violated under present social conditions. The man, who as carpenter or brick-layer leads a dissatisfied and unregulated life, may as sign-painter become a happy and useful citizen, because, in the latter case, his native ability is finding free expression and not being thwarted and stifled.

After the life-work is once chosen the individual may rightfully claim a large liberty in methods of preparation and accomplishment. He should follow the principle which governs action in the individual sphere—selecting those means which promise, in his case and with his nature, the most effectually to further his supreme aim. Of course human experience has discovered, in the case of the leading occupations, what is in general the best preparatory train-

[4] Hugo Münsterberg: " The Standing of Scholarship in America," *Atlantic Monthly*, October, 1900, p. 455.

ing, and the individual greatly economizes his own time and strength who submits willingly to such preparation and appropriates as much as possible of its benefit. But when accepted methods of preparation and practice in any trade or profession become so rigid and exacting as to cramp his originality and destroy his initiative, they lessen the individual's power of achievement, and he is justified in rebelling against them and asserting the right of his individuality to seek its own methods of accomplishment.

In other details of his conduct not related to his specific life-work, but intimately connected with himself, such as dress, amusements, and daily routine, the individual should have in a large measure the freedom to determine his action in accordance with what he believes to be his highest interest. These are not matters of great moment, but they are ways in which individuality naturally seeks expression. Hence they may assume a critical importance when an unwarranted interference in them is attempted by society, and such interference, if successful, reacts most unfavorably upon the character of the individual. In this way sumptuary and " blue " laws, such as those enacted by our Puritan ancestors, do great harm. Unfortunately, some traces of this aspect of Puritanism are still seen among us, especially in our smaller communities, where a person's attitude towards " worldly amusements " is deemed more significant of his character than his acts of justice or of mercy. The right which many Protestant communities arrogate to themselves of censoring their minister's conduct, even in the minutiæ of clothing and amusements and domestic economy, has undoubtedly lessened the efficiency of many members of the Protestant ministry, thwarting their individuality and destroying their independence, thus causing them to appear negative and colorless in their virtue.

6. **The Principle of Social Welfare.**—In the social sphere Self-realization requires that *the welfare of society be preferred to the interest of any individual.* The human individual is thus forbidden in all his relations with his fellows to utilize other individuals as means or instruments to the attainment of his own interest, but is rather enjoined to seek the interests of others as his own. This subordination of individual interest to social welfare is not in any sense a violation of the true welfare of the self. Instead it signifies the realization of the social self, and this social self is larger and more complete than the individual for the very reason that it does not center around a single individual interest, but comprehends in an organized system a vast number of interests each one of which is an end in itself. The social self is a kingdom of ends the content and value of each of which is increased by its relation to all the rest; human society is an organic system in which all the members stand in functional relation to the whole.

The principle of social welfare applies to all human action that concerns more than one individual. Of course every action of a normal human being has its reference to other individuals, but, as we have just recognized, this reference is often only indirect and implied. On the other hand, there are actions of the individual that are primarily social in their character. Such are, for instance, the activities of citizenship. In a democracy the most important of these activities is the exercise of the franchise. In his voting the individual citizen should be governed altogether by the principle just enunciated. Not the promotion of individual interest in any of its forms, but the furtherance of public welfare should be the aim of every ballot cast. This moral issue which is involved in every election is frequently confused where popular government is secured through the party system. In that case the individual cannot vote directly upon measures and policies, but only for party candidates who are pledged to enact certain laws and follow certain policies. Now it is unlikely that a man who thinks seriously about public welfare will agree entirely with the platform of any party. Yet, if his vote and influence are not to be entirely ineffective, he must join one of the leading parties and support it loyally. Hence election time finds the good citizen aiming directly at party success rather than public welfare. This necessity for choosing some party as best on the whole, and then of loyally supporting it, despite objectionable features in policies or personnel, does not mean, however, that the citizen shall cease to think for himself on all matters of public concern or shall hesitate to abandon his party on the instant that he is convinced that the policies of another party are more in accord with the general welfare. Unfortunately, this is just what it does mean with many citizens who substitute a blind loyalty to party for an intelligent devotion to social welfare, thus seeking the good of a group within the state rather than that of the state itself.

The same situation is reproduced on a larger scale when we think of the relation of the human individual to other individuals of different nationality—to human beings over all the world. The citizen of a modern state can exert very little direct influence for good or for ill upon the citizens of other states. The rise of the nationalistic idea in modern times seems in many ways to have increased the barriers between civilized states. But the rise of the nationalistic idea has been accompanied by the inception and growth of *internationalism*—the belief that the single state has an office to discharge in the family of nations. Hence while the individual citizen can do little directly to affect the destinies of the millions of human beings living outside his own state, he can have a share in determining the policies of his own nation, which, acting in its national capacity, may affect profoundly the welfare of humanity over all the world. The principle of social welfare, applied here, shows it to be the duty of the citizen to favor those measures which promise to further, not the well-being of his own nation merely, but of all the nations, of mankind universally. There is no reason to doubt that such internationalism will be as effective in benefiting humanity as would a humanitarianism which leveled all national barriers. For, in acting at a distance and in a large way, the organized agencies of government are more adequate and efficient than the effort of single individuals or associations of individuals. At the time of the earthquake of 1908, in Italy, much valuable assistance was rendered through individual initiative and coöperative enterprise; but none so prompt and effective as that of the government, which diverted a loaded naval supply-ship to the relief of the starving sufferers.

7. **Maxims of Individual Interest: (a) Maxim of Prudence.**—But the idea of Self-realization when interpreted in the light of human experience is capable of supplying more explicit and detailed criteria of right and wrong, whose bearing upon the questions of daily conduct is direct and obvious. Let the two principles just explained, those of individual interest and social welfare, be applied within their respective spheres, and the result is in each case two corollaries or maxims. These maxims express the requirements of Self-realization in successive stages, and each constitutes within its own province the determining principle of moral judgment.

In the individual life Self-realization calls first for the regulation and adjustment of those sentient impulses which are the common heritage of mankind. Now of all the natural instincts of man that which, when raised to the level of conscious aim, is most comprehensive in its scope, is the instinct of self-preservation. At first merely a desire for present security and well-being, it develops, with the growth of intelligence, into the purpose to have comfort and pleasure throughout the natural lifetime. Its object, the individual in his physical existence, endures throughout a period of years, and is permanent compared with multitudinous objects of natural desire which are varying and transitory. Within this inclusive purpose, then, fall the objects of the other natural instincts which have been developed as means to individual survival, like those of food, acquisition, resentment, etc. Being thus inclusive of all such objects in the degree to which they contribute to man's comfort and well-being, this purpose represents the system of natural goods, and, within its own province, the Ideal of Self-realization. Hence the first maxim in the individual sphere is that *survival and future pleasure should be preferred to the gratification of any desire or desires.*

There is slight reason, it may appear, to enjoin human beings to seek their own comfort and pleasure. Prudence is easily learned, and the burden of ethical teaching must be to recommend the subordination of prudential considerations to the larger personal and social ends. Yet as limited and circumscribed as is its cause prudence constitutes an end much larger and more significant than many of the ends to which it is often subordinated. Such objects are, for example, wealth and reputation, when these are sought for themselves, and not as part of some far-reaching plan. To be sure, a certain amount of property and a good reputation are important aids in the attainment of comfort and security, and, in so far as they are thus sought, their pursuit is justified. But from being at first sought as means they become, in many cases, ends in themselves sought for their own sake and to which the comfort and pleasure of living are ruthlessly sacrificed. This is particularly true in a country like our own, where the individual's sphere of activity and social standing are not pre-determined by his birth and early surroundings. The appearance of unlimited opportunity begets a spirit of restlessness and dissatisfaction with present conditions which leads the individual to seek wealth and reputation, not from any appreciation of the larger possibilities of life which they may open, but simply from a desire to "get on." To this desire, eager and consuming, all the simpler joys of living are sacrificed—the comfort of the fireside on winters' evenings in company with interesting books or truly congenial friends, the enjoyment of the summer's holiday out-of-doors, the pleasures of unimpaired digestion, and the solace of refreshing sleep. Spencer remarks upon the folly of the husband and father. who, in order to increase the income of his family, applies himself so unremittingly to his business that his health is broken down or his life shortened.[5] How much more foolish is the individual who brings these results upon himself not because of devotion to his family but merely from a desire to surpass his acquaintances in wealth or rise above his parents in social position!

8. (b) Maxim of Idealism.—In addition to his natural instincts the human individual possesses, as we well know, certain spiritual capacities which require for their satisfaction the attainment of ideal objects, such as Truth and Power and Beauty. To realize himself fully it follows, then, that the individual must seek and attain not only material well-being but also personal culture. Now these ideal ends which man in his spiritual capacity pursues are, as has been previously shown, more comprehensive and far-reaching than any of the objects of natural instinct, even that of the instinct of self-preservation itself; because such ideals as Truth and Beauty are not limited in their scope to the period of the individual's natural lifetime but include the existence and activity of many generations

[5] SPENCER: *Data of Ethics*, § 72.

of men. Hence the individual who devotes himself to a realization of these ideals identifies himself with the cause of spiritual progress which unites men of all ages as loyal adherents and fellow-workers. We may therefore set down as the second maxim of Self-realization in the individual sphere that *the attainment of the ideal objects of intelligence and personality should be preferred to the promotion of material well-being and the gratification of natural desires.*

The grounds for this maxim should be made perfectly clear. The one and only reason why from the standpoint of Self-realization the exercise of man's spiritual capacities is better than the gratification of his natural desires is that such spiritual activity results in a larger and more comprehensive life. Thus the attainment of ideal ends, intellectual, practical, and æsthetic, represents the realization of the whole self, in contrast to which the material comfort and pleasure stand for the interest of the partial self. The life of spiritual attainment and personal culture is to be preferred morally because it is a larger and a fuller life than that of physical gratification and well-being. This is easy to see when we contrast the life of the cultivated man of affairs with his broad outlook and lasting achievements to that of the unlettered peasant with his narrow horizon and rude pleasures. But it is not so easy to see when the life of the successful man of the world and that of the struggling artist or obscure scholar are compared. Particularly is this true at present when improved facilities of transportation and communication, and the development of the arts of printing and photographic reproduction, have made it possible for a man possessed of good health and riches to travel over the entire world and to possess what books and works of art he pleases. It is difficult indeed to believe that the career of such a man, widely traveled and surrounded by all the fruits of culture, is not larger and fuller than that of the artist or investigator who has never been able to travel outside his own country and can scarcely supply himself with the books and appliances which his work necessitates.  Now the advantages of travel and the possession of books and pictures in stimulating even a belated growth of intelligence and taste are not to be overlooked on the one hand, nor is the limitation which the lack of these things imposes upon the most fruitful and promising spiritual activity to be neglected on the other.  Yet the law inexorably holds that the breadth and fullness of human life is directly proportionate to the amount of spiritual activity exercised in it.  The uncultivated man may travel to every quarter of the globe and all that his travel will yield him is a succession of unrelated impressions which soon become vague memories or are forgotten altogether.  He cannot make the objects he sees *his own* because his mind furnishes him with no background of historic associations or value judgments with which to connect them.  His varied and interesting experiences do not become a permanent addition to his life, for he has built up by his own thought and study no system of ideas within which the new experiences can be given a fixed and definite place.  Such a person may buy books by the ton and pictures by the gross, but these will remain simply material objects without a trace of profound meaning or subtle suggestion.  The scholar, artist, or investigator, on the contrary, although he possess few or comparatively none of these advantages, has through the exercise of his intellectual powers, creative ability, or artistic skill, so correlated his ideas and organized his experience that his life is extended in space and time far beyond the limits of his geographical location or natural existence, understanding the past in its relation to the present, viewing other worlds than his own, and penetrating to the deeper and essential meanings of things which do not appear on the surface but reveal themselves to rational insight and æsthetic intuition. The career of the philosopher Immanuel Kant is instructive in proving that the breadth and fullness of a human life is determined rather by cultivation of spirit than by any external advantages or possessions whatsoever. During the whole period of his maturity Kant was occupied with the methodical discharge of the routine duties of a university professor. He seldom left the university town of Koenigsberg and never went outside his native province in Germany. Yet he possessed such an inquiring mind and so comprehensive an intelligence that his reading and thought extended far beyond the subject of his special interest, philosophy, to all questions pertaining to the earth and its inhabitants. Hence in addition to his epoch-making work in philosophy he wrote treatises on the history of the earth, upon the origin of the different living forms, and upon the relations of the various races of men. These latter rank among the most important contributions of the eighteenth century to our knowledge of the natural world and anticipate in a remarkable way the evolutionary conception of the succeeding century. Thus Kant, secluded throughout life in an insignificant German town, and hampered by the exactions of an academic routine, attained a fuller knowledge of the natural world, its facts and its forces, than many a contemporary who, blessed with rank and fortune, was able to travel over Europe at will, viewing its most interesting localities and interviewing its most illustrious personages.

9. **Maxims of Social Welfare: (a) Maxim of Altruism.**—In the social sphere the primary adjustment is between single individuals or persons. The individual comes into contact with other persons like himself before he enters into conscious relations with the larger social groups such as the community, the " public," the nation, or

humanity. In all the stages of individual development the self is of course associated with others. Material comfort and pleasure are obtained by the individual only by association with other individuals in procuring the means of subsistence and maintaining the conditions necessary for human existence. In this case, however, the social relationship enters as a means to the survival and material well-being of the individual. To a still greater degree does the achievement of the aims of intelligence and personality involve the coöperation of many individuals in the fields of art and science and invention. But here the individual is brought into contact not with the lives of others in their entirety, but only with such parts as are connected by the bond of a common interest with his own. Thus a man can achieve professional success only through coöperation with his professional colleagues: but he is interested in them not as *men*, but as physicians or lawyers or engineers. It is this fact to which Mr. Chesterton refers in his picturesque and forcible way when he asserts that the social life of the large community like our modern city is much narrower and more limited than that of a small community. For in the large city we come into association only with those who have aims and interests identical with our own, while in the small community we are forced to come to terms with individuals in the totalities of their natures, which are always different from and, at some points, antagonistic to our own.

" We make our friends, we make our enemies; but God makes our next-door neighbor. Hence he comes to us clad in all the careless terrors of nature; he is as strange as the stars, as reckless and indifferent as the rain. He is Man, the most terrible of beasts. That is why the old religions and the old scriptural language showed so sharp a wisdom when they spoke, not of one's duty towards humanity but of one's duty towards one's neighbor. The duty towards humanity may often take the form of a choice which is personal and even pleasurable. That duty may be a hobby; it may even be a dissipation. . . . The most monstrous martyrdom, the most repulsive experience may be the result of a choice or a kind of taste. . . . But we have to love our neighbor because he is *there*—a much more alarming reason for a much more serious operation. He is the sample of humanity which is actually given us. Precisely because he may be anybody he is everybody. He is a symbol because he is an accident." [6]

The maxim which the principle of social welfare (and ultimately the Ideal of Self-realization) supplies for the directing of conduct in this adjustment of differing individualities is that *the individual should prefer the interest of another to his own interest.* Now it has been previously made clear that for a man possessed of the instinct of sympathy and of an intelligence to which his own personality is revealed as a universal principle present equally in the lives of all other self-conscious persons, the interest of every other human individual is an end of equal value with his own. Hence the individual does wrong when he treats another individual as a *means* to his own ends, subordinating the interest of another to his own. The reason for this is apparent when in case of conflict the interest of the *alter* is greater than that of the *ego;* for when, in such emergency, we prefer another's interest to our own we are attaining a greater good, realizing our own larger selves. Perplexity may arise, however, when the conflicting interests of *ego* and *alter* are, as far as honest thought can decide, equal in amount and importance. Why, it may be asked, when *ego* and *alter* have equal interests at stake, is it attaining a larger good to sacrifice my interest to that of another than to sacrifice his interest to mine? Only one interest can be attained: the other must be thwarted. It is asserted that both have equal value, and

[6] CHESTERTON: *Heretics,* " On the Institution of the Family," p. 185.

the same right to attainment. Let this be granted, and readily—why then should not mine be the one that is attained and the other's the one that is thwarted? There is genuine difficulty in such cases, but it is not insuperable. From the standpoint of Self-realization a form of conduct is preferred as better only as through it the self attains a larger and more inclusive end. When in the circumstances above described the individual subordinates his interest to that of another, his own interest is not entirely thwarted. It may be in so far as the attainment originally sought for is concerned. But when voluntarily sacrificed to another's good the interest of the *ego* is converted into a means to the promotion of the *alter's* interest and lives again in its complete and successful attainment. The same is not true in the contrary case where another's interest is made subordinate to one's own. The interest of the *alter* may be forcibly subordinated to the interest of the *ego,* but it not voluntarily sacrificed to it. No individual has the power to cause the aims and interests of others to sacrifice themselves voluntarily to his own interests and ambitions. Hence in the first case the conflicting interests merge, the one entering into and completing the other; in the second the one is attained at the expense, and to the exclusion, of the other. Manifestly it is in the former alternative that the self attains the larger and more inclusive end, and it is this course only which it is right for the individual to take.

Instances in which the opposing interests are exactly equal are extremely rare, however; and the difficulty just considered is more one of theory, perhaps, than of practice. Usually it is amply sufficient if the individual recognize that the interests of others have equal value with his own and then, in particular cases where the interests of *ego* and *alter* come into conflict, try earnestly to discover which is the larger good. If study of the situation shows that he has himself much more at stake than his fellow, the individual is justified in preferring his own interest. In all other circumstances he is morally bound to seek the other's good. But this obligation of the individual to interest himself in desires and ambitions which are frequently unattractive or even distasteful does not, as would at first appear, act as a check to his own development, thwarting his aims and impoverishing his life. It has just the opposite effect, by opening to the individual new sources of interest and capacities for action. When we seek the interests of others they, by virtue of being different from and antagonistic to our own, communicate to our lives a fuller and more varied content. The fullness or variety of any individual's life is measured largely by the degree to which he has, in domestic and social life, interested himself in the hopes and plans of others, participating in their efforts and sharing their successes. To seek the interests of others, therefore, so far from hampering or impoverishing the life of the self, is the most effective means to broaden and deepen it.[7]

10. (b) Maxim of Humanitarianism.—The social relationship is not limited to the association of individuals who come into direct contact with one another. For to the human individual as an intelligent person all conscious personality has the same absolute worth. Hence the welfare of humanity in the larger social groups of the community and the state and the world becomes an object to be sought for, although here a personal contact of all the individuals involved is manifestly impossible. And since

[7] Theodore Roosevelt brings out most forcibly the interest and value which attaches to each individual among the mass of our fellow-citizens if we take the trouble to investigate it. In his article, "The Coal Miner at Home," he says: "I think that those who preach to the educated man—to the graduate of a particular school or college—about his duty to the country often tend to lay the emphasis on the wrong side. If he remains aloof from his fellow-citizens, the damage done is really not as much to them as to him, and he is the man who suffers most."—*Cf. Outlook*, December 24, 1910, pp. 900-904.

all persons are alike *ends* whose interest is to be pursued, the most inclusive object is that which embraces in its realization the welfare of the largest number of persons. Most comprehensive of all objects in the social sphere is, therefore, *humanity,* the welfare of human personality universally. It follows then that the second maxim in the social sphere is that *the welfare of humanity should be preferred to the interest of any lesser number of individuals.*

The first duty of the individual in the social sphere is to seek the good of other individuals with whom he is acquainted. This means that he shall strive incessantly to extend that personal development and cultivation which he seeks for himself to the members of his family, his circle of friends, and those with whom he is professionally associated. Such effort has frequently been successful in human history, and small groups or classes have arisen which, through coöperative activity and mutual encouragement, have attained a high level of personal culture in the various fields of spiritual achievement such as art, science, literature, etc. But the culture of these small groups has usually been at the expense, rather than for the benefit, of existing humanity. A much larger number of their fellow-men have been condemned to lives of ceaseless and spirit-killing toil in order that a selected few should have the needed leisure and appropriate surroundings for the exercise of the higher psychic powers of human nature. It was thus in ancient Greece where the labor of thousands of slaves provided a small number of citizens with the means of subsistence and thus made possible their incomparable intellectual and artistic achievement. The same condition has existed, though to a less extent, in many modern states in which the presence of a hereditary aristocracy has led to a restriction of culture, as a privilege of the select few born into this class. Up to the time of the French Revolution the great mass of toilers with few exceptions bore this arrangement uncomplainingly, being led by social tradition and religious superstition to believe that the lot to which God had ordained them was to labor unremittingly that a few of their fellows might enjoy the better things of life. But during the past century the proletariat has been awakening, its attitude has entirely changed, and it will no longer submit willingly to a régime that restricts the benefits of culture to a chosen few. As Eucken says: '' Hitherto spiritual conflict has usually been confined to the limited arena of cultivated society, and the general mass of mankind has not been much affected. Now, however, the people are pressing forward; they not only demand a voice in the settlement of ultimate questions, but require that the whole structure of society shall be regulated with reference to their opinions and interests. They are very liable moreover to that harsh intolerance which always characterizes big mass movements.'' [8]  It is plain then that the work of extending to all humanity the opportunity for real cultivation of spirit —to each man according to his capacity—must be undertaken more vigorously and on a larger scale than ever heretofore. For the days of privilege are numbered, and the sort of spiritual expansion which is possible in a few only at the cost of a corresponding limitation in the many, will not be permitted to exist much longer on the earth. Culture must now, if ever, be justified of her children, and those of her exponents do her indeed a poor service who assert that she is essentially selective and opposed to the spirit of democracy. For if culture is identified with privilege she is destined to be swept away by that movement for human brotherhood and social equality which is slowly beginning and gathering momentum, but which when it gains its full force shall sweep all else before it. Far

[8] EUCKEN: *The Problem of Human Life,* Eng. trans., p. 566.

terest to the welfare of his fellows—that every man's interest was his good and the law of the state represented the interest of the strongest individuals. The illustrious contributions of Socrates, Plato, and Aristotle, to ethical theory were prompted by a desire to find rational grounds for a social obligation supreme over all considerations of individual interest. But while the insight of these great thinkers was more illuminating and profound than the shallow and dogmatic pronouncements of the Sophists, still they were only partially successful in solving the problem. They agree in basing social obligation on the faculty of reason common to all men—holding that if men would take the trouble to think clearly concerning human life and conduct they would be convinced that the interests of all individuals in the state are identical and hence that any individual who serves community or nation is thereby attaining his own private interest. They were able to demonstrate that such a community of interest existed, however, among a comparatively small number of fellow-citizens, only; much larger classes such as women, slaves, and barbarians, being left partly or wholly out of account. Hence the problem of the larger social obligation extending to all fellow-humans was left unsolved. It remained for Christianity to enforce this obligation in its fullest extension, making self-sacrifice the keynote of its teaching and communicating to mediæval and modern morality a negative and ascetic tone which contrasts sharply with the freedom and spontaneity of Greek life. In justification of thus enjoining the individual to sacrifice his interest to the good of humanity there is clearly suggested in the Christian gospel a view of human nature and human life much more adequate and profound than that of Greek philosophy. But this has been so often confused by exponents of Christianity with merely a supernatural sanction of morality which recompenses the individual in a future life for the pain and privation undergone in the discharge of duty here, that the whole problem must be considered afresh by present-day Ethics and, if possible, a solution found which will agree with modern conceptions of man, his social relations, and his place in the world.

2. **Self-Sacrifice, if a Duty, Must Be of Ultimate Benefit to the Individual.**—The problem of self-sacrifice arises from the presence in man's moral experience of two sets of facts neither of which can be disputed, but which seem to contradict and even to exclude one another. The first of these facts is, that whatever it be that conscience requires of man, it is for his real benefit to recognize and fulfil this obligation. This identity of the Good with the highest interest of man has been sufficiently emphasized in previous pages. In the case of self-sacrifice it seems an indubitable fact, therefore, that—no matter how extreme the sacrifice—if it is a duty, then it is the fulfilment of the individual's own good. Even the extreme of self-sacrifice recommended by Christianity must thus be regarded as a method of self-realization—just as much as the observance of the mean, or the attainment of a harmony, in conduct, was to the Greek moralist. In this connection Green says with his usual discernment:

" It is not because it involves the renunciation of so much pleasure that we deem the life of larger self-denial which the Christian conscience calls for, a higher life than was conceived by the Greek philosophers; but because it implies a fuller realization of the human soul. It is not the renunciation as such but the spiritual state which it represents that constitutes the value of a life spent in self-devoted service to mankind; and it represents, we must remember, not merely a certain system of desires and interests, on the part of the persons who make the renunciation, but certain social development in consequence of which those desires and interests are called into play." [1]

[1] GREEN: *Prolegomena to Ethics,* § 273, p. 332.

**3. Self-Sacrifice, if Genuine, Must Involve Real Loss to the Individual.**—A second group of facts which are equally important seem to show that moral value attaches only to such " self-sacrifice " as entails real loss. When this aspect of the subject comes home to us in full force, it becomes impossible to treat self-sacrifice as an incident, merely, in self-realization. Moral experience teaches us that self-sacrifice is a real surrender of personal interest involving the pain of irretrievable loss and calling for genuine heroism. Shall we understand it then as a temporary discomfort due to the denial of present desire for the sake of future well-being? This is to make self-sacrifice a part of enlightened prudence. Such an interpretation appears to contravene the plain teaching of moral experience and to rob this vitally important feature of morality of its true meaning. It was this aspect of the subject which impressed Leslie Stephen, who believed that morality has been developed as a means for securing *social* as distinct from *individual* survival, and that the obligation to altruism can never be reconciled with individual interest. Certainly his remarks upon this subject contain much shrewd sense:

" When we listen to the careful demonstrations of the reality of benevolence, when we are told again and again that a man may, and in fact does, sacrifice his own happiness to the good of his fellows, we are edified and convinced. But we receive something of a shock when the edifying moralist suddenly turns round and tells us that the sacrifice is only temporary, that is to say, that it is after all unreal. It is still more surprising when this is presented, and precisely by the moralists who profess to take the loftiest theory, not merely as expressing the fact, but as an *a priori* truth deducible from the very nature of things. For what can this be but to fall back upon the purely egoistic doctrine." [2]

[2] STEPHEN: *Science of Ethics*, ed. of 1882, p. 430.

**4. The Conception of Organization Furnishes the Solution of the Problem.**—How shall we interpret self-sacrifice so as to harmonize these discordant facts? The conception of moral development as a progressive self-organization through the instrumentality of volition gives us the key to the puzzle. For all organization, not only in the development of conscious intelligence, but also in the evolution of all living matter, involves two opposite and complementary aspects. On the one hand there is *differentiation* or the division of the whole which is being organized into disparate parts. Thus the evolution of the organism is accompanied by a multiplication of cells and structures, the development of consciousness by a diversification of ideas and experiences. On the other hand and equally prominent is *integration*, in which the independence of these parts is canceled and they are adjusted within a comprehensive whole. Thus organic evolution is accompanied by an increasing inter-dependence of tissues and organs, and personal development by a more and more perfect correlation of the contents of consciousness. These two aspects of differentiation and integration characterize evolution universally and may be accepted as essential features of all growth, conscious and unconscious. And in this fact that all growth, as an organizing process, encourages the development of parts in independence of one another and of the whole to which they belong, while it also destroys this independence and subordinates the parts to the good of the whole, we have a possible explanation of the presence and importance of self-*sacrifice* in moral development.

**5. All Organization Involves the Sacrifice of the Part to the Whole.**—Such sacrifice of parts to the whole prevails throughout the field of organic evolution. The single organism is a colony of cells and tissues crowding one another for place and competing with one another for food. Yet the health of the organism and the proper balance of its functions necessitate that the activities of these constituent parts be strictly limited and that they be prevented from attaining their maximum of size and strength. Frequently in the life-history of organisms structures are developed to completeness and maturity simply as a means to the inception and growth of other structures more important to the existence of individual or species.[3] Then, when these latter are produced, the former—like a temporary scaffolding—are destroyed. Striking instances of such sacrifice of one part or member of a living organism to the welfare of another or of the whole have been observed. Evidently the familiar statement has more than a figurative meaning which compares the act of self-sacrifice to the dying of the seed that the young plant may live and grow. Turning from ontogeny to phylogeny we find that the evolution of the species is accomplished by a process of struggle and selection in which the individual is sacrificed to the welfare of his race or species. Individuals are born in much greater numbers than the environment can support and then a large majority of these are exterminated, often suffering painful deaths, in order that only the individuals possessing the best natural equipment shall survive and reproduce their kind. An analogous process of competition and resulting selection goes on among the species in their turn, many living forms suffering extinction in order that a more perfect adaptation of the existing forms of life to the resources of the environment shall be secured. Many species seem to be developed simply as bridges from the parent form to the one still more divergent and then to

[3] A beautiful case is that of the "nurse-cells" which in some insect and other forms surround the young egg-cell and nourish it. The egg-cell grows rapidly at the expense of the nurse-cells, which, being steadily depleted, become mere rudiments attached to the egg-cell and then finally disappear. (WILSON: *The Cell in Development and Heredity*, p. 151.)

be eliminated in competition with these two.  Thus we see that throughout the entire field of life evolution as a progressive organization involves the complementary processes of differentiation and integration, in which parts are developed in distinction from the whole and, at the same time, this independence is canceled in a subordination of all parts to the good of the whole.  In all these cases of the sacrifice of parts or members to the welfare of the whole undergoing development, it is worth noting that the benefit of the whole to which the sacrifice of the parts is instrumental accrues only *after* the part has been suppressed or destroyed.

6. **Self-Mastery.**—The evolution of intelligent consciousness is achieved by volition which is itself an organizing agency.  The work of volition displays those two features of organization just mentioned—more strongly emphasized, however, and set in sharper and clearer relief.  Self-organization begins with a differentiation or diversification of conscious life.  Volition first expresses itself in differentiating out of a mass of instinctive tendencies a number of separate desires, each having a distinct object and employing special methods in its pursuit.  The differentiation of these desires is the first step in self-organization and the pre-requisite of all further moral development.  For the individual to be conscious of certain definite needs, for him to desire certain special objects as ends, and also to have knowledge of the ways of gratifying these desires, of availing himself of the resources of the objective world —this ability, while it occupies the very lowest place in the scale of moral excellence, is still the absolutely indispensable foundation upon which the higher development rests.  The individual who is too dull to have any definite desires, too listless to make any special demands upon the world, and too incapable to secure the few objects he does desire is, morally speaking, the one absolutely hopeless

case. It is necessary to Self-realization, then, that a number of different desires and purposes be developed within the consciousness of the individual, and that each of these desires should acquire a certain strength and independence.

But organization requires that this process be supplemented by a complementary activity of correlation and adjustment in which these different desires are subordinated as means to larger ends. It is a natural, an inevitable, consequence of raising a desire to clearest consciousness and adding to this consciousness a knowledge of the most expeditious method of gratification, that the desire in question should insist upon its own gratification regardless of any other considerations whatever. The result of the primary differentiating of desires within the individual is thus to put him at the mercy of a number of eager and aggressive impulses, each of which is clamoring for its own satisfaction to the exclusion of the others. Hence volition is compelled to undertake the work of suppressing these desires in their independence and isolation —only permitting them to exist as they are made conformable to the total interest of the individual. This repression which, from the standpoint of the single desire, may be injurious and destructive, is strongly resisted. Volition is compelled to overcome this resistance and forcibly to restrain the rebellious desire or purpose. Such forcible restraint causes distress and pain to the individual; since the desire which is subjugated after struggle is a part of himself and he suffers both the distress of a nature divided against itself and the pain of a consciousness deprived of its usual gratification. This form of self-sacrifice which arises from the necessity of integrating all single desires and purposes within the unity of the individual life may be called *self-mastery,* to distinguish it from *self-sacrifice* proper, which will be later discussed. Plato treats of this subject of self-mastery in a well-known passage of the *Republic*.  Socrates is made to remark upon the paradox involved in the expression " master of himself." " For the man who is master of himself will, also, I presume, be the slave of himself, and the slave will be the master.  For the subject of all these phrases is the same person." [4]  The use of such an expression is due in the opinion of Socrates to the presence in human nature of two principles, a good and a bad, and a man is said to be master of himself when the good principle is master of the bad.  He further maintains that, of these two principles which are in constant conflict, the good is the rational and the bad the sentient or irrational part of our nature; and this is generally true because the ends of reason, being concepts, are larger and more inclusive than the particular objects of sensuous desire.

Self-mastery does not usually consist, as we might suppose, in a certain amount of compulsory restraint placed upon all desires equally, in the interest of individual well-being.  The fact is that in most cases the great majority of desires submit without much resistance to subordination and control, and the rebellion is concentrated in a few desires (or perhaps just a single one) especially strong and insistent in the particular individual—his " besetting " sin or sins, as the expression is.  With such desires man must fight, and over them he must triumph, if he is to realize himself as an individual.  Of course, any desire may prove thus difficult to control, but there are certain impulses and appetites which seem particularly liable to make trouble with all human beings.  Such is the appetite for stimulants and narcotics which because uncontrolled has ruined the life of many an individual.  Our literature contains many descriptions of the agonizing experiences of individuals who have fought desperately with the craving for alcoholic drink and finally have conquered it—and mastered themselves.

[4] *Republic*, 431 A.

The passion for gaming and the desire for sexual gratification belong to the same class of appetites which often possess exceptional strength and which, unless closely restrained, will escape from control. Nor is the total interest of the individual to which all the single desires are made subservient, always represented by the demands of all his desires and purposes in their organized unity. Just as the resistance of the different parts, to such an adjustment, may be concentrated in a single desire, so the good of the individual as a whole may be represented by a single purpose or desire. Thus the part and the whole confront one another in the guise of two conflicting desires, and self-mastery consists in the victory of the one over the other. To take a concrete instance chosen almost at random from a large and important class, the total interest of an individual may be represented by a comprehensive purpose to achieve success as an artist, thus realizing marked creative ability and gratifying a strong love of beauty. The chief obstacle to the realization of this purpose in a youth or young man may reside in the presence of strong sexual and social impulses which conflict with the larger purpose because they resist that postponement of marriage and domestic life which a long period of preparatory study and travel, would entail. Here self-mastery, the attainment of the more comprehensive good, demands that the desire for immediate marriage and a home, be subordinated and its gratification postponed, in order that the larger end be pursued which, if realized, will provide for a more permanent and adequate satisfaction of these desires as well.

Self-mastery—self-denial—prove then to be instrumental to self-development. In these experiences, painful as they are, the individual gains and not loses. Yet it must not be forgotten that he does not experience the gain when he suffers the loss. The attainment of the larger interest does not occur simultaneously with the loss of the desired object. If it did, the pain of deprivation might be canceled and overcome by the satisfaction of a larger attainment. But the condition of achieving the greater goods is that the lesser goods shall first be surrendered. The pain of denial and deprivation must be endured before the satisfaction of a full and harmonious expression of individuality can be experienced. Moreover, the satisfaction of fulfilling the larger aims of his entire nature cannot even be imagined adequately by the individual, because this is a satisfaction, not of his nature as it is at present but of his present nature after it has been changed by just such painful adjustments as he now is making. Moral development requires the sacrifice of objects proved in experience to be good, on behalf of others which might not at present be satisfactory even though successfully achieved. The ambitious boy abandons amusements which give him keenest delight in order to acquire information and training in a field of activity whose significance he does not clearly understand and whose value he does not fully appreciate. But thus it is with all growth, spiritual as well as natural, the interest of an assured present is sacrificed to a larger future which is yet to be.

7. **Self-Sacrifice.**—The very process of integration which we have been describing—of activities within the life of the individual—is itself a differentiation. For it is through such an adjustment of different desires and impulses that the nature of the individual is organized and his abilities all directed towards the attainment of some supreme aim or life-purpose. Knowledge of such overmastering interests in himself makes the individual conscious of the dominance of similiar aims and ambitions over the lives of other individuals. The respective interests of self and others soon show themselves to be discordant. Self-organization, or Goodness, then necessitates another process of integration,

this time upon a larger scale, the adjustments of these warring interests within the unity of an organized social system. When, in the course of moral development, the necessity thus arises for the individual to subordinate that interest which he has come to identify with himself, to the welfare of others,—then self-sacrifice proper first enters the moral life. Previous to the emergence of individuality through the coördination of the various desires, true self-sacrifice is impossible, for the self-in-its-unity has not yet attained to conscious expression. Hence neither the child nor the savage is capable of self-sacrifice in the full meaning of the word, since the individuality of neither has come to conscious existence through the adoption of plans and purposes which he recognizes as his own and distinct from all others. This awakening of individuality to consciousness of itself comes in the history of the race when, owing to a developing intelligence and easier conditions of life, men refuse to be bound longer in their conduct by tradition and custom, but assert their rights as individuals to choose, each of them, the manner of life which appeals to his intelligence and suits his taste. It occurs in the development of the individual when, at the period of adolescence, the youth is unwilling to be dominated longer by the practices and point-of-view of his family, and considers plans and adopts purposes which he proposes to pursue as an independent individual.

Just as much as the total interest of the individual is, through its greater complexity and superior organization, stronger and more compelling than any one of his single desires, so much the greater is the power of resistance it shows when attacked. Hence the subordination or suppression of self-interest is a greater task, calling for more effort and persistence than that of self-mastery, and it is accompanied by struggle and suffering correspondingly more intense. The individual who feels the obligation to sacrifice his interest—his most cherished hopes and plans—for the good of another faces the gravest crisis of the moral life. His soul is the scene of a mighty conflict upon the issue of which may hang his moral salvation. Our recognition of the high moral worth of self-sacrifice, as well as our appreciation of its almost insurmountable difficulty, is witnessed by the spontaneous burst of approval and admiration that greets every notable instance of it which is brought to public attention. Indeed the public praise and eulogy—in newspaper, pulpit, and periodical—of those who have under unusual circumstances sacrificed property or health or life for the sake of others' welfare, may lead us to think of self-sacrifice as something which occurs only under extraordinary conditions and in a dramatic setting—as when the engineer dies at the throttle in saving the train, or a miner risks his life in returning to a burning mine in order to rescue his injured comrade, or the sailor insists that his shipmates go first in life-boat or breeches-buoy and is left to freeze or drown. But self-sacrifice, in order to be genuine, requires no dramatic setting, no wide publicity—it need in fact be known to no one except the individual who is undergoing it. Such self-sacrifice is constantly occurring with no blare of trumpets or bursts of applause, but just as a part of recognized duty—hard, but cheerfully or stoically endured. Thus there are parents working to the breaking-point and foregoing nearly every rightful pleasure, in order that children may be educated; there are sons and daughters giving up plans and ambitions which seem to mean more than life itself to them, in order to care for an aged or infirm parent; there are physicians wearing themselves out in the relief of pain and the curing of disease among their fellows; there are ministers and teachers expending their intelligence and energy without stint in ministering to the souls which have been committed to their charge. What Pro-

fessor Royce says about loyalty in this connection is also
true of self-sacrifice which is an essential part of all true
loyalty.

" My own mind also chooses some of the plainest and ob-
scurest people whom I chance to know, the most straightforward
and simple-minded of folk, whose loyalty is even all the more sure
to me because I can certainly affirm that they at least cannot be
making any mere display of loyalty in order that they should
be seen of men. Nobody knows of their loyalty except those
that are in more or less direct touch with them; and these usually
appreciate this loyalty too little. You all of you similarly know
plain and wholly obscure men and women of whom the world has
not heard and is not worthy, but who have possessed and who have
proved in the presence of you who have chanced to observe them a
loyalty to their chosen causes which was not indeed expressed
in martial deeds but which was quite as genuine a loyalty as
that of a Samurai or as that of Arnold von Winkelried when
he rushed on the Austrian spears. As for ordinary expressions
of loyalty, not at critical moments and in the heroic instants that
come to the plainest lives, but in daily business, we are all aware
how the letter-carrier and the house-maid may live, and often
do live when they choose, as complete a daily life of steadfast
loyalty as could any knight or king." [5]

With these facts before our minds we condemn as the
veriest sophistry any view which does not admit that the
sacrifices exacted by duty are real, or attempts to explain
them as part of a larger prudence or as the gratification
of sympathetic or social impulses. Such interpretations of
self-sacrifice do not explain it: they explain it away. Self-
sacrifice is a means to Self-realization? Yes, assuredly!
But it is not the sacrificed self which is finally realized.
It is not the surrendered interest—the unfulfilled ambitions, the thwarted aims, the lost hopes—which are triumphantly attained. No, it is the self whose character
has been transformed through the ordeal of suffering and

[5] ROYCE: *Philosophy of Loyalty*, pp. 112-13.

sacrifice that is finally realized: it is an interest which has been altered and enlarged by denial and deprivation that is triumphantly attained. Self-sacrifice is then a real " dying to self " in which the pangs of dissolution undergone by the old nature are the birth-pains of the new. " The higher or personal self can be realized only through the death of the lower or individual self, as lower and merely individual." [6]  " The individual must die to an isolated life—i.e. a life for and in himself, a life in which the immediate satisfaction of desire, as his desire, is an end in itself—in order that he may live the spiritual life, the universal life which really belongs to him as a spiritual or self-conscious being." [7]  It is necessary that the limitations of a narrow and exclusive individuality shall be overcome if man is to realize the larger possibilities of his nature. But such individuality maintains its independence and isolation with utmost stubbornness. It must be crushed and broken, therefore; for thus only can it be rendered pliant and adaptable—capable of adjustment along with the differing interests of other individuals within a comprehensive system of social ends and activities. As long as Self-realization compels man to make this adjustment, it will remain a severe ordeal fraught with spiritual struggle and soul agony. Self-sacrifice cannot be expelled from human life, then; but seems destined to remain one of the most profound and searching—as well as the most characteristic—experiences in man's moral life.

8. **Is Self-Sacrifice Due to Merely Temporary Maladjustment?**—While the social adjustment of individuals whose desires and ambitions are at variance with the good of society is difficult and exceedingly painful, is it not sure to become much easier and less painful as moral development proceeds? In the course of social evolution are not man's social instincts and impulses certain to

[6] Seth: *Ethical Principles*, p. 207.     [7] Caird: *Hegel*, p. 213.

be so far strengthened, and his understanding of the advantages of coöperation so much increased, that he will seek others' interests as naturally and spontaneously as his own? Herbert Spencer looked forward to such a state of human society in the far distant future, in which there would be no more need of self-sacrifice, and the conflicting claims of egoism and altruism would be completely reconciled. In his own words:

" From the laws of life it must be concluded that unceasing social discipline will so mold human nature that eventually sympathetic pleasures will be spontaneously pursued to the fullest extent advantageous to each and all. The scope for altruistic activities will not exceed the desire for altruistic satisfactions." [8]

Confining ourselves just now to the trend of social development and the direction of civilization as we can observe them—and not asking whether the laws which govern moral development as a progressive self-organization permit of the elimination of self-sacrifice—we find slight reason for expecting that such a condition of ready-prepared social adjustment and harmony will come in the near or distant future. It is true that man becomes more socialized as civilization advances. We are less confident than Spencer was that his experience of the benefits of social life and his acquisition of habits socially useful are modifying his native instincts and impulses in any decided or revolutionary fashion. There is no doubt, however, that as he becomes further civilized man gains a more adequate knowledge of his community of interest with his fellows and a more intelligent appreciation of the importance and value of social organization and social service. Such knowledge of social relations, being transmitted through training and education from one generation to the next, steadily

[8] SPENCER: *Data of Ethics*, § 95, p. 294.

accumulates and must, it might appear, make altruistic action easier and the social adjustment more natural and spontaneous. Hence we should expect to find the citizen of a highly civilized state more willing to serve his nation at the expense of private interest than the member of a society not so highly civilized. Unfortunately the facts are otherwise—or partially so—owing to the operation of other factors which have a contrary influence. For the mental development which accompanies advance in civilization not only leads to an increased sense of social obligation but it also makes clearer and more acute the consciousness of individual interest. The stimulation of intellectual and imaginative faculties in an advanced civilization gives to the individual a much more vivid and realizing sense of his own interest—present and future. His imagination enables him to enjoy in anticipation the pleasures of fulfilling his ambitions—and equally to suffer in apprehension of the failure of his plans and the frustration of his purposes. An increased sensitivity to pain seems to be an accompaniment of civilization, due both to added power of imagining it beforehand and to a more delicate sensibility which has resulted from easier conditions of life. Hence the citizen of a half-civilized state might, and probably would, respond more readily to the call to take up arms and suffer danger, pain, and possible death, for his country, than would the educated man of modern society. And this would not be because he had a clearer or more intelligent conception of his duty as a citizen but because he had less ability to imagine the hardships and sufferings he would have to undergo on the one hand, and the satisfactions and successes he might be compelled to forego, on the other.[9] Yet the outcome is that he can

[9] Compare this statement of Aristotle (*Nicomachean Ethics*, Bk. III, Chap. XII) : " If then the case in regard to courage is similar to this, death and wounds will be painful to the courageous man and involuntary; but he will endure them because endurance is honorable

be depended upon to sacrifice himself as an individual, more willingly, suffering peril and death in his country's cause with less hesitation, than his civilized descendant. These facts have caused it to be alleged as a penalty of civilization that nations lose their "fighting edge." The intensifying of self-consciousness, the training of imagination, and the refinement of sensibility in the individual all tend to make him less ready to place himself at the disposal of his country as a weapon or instrument to be used in its defense. Hence, it is predicted, nations in which civilization has progressed thus far will be at a decided disadvantage in time of war and will perhaps be defeated and finally superseded by other peoples, in whom mental development has not proceeded so far as to interfere with the action of instinctive loyalty and unthinking courage. However this may be—and many other facts would have to be considered before assent were given to such a conclusion—the significance of the whole matter as it bears upon the present argument is that an increasing knowledge of the character and importance of the social relation among the individuals that compose a society does not of necessity make the sacrifice of private interests to the public good any easier for these individuals. For the same growth of intelligence that enlightens the individual concerning his social relationships gives him also a clearer conception

and avoidance disgraceful. Nay, in proportion as he possesses virtue in its fullness and is happy, will be his pain at the prospect of death; for to such an one life is preëminently valuable, and he will be consciously deprived at death of the greatest blessings. But, painful as such deprivation is, he is none the less courageous, nay perhaps he is even more courageous, as he willingly sacrifices these blessings for noble conduct on the field of battle. It is not the case, then, that all virtues imply a pleasurable activity, except in so far as one attains to the end. Still, it is true perhaps, after all, that people who enjoy a happy life are not such good soldiers as people who are less courageous but have nothing to lose, as these last are ready to face any danger, and will sell their lives for a small sum of money" (Welldon's trans., p. 89).

of his interests as an individual and an added power of imagining his own successes and failures. Thus self-sacrifice becomes no easier, and may even be rendered more difficult and painful.

9. **On the Contrary It Is a Necessary Factor in Self-Organization.**—Self-sacrifice has been interpreted as the surrender of the narrower purposes and ambitions with which individuality has identified itself in order that the larger ends of the social self may be realized. Such an interpretation should satisfy all persons who believe in the reality of self-sacrifice—except, to be sure, those who, like Leslie Stephen, believe that self-sacrifice, in order to be real, must involve final and irretrievable loss to the self. From this extreme standpoint, if self-sacrifice is regarded as instrumental in self-realization, its meaning is entirely destroyed and it is degraded into a form of self-interest. Thus if one who sacrifices his plans and purposes for another's benefit is aiming at his own self-realization his sacrifice is not genuine and his conduct is merely prudent. And moral enlightenment is all that is necessary to remove as groundless from the experience of man any feeling of pain or sorrow in the subordination of private interest to social welfare and to create instead the pleasant consciousness of securing his own good. This position would be justified if our actions were in every case inevitably determined—as Socrates, for example, believed—by what we, upon solely intellectual grounds, thought was for our highest interest. Then certainly virtue would be knowledge and our pursuit of the largest good would be simply an affair of intellectual enlightenment. But the facts are nearly the reverse. Man's action is not necessarily determined by what he believes to be true from the exercise of his reason, and in independence of action. Rather is his knowledge determined by his action, his conception of truth dependent upon his conduct with its experiences of

success and failure. The true idea is the idea that can
be realized, i.e. that satisfies volition in increasing the
fullness and variety of self-conscious life. Hence the
largest knowledge at the command of any human individual
—the body of accepted truths in any generation—but sums
up the results of human achievement in the past. The
science of Ethics is thus a systematic reflection upon the
experience of man in organizing his life and thus fulfilling
the power of self-development resident in his own will.
Now the individual must act with the fullest knowledge
available if his action is to build upon his own experience
and the experience of his fellow-men. But to new situations in which the individual finds himself this knowledge
is never adequate; since it can receive conclusive verification only in his own experience and the prospect of further
development open before every human being involves the
possibility of entirely new and unexpected experiences.
Hence at each successive step in his moral development
man is compelled to abandon objects which his experience
has shown to be satisfactory for the sake of others whose
reality and value await their final verification in the results
of the action which he is then undertaking. Such acts
are primarily ventures of will and not expressions of
knowledge; and they are of necessity painful, because they
call for the negation of objects through which the self
itself has found expression—thus putting its very existence
in jeopardy in order that other and larger objects may
be sought and, if possible, attained. Self-sacrifice is the
greatest as well as the most painful of these ventures,
requiring the surrender of objects on which the existence
and integrity of individuality itself seem to depend, as
the condition of pursuing social ends which are untried
and hence in character and value uncertain. Thus self-
sacrifice is revealed as a necessary consequence of the
fundamental fact of morality, that moral development is

an organization of conduct achieved by volition and not an organization of ideas accomplished by thought and reproduced in action.

**10. Optimism and Pessimism.**—Self-sacrifice appears as one and perhaps the most important of the adjustments of parts to the whole which are effected by volition in the course of its organizing activity. Viewed from this standpoint, but with a slight change of angle, it may be regarded as a consequence of the maladjustment which actually exists within the nature of man and throughout the world of human experience. The existence of such maladjustment, deep-seated and thorough-going, cannot be disputed. The presence of moral evil, springing from the opposing interests of individuals in society and the conflicting tendencies within these individuals themselves, testifies to its presence in the nature of the human individual and in human society. The existence of physical evil likewise, the indescribable suffering and painful deaths inflicted upon countless thousands of innocent human beings by the forces of nature in fire and famine, flood and storm, earthquake and volcanic eruption, proves that the natural universe is not adjusted to the needs and purposes of man. It is this maladjustment with which intelligently directed will is contending in the evolution of human life and conduct, and which it has been able in a measure to overcome. This process is necessarily painful. But suffering cannot be escaped in any event; it must follow from the lack of adjustment and harmony in the actual nature of things. In the organization of life through the instrumentality of volition, we see this pain and suffering made a means to a larger satisfaction, however, the extent and fullness of intelligent life being increased by the number and variety of originally conflicting elements that have been adjusted within it. Such an understanding of moral development leads us to a view of the world of human experience that is between the extremes of optimism and pessimism. Extreme optimism would deny that there is any disorder or maladjustment inherent in the nature of the world. What seems to be such must be, from this point of view, purely *temporary* and presently to be done away with, or only *apparent*, i.e. due to our failure to understand the world completely, and sure to disappear when we gain a fuller knowledge. Extreme pessimism sees only disorder and conflict in the world of human experience and believes it to be impossible for man to introduce into it any real consistency or derive from it any genuine satisfaction. Now the true view lies between these two extremes, in a qualified optimism. It is difficult to see how any one not superficial in his thought or else wilfully blind, can deny that evil, due to radical maladjustment, is inherent in the actual world. The insight recently gained by science into the causes operative in organic evolution adds to the evidence already more than sufficient which human experience has furnished on this point. In the process of natural selection the evolution of species is secured at the expense of the individuals which compose it, the majority of those born in each generation suffering death and often cruel death before reaching maturity in order that only the minority who are best adapted to the conditions of life shall be allowed to breed and thus determine the character of the species. Yet there is another side which is equally prominent and equally worthy of emphasis. Our increased knowledge of organic evolution and of the history of human morality—of universal evolution, in fact—sets in stronger relief than ever the fact that this maladjustment is being overcome, that harmony and order are being won through pain and struggle. The discovery of natural selection was not needed to teach us that warfare is incessant and cruelty prevalent in the organic world, that the law of the jungle is the law of tooth and claw, that nature on its face so peaceful and " bright with gladness " is the scene of constant turmoil and destruction.[10]  But we are indebted to science for the knowledge that this suffering is not useless and not meaningless, but through its instrumentality adaptation is being secured and evolution is proceeding.  In the sphere of intelligence and personality likewise a survey of moral development shows us how in the process of self-organization man, by suppressing his single desires in their independence, gains control over his entire nature, all of whose different resources are thus put at his command; by sacrificing his interest as an individual he gains entrance into a larger life which provides a wider and more varied field for the exercise of his own powers; and by seeking to understand, and adapt himself to, the laws and forces of the universe, he allies himself with the process of universal evolution and the cause of world progress.

11. **Conclusion.**—In the only world we human beings know the cost of progress is pain, and suffering is an accompaniment of evolution.  Moreover, mental development in man has for its penalty an increase of this suffering— present pain being more acute and highly focalized in his consciousness, while that of the past is preserved in memory, and that of the future anticipated in imagination.  Yet for this, his superior intelligence more than recompenses him by revealing with increasing fullness the stupendous results which are being achieved through the toil and travail of the world—reproducing in his conscious life the main stages of universal evolution, and awakening within his soul some appreciation of the significance and value of the ends that are being realized therein.

[10] *Cf.* DARWIN: *Origin of Species*, Chap. III.

# CHAPTER IV

## SELF-REALIZATION AND THE MOTIVE OF GOODNESS

**1. The Motive of Good Conduct.**—The motive of conduct has been defined as that idea which as an end attracts the self to action in its pursuit. The motive of good conduct is, of course, the idea of the Good. The Good is now understood to be Self-realization. We have in the present chapter then to consider the adequacy and efficacy of Self-realization as the motive of good conduct. There are many motives which actually impel men to action, varying in comprehensiveness and power from the particular object of the individual's momentary desire to the great cause which commands the devotion of tens of thousands in successive generations. Among these different motives three stand out as predominant in the influence they exert upon human conduct. They are—love of self, sympathy for others, and fear of God. It will be found helpful to discuss these leading motives singly—first, the egoistic or self-interest; second, the altruistic or sympathy; third, the religious, or reverence: and then to consider Self-realization in the capacity of motive, as related to each of these three. Thus we may hope to gain a true idea of the potency of Self-realization as an impelling principle in the conduct of men.

2. **The Egoistic Motive: Self-Interest.**—Certainly the love of self, or "self-interest," is a controlling force in human life and affairs. So important a part does it play that many moralists have regarded it as the sole motive actuating man's conduct. "Of all the voluntary acts of man the object is some good to himself,"[1] says Hobbes, and by this he means that man seeks his own pleasure and that only, in all that he does. Accordingly, Hobbes and the school of Egoistic Utilitarians which he founded sought to explain all the actions of men—even those which appear most unselfish, or, it may be, self-sacrificing—as expressions of self-interest. "Pity," says the philosopher in question, "is imagination or fiction of future calamity to ourselves, proceeding from the sense of another man's calamity."[2] Charity or good-will, he thus explains: "There can be no greater argument to a man of his own power, than to find himself able not only to accomplish his own desires but also to assist other men in theirs: and this is that conception wherein consisteth *charity*."[3]   Reverence is also interpreted in terms of self-interest as "The conception we have concerning another, that he hath the power to do unto us both good and hurt."[4]   Thus to resolve all the springs of human action into forms of self-interest seems to present thought a gross exaggeration of the importance of this motive and a perversion of the plain facts of moral experience. Indeed some students of morality to-day not merely deny that self-interest is the sole motive but question whether it is even an important motive in the conduct of man. These thinkers maintain that a true psychology of action shows that the human will is directed primarily upon external objects and not upon subjective states, such

[1] HOBBES: *Leviathan*, Part I, Chap. XIV.
[2] HOBBES: *Human Nature*, Chap. IX, § 10.
[3] *Ibid.*, § 17.
[4] *Op. cit.*, Chap. VIII, § 7.

as the pleasure or comfort of the self.[5]  Thus the man whose conduct appears most selfish is probably moved by the idea of food or of drink, of the most comfortable seat or the finest view, rather than by any idea of his own pleasure.  Now it is undoubtedly true that the human will is first attracted by such external objects as promise to satisfy its natural desires.  But it is also a fact that the instinct of self-preservation leads man to seek to prolong and to renew pleasant experiences, and to curtail and to avoid those that are painful.  Hence objects which experience shows will yield pleasure are sought as *pleasurable,* while those that have been found to bring pain are avoided as *painful.*  Thus far the facts can scarcely be disputed. When we consider next that self-consciousness develops in due time, bringing with it a recognition of individuality in its exclusive character, we see how the motive of self-interest takes form and acquires great power as a spring of action.

In this motive, the idea which impels the individual to act is not that of his own pleasure in the abstract, but rather the idea of some object or objects, attractive because known to be a source of individual enjoyment.  The man whose conduct is actuated entirely by self-interest is not wholly absorbed in increasing his own pleasure, thought of as a subjective or psychological state.  Such a character scarcely exists outside the books of ethical theorists.  But love of self is a leading motive in human conduct, nevertheless; and some men's lives seem completely dominated by it.  What such individuals seek is money, or land, or power, or some other object, *which they imagine themselves as enjoying.*  Thus the moving-spring of their action may with truth be said to be their own enjoyment or comfort. We may therefore accept Sidgwick's statement, as correct in substance at least, when he says that the object of self-love is " the kind of feeling we call pleasure taken in its

<hr>

[5] DEWEY AND TUFTS: *Ethics,* p. 379.

widest sense and including every species of delight, enjoyment, and satisfaction, except in so far as any particular
species may be excluded by its incompatibility with some
other greater pleasures." [6]  The object with which the anticipated enjoyment is identified may be a material one,
or it may be the ideal object of some spiritual capacity,
such as the discovery of truth in the intellectual, or the
attainment of beauty in the æsthetic, sphere.  In such case,
however, the ideal object is sought by the individual merely
as a means to his own enjoyment; and, since the ability of
such larger ends to yield pleasure in their attainment is
less obvious and certain, self-interest usually prompts to
the pursuit of the narrower objects of natural desire.
Aristotle recognizes that two meanings are given to the
term self-love—the word in its more restricted and also
more common signification being properly applied to
" people who assign themselves a larger share of money,
honors, and bodily pleasures, than belongs to them." [7]

When the motive of self-interest is defined as the appeal
which the idea of his own comfort and pleasure makes to
the human individual, few indeed will deny its power and
efficacy as a dynamic in the field of conduct.  While the
statements of those moralists who explain all the deeds of
men as due to the working of self-interest are justly condemned as cynical and exaggerated, still their general plausibility and partial truth bear witness to the extensive influence of this motive.  When joined with an intelligence that
foresees consequences and understands the larger relationships of human life, it is capable of imposing a thorough and
far-reaching regulation upon the conduct of man.  Self-
interest enjoins strict temperance upon the man who foresees the injurious consequences of excess.  Comparatively

---

[6] SIDGWICK: *Method of Ethics*, p. 88.
[7] ARISTOTLE: *Nicomachean Ethics*, Bk. IX, Chap. VIII (Welldon's trans., p. 300).

little knowledge is required to show the individual that since his own security and comfort are dependent upon the maintenance of the social and political orders, it is for his interest to support their authority.  The lesson that honesty (at least in the sense of an outward observance of others' property-rights) is the best policy, is easily learned. Thus love of self becomes a great conserving agency in human society which no ethical theory can afford to neglect, making for steadiness of purpose in the individual and stability in society.

Not confining ourselves to the positive contributions to social welfare which an enlightened self-interest will prompt, we may notice further the benefits which accrue to society incidentally from the operation of this motive, even when the thought of the individual is altogether concerned with his own enjoyment.  The man who is impelled by love of self to preserve his bodily vigor and mental capacity while accumulating sufficient property to provide for himself during his old age, at least relieves society of the burden of caring for him in his declining years.  Moreover, that normal degree of self-interest which leads the individual to seek healthful amusement and to keep his bodily functions vigorous is productive of a cheerful disposition and a flow of animal spirits which are contagious and themselves a contribution to social welfare.  As Spencer says, in defending the rights of egoism to a place in a well-ordered and socially efficient life:

" The conclusion forced on us is that the pursuit of individual happiness within those limits prescribed by social conditions, is the first requisite to the attainment of the greatest general happiness.  To see this it needs but to contrast one whose self-regard has maintained bodily well-being, with one whose regardlessness of self has brought its natural results; and then to ask what must be the contrast between two societies formed of two such kinds of individuals.

"Bounding out of bed after an unbroken sleep, singing or whistling as he dresses, coming down with beaming face ready to laugh on the smallest provocation, the healthy man of high powers, conscious of past successes, and by his energy, quickness, resource, made confident of the future, enters on the day's business not with repugnance but with gladness; and from hour to hour experiencing satisfactions from work effectually done, comes home with an abundant surplus of energy remaining for hours of relaxation. Far otherwise is it with one who is enfeebled by great neglect of self. Already deficient, his energies are made more deficient by constant endeavors to execute tasks that prove beyond his strength, and by the resulting discouragement. Besides the depressing consciousness of the immediate future, there is the depressing consciousness of the remoter future, with its probability of accumulated difficulties and diminished ability to meet them. Hours of leisure which, rightly passed, bring pleasures that raise the tide of life and renew the powers of work, cannot be utilized: there is not vigor enough for enjoyments involving action, and lack of spirits prevents passive enjoyments being entered upon with zest. In brief, life becomes a burden. Now, if, as must be admitted, in a community composed of individuals like the first the happiness will be relatively great, while in one composed of individuals like the last, there will be relatively little happiness, or rather much misery; it must be admitted that conduct causing the one result is good, and conduct causing the other is bad." *Data of Ethics,* § 70.

3. **Inadequacy of the Egoistic Motive.**—After doing full justice to the actual importance and ethical value of the motive of self-interest, we must admit that when this motive is allowed to rule alone in human conduct or to dominate all other motives, it not only proves itself inadequate but also positively ruinous in its effects, stunting and deforming the nature of the individual, checking and subverting social progress, and endangering human welfare. The defect of self-love may at first appear to be of a purely negative character—that it is not sufficiently inclusive, but confines itself to the happiness of the individual. Beginning thus with a passive neglect of others' interest, to be sure,

—when it is given the opportunity to grow and expand through continuous exercise,—this motive leads directly to an active violation, and finally to a complete annihilation, of the rights of others. The worst feature of the life entirely controlled by self-interest is not, therefore, that it seeks wealth and honor and pleasure which it does not propose to share with others, but that in an increasing degree it seeks to use other human beings as instruments in the amassing of wealth, as stepping-stones in the acquiring of reputation, as tools in the gaining of pleasure. The ethical problem would be simpler if such uncurbed and ruthless selfishness always defeated its own ends—bringing satiety and disgust, a sense of estrangement from fellowmen increasingly painful, and a growing feeling of regret over the suffering caused to others. Unfortunately this is not always true. History affords conspicuous examples of monsters of selfishness who throughout a long life have used intelligence and skill in preserving their bodily vigor, husbanding their financial resources, and maintaining their reputation and influence over their fellows, all in order that they might the more fully gratify their private lusts. No, the fundamental fact is that self-interest in the sense of individual enjoyment, and the largest human welfare do not always coincide. The attainment of the latter often —usually, it seems—requires the sacrifice of the former. The motive of self-interest cannot be relied on, consequently, to furnish the dynamic for *good* conduct, conduct that shall have for its aim the realization of all capacities of human personality. The short-sightedness and folly of appealing to this motive when the desire is to promote social efficiency and personal development, have recently been demonstrated in this country. For decades the gospel of " success " has been preached to American youths in school and in home, from lecture platform and magazine page. The success which was thus glorified in the mind of the growing boy was generally a purely individualistic one: his imagination was stimulated by tales of the making of enormous fortunes, the building up of extensive industries, and the attainment of supreme political power. The anti-social character of such teaching remained for long unnoticed; for the settlement of a new country placed an especially high premium upon individual initiative and aggressiveness, and the exploitation of undiscovered resources or the organization of new industries which were incidental to the acquisition of private fortunes, seemed to constitute a sufficient social justification. But now that the country is nearly all settled and some of its resources show signs of exhaustion, on the one hand, and the ability of favored individuals to exploit the land and its resources has been tremendously increased by combinations of capital, superior organization of industry, and better facilities of production and distribution, on the other, things assume a different complexion. The further depletion of national resources which belong to the whole people by a few individuals for their own enrichment appears no longer as a case of commendable initiative and enterprise but of deplorable rapacity and greed. In fact the " enterprising " business man is now seen as the commercial pirate, and the " shrewd " politician who works with him (and upon him) as the political free-booter. Of the two characterizations perhaps the latter is the truer, but both are extreme. One lesson should be learned, however; that if we would lay the foundations of democracy and social justice deep in the character of our people, we should not attempt in our teaching of youth primarily to arouse individual ambition through appeal to the motive of self-interest, but rather to develop an interest in civic problems and a capacity for public service, by an appeal to that sentiment of comradeship and capacity for loyal devotion to ideal causes which is latent in all normal human beings.

4. **The Altruistic Motive: Sympathy.**—The failure of egoistic interpretations of morality such as that of Hobbes to win general acceptance is due principally to the recognized presence in human nature of an altruistic tendency which makes others' welfare in itself attractive as an end of action. Against this fact of the existence of an altruistic or social motive in the nature of man, as against an impregnable rock, all egoistic theories are shattered in pieces. While the existence of an altruistic motive had been recognized by earlier thought, it remained for the biological studies carried on in the last century under the inspiration of the idea of evolution, to establish the true importance of this motive for human conduct and to give it unquestionable scientific standing. Darwin, as is generally known, found in the social instinct which man inherits from the lower animals, the foundation of human morality. This instinct, he believed, was an extension of the parental and filial affections which are rooted as deep in the nature of the organism as the instinct of self-preservation itself.[8] He thought it highly probable that " any animal whatever, endowed with well-marked social instincts, the parental and filial affections being here included, would inevitably acquire a moral sense or conscience as soon as its intellectual powers had become as well, or nearly as well, developed as in man."[9] Those practices and beliefs which originate in this instinct and consequently tend to promote social welfare would, he believed, be favored by natural selection because they make a group stronger and more efficient in its struggle with other groups.[10] Other writers, following Darwin and approaching Ethics from the biological standpoint, sought to show with increasing fullness and detail how human morality had grown out of this social or sympathetic instinct. Leslie Stephen explained morality as

[8] DARWIN: *Descent of Man*, Chap. IV.    [9] *Ibid.*
[10] *Op. cit.*, Chap. V.

the condition of social health and survival. Mr. Sutherland in his compendious work *The Origin and Growth of
the Moral Instinct* reviews the whole course of moral development, endeavoring to prove that it consists essentially
in an extension of the instinct of sympathy, which is itself
derived from the parental instinct. In the words of this
writer, who gives the most complete exposition of the view
we are considering, " Moral conduct is that conduct which
is actuated by wise sympathy. Sympathy, of course, is the
natural capacity of being pleased at the pleasures and
pained at the sufferings of others. Sympathy is wise when
it sacrifices no ultimately greater happiness of others for the
sake of a smaller but more immediate happiness." [11]
Hence Mr. Sutherland is led to maintain that " An efficient
degree of sympathy will, and among the mass of mankind
actually does, provide an adequate morality without a great
admixture of other qualities." [12] With reference to moral
development, it consists, he asserts, in a growth of sympathy which involves both a widening and a deepening.
Arising in family life out of the parental and sexual instincts, sympathy first spreads to all members of the tribe
where it is deepened and strengthened through the increasing friendliness and devotion of fellow-tribesmen. Then
its area is extended beyond the tribal bounds, first in
toleration, then in friendliness, and finally in universal
human brotherhood.[13]

Moralists of the school just referred to have done a
service of inestimable value to ethical reflection. They
have established beyond possibility of further doubt or
question the existence and importance of an altruistic
motive in human conduct. By their historical and ethnological researches they have demonstrated the preëminently

[11] SUTHERLAND: *Origin and Growth of the Moral Instinct,* Vol. II,
p. 19.
[12] *Op. cit.,* Vol. II, p. 9.
[13] *Ibid.,* Vol. I, p. 369.

*social* character of morality from its earliest beginnings; thus a death-blow has been dealt to all egoistic theories whether of a naturalistic or theological character. Moreover they have summoned the incontrovertible facts of Biology to show that altruism is as authentic and necessary a product of the organic evolution as is egoism. While the range or meaning of benevolence is not limited by the scope of the instinct in which it originated, still it is reassuring to know that the instinct of sympathy is as deeply rooted in human nature as the instinct of self-preservation. The fact that sympathy is not a derivative or secondary product gives an additional warrant for those developments of intelligent altruism which pass altogether beyond the limits of organic adaptation. With reference to the importance and value of the motive of sympathy in the field of human life and conduct, it is scarcely possible to exaggerate. In many periods of human history, it alone has thrown a cheerful kindly light in scenes of darkness and disorder where insatiate greed and brutal passion have vaunted themselves. Although it does not possess the breadth and elevation characteristic of the self-sacrificing devotion of patriot or martyr to his ideal cause, yet sympathy has a spontaneity and readiness about it that renders it a peculiarly gracious and inspiring element in human life. It creates an atmosphere in which good deeds and noble aspirations flourish. Upon the subject the words of Mr. Sutherland may again be quoted with heartiest approval:

" So too with our social relations, duty makes a substitute, but only an indifferent substitute, for kindly sympathies. The man who does what he ought to do, though actuated by no feeling of gladness in giving happiness, no sense of compassion for the sorrows of others, may indeed make a good enough citizen. But if he reluctantly help another out of a ditch because it is his duty to do so, instead of cheerfully giving a hand because eager to help, the quality of the resulting morality is very inferior. The man who is incapable of a warm friendship or a noble enthusiasm of patriotism or the glow of benevolence is in so far a poorer type. Though upright he is frigid; though courteous he is stiff. We all think him a good man, but our hearts never gladden at his approach. Whereas the man whose life finds the spring of its goodness in active sympathy brings happiness wherever he goes, and his morality is contagious." [14]

### 5. Inadequacy of the Altruistic Motive.

—Although it seems frequently to constitute the redeeming virtue of man's nature, this altruistic motive, if allowed to rule without check or control, produces a life as incomplete and one-sided, if not as perverted and monstrous, as that dominated entirely by egoism. For altruism, when it is not balanced by the opposite tendency or included within a principle of action comprehensive enough to embrace them both, defeats itself. In the first place, a person who is so far preoccupied with the welfare of others as to neglect altogether his individual interest will soon find himself lacking the ability to give further help, and will finally become a care and a burden upon those whom he wishes to benefit. Thus the head of a family whose incessant exertions on behalf of wife and children leave no time for rest or recreation is in danger of being incapacitated in middle life and becoming an invalid to be supported by the labor of those whom he would serve. Or, think of a man in a position of great social or political responsibility upon whose wisdom and skill the continued prosperity and moral betterment of hundreds of thousands of his fellow-beings depend. Let such a man become so absorbed in his plans for others' good that he forgets the limits of his own strength and breaks his health down, or heedlessly exposes himself, contracts pneumonia, and dies; the objects of his devotion, the men and women who are dependent

[14] SUTHERLAND: *Op. cit.*, Vol. II, p. 8.

upon him, will pay the penalty of his exaggerated altruism. Hence the cause of altruism itself justifies a moderate and healthy egoism—an indulgence of desires for rest and recreation, for appetizing food and comfortable clothing, and all other objects which contribute to individual strength and efficiency. Then, secondly, unbalanced altruism defeats itself by encouraging an extreme of egoism in those to whom it ministers. How often do the unwearied efforts of a devoted wife and mother to increase the comfort and happiness of husband and children encourage a deplorable selfishness in these members of her family! A similar result is frequently observable where an unrestricted generosity leads to the distribution of bounties without the expectation or desire of any service in return. The effect seems usually to be the fostering of selfishness in the recipients—their appetite for further benefits is whetted, and their willingness to render adequate service in return is correspondingly diminished. Self-respect is lost and pauperization begins.

Even within the field of altruism proper the instinct of sympathy, when it is not reinforced by other factors and abilities, proves to be an insufficient motive. Like all other organic instincts it responds only to its proper stimulus, and this stimulus must be a particular object or event. Thus sympathy is elicited by the pleasure or pain of fellow-beings when this is seen, or otherwise perceived. Hence it is naturally circumscribed in the scope of its object to individual cases and particular occasions. True, it may, through the help of memory and the imagination, be extended to cover the future happiness or misery of particular persons. Yet it remains too limited in its influence to move men to the service of ideal causes representing some general aspect of human welfare—like the moral awakening of a nation, or the establishment of peace throughout the world. Furthermore, sympathy, because an organic reaction, will be determined as to intensity and duration by the physiological condition of the subject as well as by the character of the stimulating object. Thus the amount of sympathy which the same situation arouses in any individual will vary from time to time, depending upon the condition of his health, his mood, the time in his day, etc. Hence sympathy has not motive-power sufficient to inspire devotion to a social end which can be realized only by small degrees but must be steadily pursued, such as the good of a city or the welfare of an institution. Mr. Sutherland himself recognizes its defects as a motive.[15] It is capricious in its play, he admits, varying from person to person, and in the same person from time to time. It is dependent for its strength upon external and accidental conditions such as the good humor of the agent, and the beauty or attractiveness of the object. Hence—his conclusion is—while sympathy supplies the motive-power, the sense of duty is required as a kind of fly-wheel to steady its spasmodic energies. This sense of duty he explains as methodized sympathy, it is true; but the important point for our notice is that even this champion of sympathy is forced to confess that in its natural manifestation and without being supplemented by other faculties, it is inadequate as a motive of good conduct. The limitations of sympathy as a motive of altruistic conduct are well illustrated by a too-familiar type of political leader in our cities. The ward " boss " often owes his influence in his district largely to his ready kindness. To no cry of suffering or distress can he turn a deaf ear and his constituents when in trouble can appeal to him with the assurance of meeting quick sympathy and substantial aid. He is loyal to active supporters, keeping every promise made to them; for his friends he has a genuine affection and safeguards their interest as his own.

[15] SUTHERLAND: *Op. cit.*, Vol. II, p. 30.

But at the same time he is absolutely without a sense of the larger social obligation. He will " sell out " his city without a qualm and betray the interests of its people for the profit of a privileged few.

**6. The Religious Motive.**—Religion must now be considered as furnishing man with a third great dynamic to action. For the " fear of the Lord " is not only the " beginning of wisdom "; it has always been a powerful incentive to good conduct. We shall not have to discuss the question whether the religious motive, like the other two just described, originates from a primary instinct or inherent faculty of human nature. Sufficient for purposes of our discussion is the fact now well-established that a religious tendency or " sense " is practically universal among mankind. Recent studies of the history and development of religion agree in their emphasis upon two points: first, that religion is an outgrowth of man's consciousness of value; and, second, that religion, especially in its beginning, is primarily social both in origin and reference. A recognition of these two facts paves the way for a clearer understanding of the function which religion discharges in moral development. The object which underlies all forms of religious thought and belief is the *universe* —the all-encompassing reality. Thus religion has been lately defined as a " feeling of harmony between ourselves and the universe." [16] Of course a clear conception of the universe as such does not enter into all religious belief; rather is the object of belief and worship often a very insignificant part of it—a carved stick, a solitary tree, a species of animal. But these objects are all thought of as endowed with what a recent writer on the subject has well called a " mysterious potency " which they derive from the great hidden forces of the universe, the total scheme

[16] McTaggart: *Some Dogmas of Religion*, p. 3.

of things.[17]  In this way they become *divine*.  Now man's
attitude toward these his divinities is that of valuation.
He regards them not merely as facts which exist, but in
a certain sense as ends which he desires to achieve; that
is, he believes that their favor and assistance may be won,
and that if he complies with certain conditions the superhuman power of these divinities—and they represent always
the great hidden forces of the universe—may be enlisted
in his service to secure the greatest goods of life.  These,
the greatest goods of life, are always conceived, during
the earlier stages of human development, in social terms,
and represent, under the varying forms of the imagination,
the best welfare, largest power, and longest life, of the
tribe itself.  Thus religion appears to be in its essence a
belief that the powers of the universe are, or may be, allied
on the side of the Good—of the highest human welfare.
It is, in short, a belief that Universal Reality is good.  The
same conclusion is reached by a somewhat different path
when we agree with Höffding in defining religion as " faith
in the ultimate conservation of values." [18]  From this
standpoint, religion is exhibited as the belief not that
Reality is good but that Goodness is Real.  Yet if, in accordance with the second form of statement, our religion
consists in the belief that those ends and ideals which we
value most highly are conserved and provided for in the
nature of things, what is this but belief that the universe
or reality is good?  Thus the second proposition may be
accepted as the simple converse of the first, a belief in the
goodness of reality implying a faith in the reality of
goodness.

If religion is such an adjustment between the good of
man and the nature of the universe it is plain that religious belief may furnish a strong support, a powerful

[17] IRVING KING: *Development of Religion*, Chap. VI.
[18] HÖFFDING: *Philosophy of Religion*.

incentive, to good conduct. For if the Supreme Power of the universe is allied with the cause of goodness, the man who performs a good act has the universe behind him. Even though the act appear to be one of absolute self-sacrifice yet the individual cannot really lose, since God is on his side. Hence religion has exerted tremendous influence throughout the whole course of human history in impelling individuals to surrender their private interests to the welfare, or supposed welfare, of the group or nation. This influence has not always been exerted for the true good of man, or his genuine development, however. Often, too often, it has supplied an external and artificial sanction for a conventional morality long outgrown, but which, partly through the aid of religion, is able to preserve its authority and block all progress. Such is the case in Russia to-day, where the influence of religion and the Orthodox Church is exercised effectively to maintain in existence and power an antiquated and barbarous régime. These facts prove the inadequacy of religion as a motive of good conduct, when acting alone and not including an intelligent self-interest and a due regard for the welfare of others. When unaccompanied by an insight into the dependence of the Good upon the true interest of the individual and the real welfare of society, religion presents the requirements of goodness to man as if they were the commands of an external power which must be obeyed if the individual is to escape the punishment which this power can inflict, and enjoy the reward which it proffers. These rewards and punishments were at first supposed to come in the present life; but the observed facts of human existence made this view no longer possible and hence the divine judgment was postponed until after death. It is apparent that the religious motive, when its appeal is based upon such considerations, is but a disguised form of self-interest, and shares all the defects of this latter motive. The individual is moved by a desire to increase his enjoyment and to diminish his suffering, not, in this case, within the limits of his earthly existence merely, but during the future life as well. That religion may be transformed into a mere appeal to the lower kind of self-interest is proved by the frequency with which the noble Christian doctrine of self-realization through self-sacrifice has been degraded by its exponents into an arbitrary device whereby the human individual can gain Heaven and escape Hell. Further evidence to the same effect is supplied by the fact that the egoistic utilitarianism of the school of Hobbes often had recourse to theology to provide hedonic sanctions for conduct which, though necessary for social welfare, could not be shown to increase the sum-total of the individual's enjoyment during the present life. In pursuance of this method Paley defined virtue as " the doing good to mankind, in obedience to the will of God, for the sake of everlasting happiness."

7. **Self-Realization as the Motive of Good Conduct.**— Self-realization has now to be exhibited as the only adequate motive of good conduct, including the three just mentioned and raising each to a higher plane of meaning and efficiency. Self-realization does not simply combine in an external fashion the egoistic, altruistic, and religious motives; it unites them organically, making each a function of the central activity of volition and causing each to express within a certain department of human life the characteristic and insistent demand of volition for a completely organized life. Of these different motives at least two originate in native instincts which, when raised to the level of intelligent desire or purpose, express the craving of the human will for a larger satisfaction—the first in such a system of objects as will yield fullest enjoyment throughout the individual's life, and the second in such activities as will increase the happiness of other individuals

with whom he comes into contact. To the attainment of such ends are the promptings of self-interest and sympathy limited, in their natural and undeveloped form. But when the individual is illuminated by a better understanding of his capacities as a conscious person and these capacities are themselves developed through constant exercise, the two motives, egoistic and altruistic, and the religious as well, are expanded in meaning, and strengthened in power, until each expresses in its own way the supreme and unifying motive in the conduct of man as a moral agent —a yearning for the largest and most comprehensive life. The impelling force of self-love is extended beyond the boundaries of "self-interest" and is bestowed upon such ideal and inclusive objects as Truth and Beauty, which are required to satisfy the higher psychic capacities of human nature. The propulsive power of sympathy is extended beyond the happiness of a limited number of individuals and communicated to humanity—the welfare of the whole human race being rendered supremely attractive as an end of action. The compelling influence of religion is no longer limited to the enforcement of a divine command which promises punishment if disobeyed, but is extended to a divine purpose which is made inspiring by the fact that it guarantees the attainment of those ideals which man values most highly, and provides for the welfare of both the individual and the race. Thus these three motives prove to be only manifestations of the impelling power of a single inclusive object—that of complete Self-realization. They do not inaugurate three different lines of action; they all prompt to one. They represent three aspects of the one process of self-organization, and while there is a difference of emphasis in every case, each one includes and makes place for the other two. The attainment by the individual of the larger ideal objects of his higher powers, intellectual, practical, and emotional, requires from him the fullest coöperation with his fellows in a mutual sympathy and service. The promotion of the true welfare of humanity must include the attainment of the real interest of the individual himself. Finally the realization of the Divine Purpose will secure the highest well-being of self and others as integral parts of the universal order. Let us now reconsider these three motives as interpreted anew in the light of Self-realization.

8. **Self-Respect.**—Self-love, as expressing the demand of the human will for complete Self-realization, does not remain a desire of the individual for his own enjoyment through the objects which he may possess to the exclusion of all other individuals. It is rather the individual's regard for himself in the universal aspect of his nature —for the satisfaction of those capacities for intellectual attainment, for social companionship and conversation, and of those abilities for constructive and creative achievement, which are characteristic of human personality universally. These capacities require for their satisfaction objects that also are not exclusive but universal, and shared by all individuals composing the community of intelligence and personality. Self-love in this larger sense has not the subjective and intimate character of self-interest. Rather it has an objective and almost external reference, since it directs the attention of the individual to those powers and abilities in his nature which distinguish human personality as such. He esteems himself not as an individual but as a person. Self-love in this higher development is frequently called *self-respect*, and is recognized as an important factor in moral development. Self-respect is a regard for one's own worth and dignity as a human person, and a concern for the due satisfaction of the powers and capacities of intelligent personality consequently possessed. As a motive it has a powerful influence in restraining the individual from actions that are mean, tricky, and selfish,

and impels him to the pursuit of larger and more appropriate ends of intellectual and artistic activity and public service.  The force of self-respect alone has influenced men to lead clean and well-regulated lives when removed by circumstances from critical scrutiny of their fellows in the lonely outposts of civilization and has enabled them to resist the insidiously debasing effect of close contact with uncivilized or partly civilized peoples with their lower standards of conduct.  Indeed, as was explained in the preceding section, when the motive of self-love is taken in this wider meaning and understood to voice the demand of the whole self, natural and spiritual, for satisfaction, it is an expression of the moral ideal and is identical with conscience itself.  It is thus that Butler understands the principle of self-love which he makes coördinate with conscience, asserting that both " always lead us in the same way."  Aristotle, as noted above, distinguishes between two meanings given to the term " self-love."  According to one, the narrower meaning, the designation " lover-of-self " is justly used as a term of reproach, signifying selfishness and greed.  But in the second and larger sense it is applicable to the good man, for he " loves and gratifies the supreme part of his being."  " It follows that the virtuous man is a lover of self, although not in the sense in which a man who is censured for self-love is a lover of self, but in a sense differing from it as widely as a life directed by reason differs from a life directed by emotion, and as the desire for what is noble differs from a desire for what seems to be one's own interest." [19]  Hence Aristotle believes that the good man may in the true sense be a friend of himself; since friendship is based upon a recognition of personal worth and the good man esteems most highly the universal, rational principle in his nature.

[19] ARISTOTLE: *Nicomachean Ethics*, Bk. IX, Chap. VIII (Welldon's trans., p. 301).

9.  **Philanthropy.**—The altruistic motive, when it is enlightened by a true understanding of the nature and
capacities of man, undergoes a like development.  Its limits
are no longer those of natural sympathy which, at its
best, is restricted in application to the happiness of a
certain number of individuals.  Instead, altruism becomes
the love of humanity, an affection for all men, a genuine
philanthropy, which is based upon a realizing sense of the
value of every human being as possessed of the capacity
for personal development and self-realization.  Such is the
Christian spirit of love for fellow-men, the feeling of human
brotherhood springing from a recognition of the spiritual
kinship of the whole human race.  Philanthropy is thus
universal in a way that sympathy could never be—not
having to depend upon the accidents of personal contact,
individual attractiveness, and temperamental affinity, but
reaching as far as the essential characteristics of human
nature themselves go.  It is more catholic and all-embrac-
ing than the sympathy of a Walt Whitman whose liking
for his human kind led him to mingle with the jostling
throng on crowded street or ferry, for mere delight of
human presence and contact.  Even such wide sympathy
has necessarily its boundaries of time and space; it is, moreover, in a large degree a native endowment and hence cannot
be acquired by that large majority of persons who do not
by nature possess it.  Furthermore, philanthropy, in the
sense just explained, is much more effective as a factor in
moral development than even the wide sympathy of a
Whitman could be.  For such sympathy finds human beings supremely attractive as they are, with the qualities
and dispositions they actually possess.  It tends to rest
in enjoyment of the characteristics which at present exist
and is seized by no passion to change and improve the
character of men and women.  The deeper love of humanity, on the contrary, is not awakened by the existent traits

and qualities of human beings—these may be neutral or even repellent—but rather by the unrealized possibilities for personal growth and achievement which it detects and responds to, in every human individual, *qua* human. That these capabilities of higher attainment and larger life should thus prove attractive, means that they will become ends to be pursued and realized. Thus the man interested by the motive of philanthropy in his fellow-men is impelled to constant effort to bring out and make actual the potency for better things which he discovers is latent within each of them. The love which Jesus sought to arouse among men was of this sort—not a love for our fellows as they *are,* for their defects, their frailties, their sins—but for them as they *might be,* for the splendid and noble possibilities of every human self. This is the love which has inspired all great moral reformers with their visions of a regenerate humanity, of an uplifted and purified human nature—has animated all great liberators with their dreams of nations relieved from oppression and their inhabitants permitted in consequence to live larger and happier lives. The transforming effect of a love of this sort is happily illustrated in Jerome K. Jerome's pretty story or allegory, *The Passing of the Third Floor Back.* Here a " stranger " is represented as entering into association with a group of people from whom every fine and gentle trait seems to be absent and, through a love based upon an insight into their better nature and higher possibilities, awakening each to a new and higher life.

10. **Reverence.** A few words will suffice to indicate a little more fully how the religious motive is illuminated and transformed through a true conception of man's highest good. It is a psychological truism that if the commands of God are to move men to action they must, like any other object of pursuit, appeal to some part of his nature, to some tendency in himself. Now unless the requirements

of deity are believed to be based upon the highest human welfare, unless their appeal is made to that yearning of man's will for fullest Self-realization, they must make their appeal to some lower and more restricted desire. This is precisely what happens when moral laws are obeyed without any real insight into their character or questioning of their authority, as the dictates of the external power supreme in the universe and hence able to enforce its commands. Under such conditions these divine behests acquire their influence over man's will through their appeal to a desire that is comparatively low—that of gaining pleasure, the pleasure of reward, and of escaping pain, the pain of punishment. Thus the performance of duty in obedience to the will of God becomes part of a very simple and elementary egoism. The attempt may be made to avoid this conclusion by assuming that the commands of deity, unlike all other objects of thought, appeal in some mystical or supernatural fashion to a special faculty in human nature, thus deriving a unique authority. But there is not the slightest evidence in favor of such a belief. Like all other ends which we pursue and seek to attain, obedience to God must appeal to some one of our actual interests—if not to a higher, why then to a lower. Nor does a recognition of this fact deprive the divine will of its rightful authority over us. Rather do we secure for it the highest possible authority when we identify it with the Moral Ideal understood as the most complete realization of the powers of intelligent personality. The absolute worth of this object is witnessed by the feeling of reverence which it arouses within us, a feeling which is akin to religious awe, and which in its turn proves that these possibilities of higher personal development which we human beings possess are a divine birth-right and a consequence of our spiritual origin.

11. **Mixed Motives.**—It is a fact of moral experience, frequently commented upon, that men seldom act from a single motive, but are usually impelled to their action by the combined efficacy of several motives. Thus we are often—most often, it might appear—led to serve others when our sympathy for them is reinforced by a recognition that in helping them we shall ultimately be benefiting ourselves. In the same way the egoistic motive combines with the religious until they seem indeed to merge completely. On first thought this fact that an action is due to a mixture of motives may appear to discredit it—as when a person gives generously to the cause of charity, recognizing that it will improve his standing in the community, or when a man realizes high ideals of professional achievement in order to please wife or mother. Now, to be sure, it is discreditable to perform an act ostensibly from one motive which is generally admired but actually from another not given such approval, thus practising a kind of deception upon the community and winning praise which is undeserved—as when a business or professional man undertakes charitable work solely for purposes of self-advertisement. Action from mixed motives is not always blameworthy, however; it is to be regarded rather as the normal thing in conduct, indicating in the majority of cases increasing intelligence and moral development. For, as we have seen, the leading motives of human action are not necessarily exclusive and antagonistic: they turn out, when developed in all their implications, to be different expressions of the one underlying tendency of volition to seek complete Self-realization. Hence it is perfectly natural and extremely advantageous that they should supplement one another and lend their combined strength of impulsion, especially where the attainment of the good end requires severe exertion and the surmounting of great obstacles. At first the presence and influence of the two different and appar-

ently antagonistic motives may be accompanied by no consciousness of their unity in the higher synthesis of the Moral Ideal; but the experience of acting under their combined promptings, with the results achieved, will itself produce a growing sense of the harmonious coöperation of intelligent egoism, altruism, and religious devotion, in the attainment of Self-realization. As a matter of actual fact we do not by any means always disapprove of action from mixed motives. Instead, our judgments of others' conduct when we come to reflect upon them are striking proof that we do appreciate the other side of the subject just dwelt upon, viz. that the operation of several motives in place of one often indicates a better balanced and more developed character. As the genial essayist Dr. Crothers says in discussing this subject in a witty paper:

" So far as I have been able to observe, such mixed motives are the ones that take men furthest. Altruism is no exception to the general rule that a man does good work only when he likes his job. . . . We cannot abide an altruist who does not enjoy himself and who has not a sportsmanlike spirit. We resent his attempt to monopolize brotherly kindness. If he be without imagination he will insist on working for us instead of with us. He will not admit us to a partnership in good works. He insists upon doing all the self-sacrifice and having us take the ignominious part of passive recipients of his goodness. He confers a benefit on us with an air that says, ' I have come to do you good. I have no selfish gratification in what I am doing for you. But a sense of duty has triumphed over my personal inclination.' . . . The universal preference which all self-respecting people have for being helped by cheerful friends rather than by conscientious benefactors is a great limitation to all philanthropic effort. Unless we heartily enjoy ourselves other people will not allow us to improve their minds or their morals." [20]

[20] CROTHERS: " My Missionary Life in Persia," *Atlantic Monthly*, October, 1910, pp. 336-37.

## REFERENCES

Spencer, *Data of Ethics*, Chaps. XI, XII.
Sutherland, *Origin and Growth of the Moral Instinct*, Chaps. XI-XIV.
Darwin, *Descent of Man*, Chap. IV.
Hobbes, *Human Nature*, Chaps. VII-IX.
Paulsen, *System of Ethics*, Book II, Chap. VI.
Martineau, *Types of Ethical Theory*, Part II, Book I, Chaps. V, VI.
Dewey and Tufts, *Ethics*, Chap. XVIII, §§ 2, 3.
Seth, *Ethical Principles*, Part I, Chap. III, § 12.
Alexander, *Moral Order and Progress*, Book II, Chap. IV, § 3.

# CHAPTER V

## SELF-REALIZATION AND HAPPINESS

1. Pleasure as an Element in Self-Realization.—2. Self-Realization Not Identical with the Greatest Sum of Pleasures,—3. But Rather with a Harmony of Pleasures, or Happiness.—4. Happiness Thus the Feeling That Accompanies the Organization of Conduct.—5. Happiness Not to Be Accepted as the Good, Because It Is Unduly Subjective in Its Reference.—6. And It Implies a State of Passive Enjoyment.—7. Is the Pursuit of Goodness Certain to Result in the Greatest Happiness?—8. It Is, on the Assumption That Moral Purpose Is Supreme in the Universe,—9. And That Man May Complete His Moral Development in a Future Life.

1. **Pleasure as an Element in Self-Realization.**—Reference has previously been made to the fact that just as on the level of sentient life pleasure is an accompaniment of all action which is beneficial to the organism, so on the higher plane of intelligence and personality pleasant feeling is attendant upon all unimpeded and successful activity. Such activity, having its source in self-conscious volition, is directed not merely upon those objects which natural instinct makes attractive because required for the continued preservation and well-being of the human organism; it is directed also upon the ideal objects which are likewise necessary for the satisfaction of man's psychic capacities of thought, emotion, and practice. Pleasure is thus the normal accompaniment of all voluntary action when successful in attaining its object, and equally whether this object be material or spiritual. Now Self-realization as the Highest Good is just the fullest possible satisfaction of all the capacities of intelligent personality, natural and spiritual. It is evident, therefore, that pleasure is an es-

sential element in Self-realization, an integral part of the Good. We have then to take account of the place occupied by Pleasure in the good life.

## 2. Self-Realization Not Identical with the Greatest Sum of Pleasures.

—If it be true that pleasure accompanies the gratification of every desire, the fulfilment of every purpose, and Self-realization consists in the fullest possible satisfaction of all purposes and desires, the question arises— May not the Good then be conceived as the maximum of pleasure, i.e. the greatest amount of pleasure obtainable by the individual during his life? If we grant this, we find ourselves in practical agreement with the Hedonist whose contention we lately rejected as erroneous. But further thought shows us that the logic of Self-realization compels no such surrender to the claims of Hedonism: the two positions remain distinct throughout and, in certain points, fundamentally antagonistic. For the recognition that pleasure is a necessary constituent of Self-realization, the highest human good, is by no means identical with the assertion that man's good is the greatest amount of pleasure. Pleasures can thus be added only when reduced to a common denominator. And this could be accomplished solely through a separation of pleasures from the objects in connection with which they arise. Then, indeed, all qualitative distinctions would disappear and we would have left only specific instances of the same type of consciousness, the pleasant as distinguished from the unpleasant. These instances of pleasant feeling would differ only in quantity, i. e. in duration and intensity. The consistent Hedonist separates pleasures in this way from their objective conditions, admitting no qualitative differences and proposing such a calculation as will bring the individual the greatest amount of pleasure. But thus to separate pleasures from the objects and activities that produce them is to falsify the facts of experience. A pleasure thus cut away from its objective source is a psychological abstraction, not a part of our concrete experience. Pleasure always comes to us as one element in a unitary experience, it being the inner, the subjective aspect, to which the object, as the outer or external factor, is essential and complementary, the two being strictly inseparable in their intimate and organic union. When pleasure is thus conceived—not as an abstract psychological entity, *mere* pleasure—but concretely, as the pleasure of *this* object or *that* action, they do differ qualitatively. The pleasure of poetry has a different quality from that of eating, and the pleasure of benevolence from either of the other two. Now Self-realization implies the recognition of a difference in quality among pleasures, and along with this qualitative difference a difference in moral value. According to this principle, the moral value of any form or feature of conduct is, as we know, determined by the degree to which it contributes to the realization of all the capacities of the self. But, in this very respect, pleasures differ widely. Certain pleasures, although in themselves comparatively intense, tend to destroy the capacities out of which they arise and to lessen the amount of satisfaction possible to other capacities. On the contrary, other pleasures, not in themselves strong, are self-augmenting and create conditions favorable to a fuller exercise of the other capacities. Compare, for instance, the pleasures arising from action to satisfy two instincts, both natural and hence having a legitimate claim to expression, that of resentment and that of curiosity. The pleasure of anger and retaliation, if sought after or frequently enjoyed, so affects the disposition of the agent, deadening his powers and warping his faculties, that his possibilities for satisfaction in other lines of endeavor are greatly lessened. The other pleasure, though less vivid and absorbing, increases with repetition, develops into the joy of intellectual attainment and, through the added knowledge which accompanies it, assists in the fulfilment of all other aims and purposes. Measured, then, by the standard which Self-realization applies, some pleasures deserve to be approved, within this class distinctions being made of good, better, and best; while other pleasures equally deserve to be condemned as bad. From the good life the latter class of pleasures is, of course, entirely excluded; while pleasures of the former class enter in a degree proportionate to their moral value. Since Self-realization thus recognizes qualitative distinctions among pleasures and provides a criterion whereby the place of each pleasure in the good life may be determined, it is obviously in radical opposition to Hedonism, which ignores all differences in quality and proposes, by adding quantities of pleasure, to secure the greatest amount.

3. **But Rather with a Harmony of Pleasures, or Happiness.**—The Good as interpreted by Self-realization is not to be identified with a sum of pleasures but rather with a harmony or system of pleasures. To such a harmony of pleasures the word *Happiness* may appropriately be applied. When thus used, the term has a meaning quite distinct from pleasure or a sum of pleasures; since pleasures may be so joined as to constitute a true synthesis entirely different from the mechanical aggregate which results from combining them externally. Such a synthesis, as has been pointed out, is based upon an insight into the qualitative differences between pleasures, differences in the content and meaning through which one pleasure has implicit reference to another. For it is a fact that pleasures have these inner relationships and in consequence of them some pleasures reinforce and supplement one another while other pleasures are conflicting and discordant. To read an interesting novel and to stroll in the park on a summer's evening are both pleasant diversions and, when they are taken out of their setting in the life of a particular person,

there is little to choose between them. Yet the character of each is such as to make it harmonious with certain activities and enjoyments and discordant with others. For the bookkeeper whose eyes are strained and muscles cramped by the day's labor the pleasure of strolling in the park is much to be preferred of the two, because it both affords greater present satisfaction through its contrast with the mode and scene of his daily employment and also will prepare him to discharge more efficiently and enjoyably the duties of his occupation on the morrow. The other pleasure, on the contrary, would have afforded less present enjoyment through its unfavorable relation to the day's labor just past and would have diminished future satisfaction because affecting prejudicially the activity of the coming day. The case is typical and shows that the question as between pleasures cannot be settled simply by comparing the amount of enjoyment each will furnish, but involves instead a consideration of each in the total context of the individual's life, and a discovery of which one harmonizes most completely with all his other activities and enjoyments. Happiness may be understood as a harmonious arrangement of pleasures, a system or synthesis in which each of the constituent pleasures supplements and strengthens the rest.

Within such a system, no pleasure—no matter how intense—which conflicts with and weakens others, thus tending to destroy the unity and upset the equilibrium of the whole system, can find a place. But, on the contrary, pleasures in themselves weak and faint enough may be given an important place because reinforcing and reviving others. Paradoxical as it may seem, unpleasantness or even pain may have its part in producing the harmony of happiness just as a discord may enter into and, in a way, increase the harmony of a musical composition. Thus the happiness of a great love or friendship may be increased by the pain of temporary separation from the beloved, or by the suffering that may be undergone in serving him. Of course it is not true that in such cases sorrow is transformed into joy, or pain into pleasure, in the literal sense; but it is true that the unpleasant experience is intimately connected as an essential part in, or necessary means to, the realization of an object which is a fertile and inexhaustible source of pleasure, and for this reason is continually directing the attention to this object which proves on thought to be so agreeable as to cause the present pain to be forgotten. Thus the pain of separation causes the lover to think of his friend and immediately his pain is replaced by greater pleasure in the thought of their love: the suffering of the mother from weariness of her long vigil over the sick child is constantly arousing a deeper joy as she thinks that through these painful efforts his life is being preserved.

4. **Happiness Thus the Feeling That Accompanies the Organization of Conduct.**—It is clear that such a harmony of pleasures as we have been describing can arise only through the adjustment of the various activities of life— through the organization of conduct. Hence happiness may be defined not only as a harmony of pleasures but also as the pleasure of a harmonized or unified life. With this idea in mind, Mr. Rashdall says that it represents " satisfaction with one's existence as a whole—with the past and future as well as with the immediate present." [1] Now, as we are already aware, such a unity can be achieved in human life only through the continued activity of volition in subordinating particular objects of desire to more general aims and purposes and including these aims and purposes within a single comprehensive ideal. When this is done—or to the degree in which it is done—all the action of the individual has one object and his life possesses unity. The progressive realization of this ideal is of course

[1] RASHDALL: *Theories of Good and Evil*, Vol. II, p. 57.

accompanied by pleasure. This pleasure may be continuous and permanent; for, as every act contributes to the realization of the Supreme Ideal, its attainment occupies the whole of the individual's life. Unlike the narrower objects of natural desire and individual ambition, its possibilities are not easily exhausted nor is its attainment dependent upon fortune and circumstance to the degree of these lesser goods. It provides, therefore, a permanent source of joy which gives tone and buoyancy to the whole of life, tending to crowd out the pain of temporary misfortune and even to relieve the sorrows of deprivation and bereavement. The complete organization of life through a supreme and all-inclusive ideal with the consistent pursuit of this ideal is thus the source of true happiness and of that " peace which the world cannot give." History records many instances of men who have identified themselves with ideal causes and have found in their devotion a happiness which not the pain of increasing illness and infirmity or even the prospect of torture and death itself could destroy; biography tells of individuals who, restless and discontented while seeking their own comfort and amusement, discovered joy and peace in the assumption of arduous responsibility. Of course the question may be asked, " What if the Ideal prove impossible of fulfilment, what if the Cause fail? " Whence shall come the happiness of the widowed mother who devotes herself to the education of her only son and sees him turn out a weakling or a scoundrel, or of the patriot who strives all his life for the freedom of his people and at last when the opportunity of achieving it arises sees the chance lost through the cowardice or treachery of his compatriots? The only answer which can be made in such cases is that the particular cause must fail in order that a still larger good shall be realized and that the individual shall find in the eventual attainment of this larger end a source of renewed happiness.  To believe this—and still more to practise it—requires moral faith, faith that ultimately the force which makes for righteousness will prevail.  Fortunately human experience justifies this faith—although it does not convert it into a certainty.  The yearning to identify his life with an object that could not fail, to adopt as his own a purpose that was sure to be realized, led the ancient Stoic to seek peace and happiness in unity with Nature; it was the same motive which caused Spinoza to recommend to men the " intellectual love of God," a joy which arises when the finite identifies itself with the Infinite and the human individual finds his own good in the Universal Order.

There is a possible danger, however, in seeking to obtain happiness or peace through " conformity to Nature " or " union with God."  It is that the ideal attained will be one of thought merely, the discovery that Reality is one inter-related system, and that along with this intellectual insight will come a quietism in practice, and an acceptance of whatever occurs as right because necessitated by the universal system.  The realization of such an ideal satisfies man's intellectual faculty alone and fails to fulfil his practical needs which demand that the world shall be capable of mastery by intelligence, of being adapted to the requirements of conscious personality.  When the attempt is made in practice to assist in the adjustment of the world to the needs of intelligent personality—when, in other words, the individual endeavors in his small way to promote the cause of universal progress—his ideal proves far more difficult to achieve and his prospect of securing happiness through its successful attainment much less than if he were content with a purely theoretical adjustment. The objective order seems to be in some points antagonistic to the purposes of intelligence, and evil to be inherent in the nature of things.  The same objection does not necessarily apply to belief and trust in an over-ruling Providence in the Christian sense, as a source of happiness and contentment, however; for the distinguishing feature of the Christian revelation is the conception of God as the power striving for righteousness in the world, whose efforts involve suffering and self-sacrifice but whose leadership in the battle against the forces of evil gives man the assistance which he sorely needs and the practical assurance of ultimate victory.

5. **Happiness Not to Be Accepted as the Good, Because It Is Unduly Subjective in Its Reference.**—Happiness, as it has been lately defined, is evidently an essential part of Self-realization, if not actually identical with it. In fact, the two words when properly understood may seem to have the same meaning. Might it not be better then to speak of the Good as Happiness rather than Self-realization? Certainly if the word has no implications which stand in the way of its use it is preferable on grounds of being better understood and hence appealing more directly to the majority of minds. But the truth is that happiness does possess implications, does have a distinctive emphasis, which constitutes sufficient reason for rejecting it as the *summum bonum*. Its emphasis is always upon the inner, the subjective, aspect of all activity and experience; it calls attention to the effect upon the subjective consciousness of every action and achievement; it directs the thought of the self upon those inner states which may be expected to accompany the pursuit and attainment of objects. Because of these implications happiness is not well-suited to serve as the supreme end of conduct. Led to think of his own states of feeling primarily, the agent is biassed in favor of those objects which have proved themselves to be reliable sources of enjoyment. But the full satisfaction of his own will—as well as the attainment of happiness itself—requires that the agent forget himself and his own conscious states entirely

in his devotion to the object. For it is only through such free outgoing activity, unimpeded by subjective concern, that the powers of intelligence and volition in man can reach their complete fulfilment. The " paradox of Hedonism " that to secure pleasure one must forget it because, if he aims at it, he will miss it, retains force as an objection to making any form or system of feeling the supreme good. Indeed the most serious objection to Self-realization itself as the Good is that it directs the attention of the agent upon himself rather than upon the objects through which his will can gain satisfaction. This disadvantage seems to be more than counterbalanced, however, by the merit of Self-realization in emphasizing the fact that the Good is based upon the powers and capacities of the conscious self and not upon the demands of any external authority.

6. **And It Implies a State of Passive Enjoyment.**— Closely connected with the first is a second objection to accepting happiness as the *summum bonum*. In laying stress upon the subjective effects at the expense of the objective conditions of activity, such a conception of the Highest Good encourages a tendency to conceive of the Good in terms of passive affection instead of active attainment; it invites the agent to fall into a state of receptive enjoyment whenever possible and to seek to prolong and repeat such enjoyment. Certainly this is an erroneous conception of happiness and the course which it prompts the individual to pursue is mistaken; for, as the ancient moralists clearly saw, if a man thinks of his happiness as an effect produced in him by external causes he is then made dependent upon the objects without him, is rendered the slave of fortune and circumstance. True happiness, on the contrary, arises when the consciousness of the agent, absorbed in the pursuit and attainment of a chosen end which he recognizes as an integral part of

his life's purpose, is suffused by a glow of pleasant feeling which adds light and life to his thought and action. Happiness is thus inseparable from activity. This fact has caused great moralists like Aristotle to define it as a "species of activity." Not, of course, that happiness is not a condition of feeling, but that this feeling is one that arises when objects are chosen and pursued, and is present in a degree proportionate to the adjustment and organization of these various activities. Thus it is relieved from entire subservience to external conditions and made dependent upon the choice and action of the individual; it also gains from his life purpose a steadiness and permanency which raises it above the changing play of natural events. Aristotle held this view of happiness, as is evident from the following statement:

" We have formed a conception of happiness as something that is permanent and exempt from the possibility of change and because the same persons are liable to many revolutions of fortune. For it is clear that, if we follow the changes of fortune, we shall often call the same person happy at one time and miserable at another, representing the happy man as ' a sort of chameleon without any stability of position.' It cannot be right to follow the changes of fortune. It is not upon these that good or evil depends; they are necessary accessories of human life as we said, but it is man's activities in accordance with virtue that constitute his happiness and the opposite activities that constitute his misery." [2]

7. Is the Pursuit of Goodness Certain to Result in the Greatest Happiness?—Another problem related to happiness may be touched upon briefly before leaving the subject; although in this case only suggestions and not a final solution can be presented. Happiness has been described as a feeling of harmony which results from the organization of our activities. Such organization frequently requires

[2] ARISTOTLE: *Nicomachean Ethics*, Bk. I, Chap. IX (Welldon's trans., p. 24).

that our desires be denied the pleasure of immediate fulfilment in order that some larger end may be realized in
the future. The larger end—ultimately the *summum
bonum* itself—may be expected in attainment to furnish
a satisfaction so great as to outweigh, or, better, so comprehensive as to include, the gratification of the desire in
question with its attendant pleasure. All very true, *provided that the larger end is attained.* But suppose that
death intervenes and prevents this. Has not the individual really lost in happiness through his self-control and
devotion to his ideal? Moreover is it not the common lot
of those who sacrifice their immediate inclinations to the
pursuit of extensive and far-reaching purposes, to die before seeing these purposes realized? The complete organization of conduct requires the adoption of an ideal too
comprehensive to be realized in the natural lifetime of
the human individual. Hence the good man seems destined to miss the pleasure of achieving his highest aim.
How then is it possible to maintain that happiness always
accompanies self-organization? Or that goodness and happiness coincide? Immanuel Kant was impressed with the
importance of this problem and was led, by the necessity
which he felt of finding a solution for it, to introduce two of
his famous " postulates of practical reason." The demand
of the moral law that happiness shall be proportioned to
goodness justifies us in postulating, he believed, the existence of a God able to bring about such an apportionment,
and of an immortality for man in which he shall have time
enough to bring his will into perfect accord with the
moral law.

8. **It Is, on the Assumption that Moral Purpose Is
Supreme in the Universe.**—Kant's introduction of God
at just this point in his ethical system has been much
criticised and certainly this criticism is deserved if it
means that God intervenes in a mechanical fashion to

square accounts and set things right, giving the good
the amount of pleasure which they have missed in life.
But the question of the relation of happiness to goodness
is not necessarily that of the sanctions of goodness in the
way of reward conferred upon the good man by an external
power. It is a question of the ultimate ground of moral
value. Is goodness real in the sense that the man who
achieves it enters upon a larger and more permanent life
whose satisfactions are uninterrupted by physical death
or is it simply a belief produced in the human mind by
certain physical and biological forces which work upon it,
with the consequence that while it may bring about useful
adjustments it can furnish no satisfaction which extends
beyond the period of natural existence? The whole matter
goes back finally to the nature of the universe—is moral
purpose inherent in it, so that the person who attains
moral development at whatever cost of physical health or
existence acquires more reality, or is it the product of
mechanical forces solely, so that reality must be measured
altogether by the amount of physical energy and the length
of natural existence? The alternatives remain the same as
they appeared to Marcus Aurelius: "Either a Providence
or Democritus and his Atoms; and with it whatsoever we
brought to prove, that the whole world is as it were one
Citie?" But, it may be said, we have already based moral
value upon the human will. This is true; for all empirical
study of conduct must proceed from a consideration of
the demands of volition as these are revealed in human
experience. Our study of the demands of intelligent volition has brought to light this significant fact, however,—
that its ultimate satisfaction requires objects whose attainment extends beyond the term of man's natural existence.
The possibility of full satisfaction to the human will—of
complete Self-realization for man—evidently depends, therefore, upon the standing of intelligent will, of self-conscious

personality, in the universe. *Is* it the ultimate reality to which all physical forces are subordinate? Is it *not* the source of the natural universe itself? We can have no certain knowledge on this point and of course the conclusions of other sciences besides Ethics should influence our belief. Perhaps the best justification for the belief or assumption that the ground of the universe is spiritual, is the fact that in our moral lives we *do assume it.* Or, more precisely, we *act upon it.* For what other belief than that of the superior reality of spirit or personality can be reconciled with the system of moral values which we uphold, with the deliberate sacrifice of natural well-being, to ideal ends and purposes? It is a significant fact, furthermore, that those individuals who do, through such sacrifice of natural well-being, enter upon the larger spiritual life, are most firmly convinced of its reality and permanence. The supremacy of a Power that makes for righteousness in the world,—in other words, the existence of God,—seems requisite, therefore, to explain fully the facts of morality, and particularly to give a final solution of the problem of happiness in its relation to goodness. Not that God is required to reward the good and punish the wicked after death, but that the superior reality of purpose and personality over matter and mechanism is necessary to validate the assumption on which the whole of moral development is based—that the human will gains fuller satisfaction through the pursuit of ideal ends and purposes which cannot be completely realized in the present life than in the attainment of those natural goods whose possession may be enjoyed during the period of physical existence.

9. **And that Man May Complete His Moral Development in a Future Life.**—The question of immortality is also involved in the subject under discussion. And the considerations advanced as a warrant for belief in God have

equal weight in the case of immortality. The strongest argument in favor of belief in a future existence, that is, is furnished by the fact that in moral development we do surrender satisfactions which we are reasonably sure of enjoying in the present existence for the sake of ideals whose scope and extension are too great to permit of their being realized during the term of our natural lifetime. Now if death cut off all further attainment and made the complete realization of these ideals absolutely impossible, they must necessarily lose much, a great part, perhaps, of their value. Immortality has its deepest meaning and highest worth in removing from man's will the limitations imposed by the conditions of physical existence and in opening before it the prospect of a far-reaching development in a larger life. Mr. Lowes Dickinson gives beautiful expression to this idea in his recent Ingersoll Lecture: " The whole strength of the case for immortality as a thing to be desired, lies in the fact that no one in life attains his ideal. The soul, even of the best and most fortunate of us, does not attain the Good of which she feels herself to be capable, and in which alone she can rest. The potentiality is not wholly realized. I do not infer from this that life has no value if the Beyond is cut off. That, I think, is contrary to most men's experience. The Goods we have here are real Goods, and we may find the Evil more than compensated by them. But what I do maintain is that life here would have indefinitely more value if we knew that beyond death we should pursue, and ultimately to a successful issue, the chosen ideal of which we are always in quest. The conception that death ends all does not empty life of its worth, but it destroys in my judgment its most precious element, that which transfigures all the rest; it obliterates the gleam on the snow, the planet in the east; it shuts off the great adventure, the adventure beyond death." The objection may be offered that thus to regard immortality as implied by the facts of moral development is to introduce a factor into morality for which experience gives no warrant and of which we can have no certain knowledge. That we can have no certain knowledge concerning this matter of future existence is assuredly true. But it must not be forgotten that, as we have already seen, moral development is conditioned primarily not by intellect but by volition—it is a venture of will rather than an expression of knowledge. To take the first step in this development man must sacrifice a present inclination which he actually experiences for the sake of a future which is uncertain and whose existence and character no knowledge can fully reveal to him. Then in social adjustment he must surrender interests which have proved satisfying to him as an individual in order to seek social ends whose nature and ability to satisfy cannot be known before the sacrifice is made. Is it unreasonable then to suppose that moral development requires one more act of will—this time of the will to be a self whose life extends beyond the limits of physical existence—in which man's natural life itself with all its interests is made subordinate to the fuller and more lasting satisfactions of a future life? Of the character of this future life we know nothing and possibly should expect to know nothing—whether it will be eternal and without the bounds of time or will have its duration indefinitely extended, whether we shall possess individuality and enter into social relations as we now do. But the same considerations which lead us to believe in any future existence at all suggest that the form and mode of that existence will be such as to enable us to participate in the realization of those ends for which we have striven and suffered here.

# CHAPTER VI

# SELF-REALIZATION AND THE SYSTEM OF VIRTUES

**1. Intuitional and Empirical Conceptions of Virtue.—** The treatment of the different virtues or duties which are a recognized part of morality has varied in accordance with the theory of conscience, whether intuitional or empirical. Intuitionists have regarded the several virtues as habits of character whose moral worth is self-evident to the human conscience. In this view, certain forms of conduct such as courage and temperance and justice are given a peculiar authority and prestige in human life. It is, moreover, a necessary consequence of its self-evident character that this authority should be admitted universally by men of all races and times. Thus Intuitionists have been led to maintain that a general agreement exists among all human beings as to the fundamental duties or virtues. If such agreement exists it should not be difficult to discover what these virtuous practices are, and the Intuitionists have endeavored to enumerate them. But, possessing no standard of moral value in the form of an end to the attainment of which all right practices are related as means, it is not strange that these moralists, in the face of the bewildering diversity of beliefs and practices that enter into the morality of different peoples and times, should have failed in their attempt to discover and catalogue the fundamental human virtues. The Empiricist, on the contrary, believing that judgments of moral value are determined by the conditions of individual existence and social survival, does not expect to find any such general agreement among men, as to the types of conduct and character which are approved as good. He does not believe that any rule of action possesses absolute authority over the life of men, and points to the lack of agreement among races, as to what is virtuous and what is vicious, as evidence sustaining his position. He is not tempted to undertake a description or classification of all the virtues, seeing in the failure of the Intuitionist's attempt sufficient proof of the futility of such an undertaking.

2. **Virtue as Interpreted by Self-Realization.**—In this matter Self-realization as usual takes the *via media* and attains the larger truth. In accordance with this point of view, a virtue is any habit or disposition required of a human individual as a means to his Self-realization.[1] It is apparent at once that this conception of virtue allows for and explains the many and confusing differences of opinion among men as to what practices are virtuous. What is meat to one man is poison to another; yet each must have his proper means of subsistence if he is to live and develop his powers. Furthermore, the conditions of man's life, the character of the human environment, vary with every individual, every race, and every epoch; yet it is these conditions and circumstances that the individual

---

[1] The relation of duty and virtue was explained in Chap. I of Part II. These two words do not signify different things, the one an outward act, which is distinct from the other, an inward quality. Rather do they both refer to the same thing, to an activity which is judged an essential part of goodness. For convenience, the term *virtue* will be employed exclusively in the discussion which follows in the present chapter, it being understood to mean equally a habit of action or a disposition to act.

must reckon with and utilize, if he is to maintain his existence and realize his larger self. It is not strange then that what one race esteems highly as a virtue another race at a different period of development and under other conditions should regard with great disapproval and repugnance. If an Eskimo should meet the game he is hunting in unusually large numbers and under circumstances exceptionally favorable to himself, it might well be a virtuous action for him to make as large a kill as possible in order to provide food for himself and his family during the winter; but such wholesale slaughter of game by a sportsman in a civilized country would be rightly condemned and viewed with abhorrence. For the scholar who works long hours at his desk or in his laboratory it is a duty to take exercise in the open-air for a certain time each day; for the farmer who works in the fields or the mechanic whose trade is pursued out-of-doors this duty does not exist, but virtue for him consists in keeping his intellectual faculties alive by daily reading and thought.

Adopting the principle of Self-realization we are thus able to make ample allowance for the variety of conditions under which moral development proceeds and do full justice to the relative and changing character of moral distinctions; but we have also found that there are certain conditions which are essential to all human life and conduct. Every human individual possesses a set of natural instincts and a number of spiritual capacities, which relate him as a natural being to material objects and other individuals, as a conscious self to other selves in a community of intelligence and personality, as a human personality to the Universal Order and Purpose. These conditions, holding for all human beings, determine on broad lines the course of Self-realization for every one. In view of the aforesaid characteristics of human nature and human life which seem to be fixed and essential, all men must achieve a series of adjustments if they are to organize their conduct. These activities of adjustment which are necessary for self-organization in the case of every human being deserve most truly the designation of virtues. Since they are indispensable means to the attainment of Self-realization, the supreme end, they share its absolute moral worth. And as they are practices required equally of all men who would completely organize their conduct, they may be distinguished from habits of character requisite to Self-realization in different individuals and with particular societies, and be properly regarded as universal virtues. But to maintain that these habits of adjustment, necessary to complete self-organization in all men, are universal in their authority, does not mean that their worth as virtues is recognized by all peoples or observed by all individuals. For the organization of conduct is achieved through a slow and arduous development both in society and the individual; in consequence many peoples have never gone beyond the earlier stages and the first adjustments; they admit the obligation to temperance and courage but have hardly a notion of idealism or benevolence. Just to this extent, accordingly, their moral development is incomplete and self-organization unattained.

3. **The Classification of the Virtues.**—Thus to conceive of virtuous actions as necessary steps in the organization of conduct, and of the fundamental virtues as activities which the essential conditions of human life require of all men who would achieve Self-realization, gives the most satisfactory solution to the problem of the virtues and their inter-relation. Interpreting the virtues as necessary stages in self-organization they are made functions within a single process and hence joined in an organic system. Moreover, a criterion or standard is supplied by which the claims of an activity or disposition to be admitted to the class of virtues may be tested. To receive a place in the

system such an activity must be shown to be necessary to Self-realization under the universal conditions of human life. Thus the foundation is laid for a classification of the virtues which shall be systematic, comprehensive, and —most important of all—expressive of the inherent character of moral development itself.

The value of such a classification would seem to be self-evident. Yet thus it does not appear to recent writers on Ethics; in fact the whole undertaking has fallen into disfavor. Professor Dewey regards a catalogued list of the virtues with an exact definition of each as undesirable and impossible.[2] Professor Mackenzie thinks that the attempt to make a list of the particular virtues is almost frivolous.[3] The relative and changing character of moral distinctions, and the dependence of all judgments of vice and virtue upon individual opinion, are cited as showing the futility of any attempt to make a classification of the virtues which shall possess universal validity. The general acceptance of any classification, moreover, would mean that morality had become formalized and conventional; since moral development, itself living and fluent, cannot without violence be restricted to the limits of fixed forms of conduct and character. In defense of the value and importance to Ethics of defining and classifying the virtues, the reply may be made that if Ethics is to succeed in its chief purpose of describing in an intelligible and convincing fashion the essential features of the good life, it must be able to give this life some coherent form, some definite framework. Such form or framework is supplied only when we define the activities which are necessary constituents of goodness in all individuals. Furthermore, if the conclusions of Ethics are to furnish guidance in life they must contain recommendations sufficiently concrete

---

[2] DEWEY AND TUFTS: *Ethics*, p. 402.
[3] MACKENZIE: *Manual of Ethics*, p. 366.

and certain to be carried out in practice. There is danger lest present-day Ethics in its anxiety to avoid stereotyped formulas and systematic principles should leave its students with ideas too indefinite and complicated to be remembered or applied in actual life. There is cause then for the complaint of the French moralist who wrote a few years ago deploring the lack of agreement in their practical recommendations among teachers of Ethics in French universities, saying these differences of opinion furnished capital for the enemies of philosophy in ecclesiastical circles.[4] He then detailed a list of ten virtues and maintained that these at least might be generally recognized by moralists as essential to good conduct.

**4. Historic Methods of Classifying the Virtues.**—The most important, and still the most celebrated, classification of the virtues is that of Plato, who describes the four " cardinal " virtues, Wisdom, Courage, Temperance, and Justice. This classification doubtless owes its fame and continued influence to the fact that it is really organic— being based upon an analysis of the faculties of the human self and a study of the conditions of their activity in human society. Recognizing three " faculties " in the human soul, the rational, spirited, and appetitive, Plato considers that a virtue resides in the discharge of its proper office by each of these faculties, Wisdom in the control by reason of appetite, Courage in the execution by will of the commands issued by reason to sensuous desire, and Temperance in the subjection of appetite and desire to the control of reason. Justice, the virtue remaining, consists in the harmonious activity of the whole self which results from the proper functioning of each of these faculties within its own province. Justice is evidently identical with Self-realization and the three other virtues may

[4] LALANDE: " Les Principes Universels de l'Éducation Morale," *Revue de Métaphysique*, Vol. IX, p. 237.

be considered as adjustments required for this end by the essential characteristics of the human self. The classification is patently unsatisfactory, however, because it does not contain enough virtues to cover the whole field of the moral life. It has a semblance of adequacy only because justice is made to include all the social virtues. Perceiving this defect in the Platonic classification, Aristotle gives us a much longer list of virtues. But while his classification is much more inclusive and concrete than that of Plato, it is less organic and essential. He first divides virtues into two classes, intellectual and moral, the former being activities of reason alone and the latter involving both the rational and the non-rational principles in human nature and consisting in the control by reason of desire and emotion. Now the law of reason in the conduct of life is that of the organic mean, i.e. such regulation of every impulse and activity as will make it a means to the realization of the end of life itself. The moral virtues then consist in the observance of this " golden mean " in the gratification of every desire. Aristotle enumerates a number of virtues which thus represent moderation in the different departments of human nature and the various activities of human life. His account of these virtues, while always highly illuminating and instructive, contains, through its very fullness and detail, much that applies only to his own time and people. One misses, moreover, a unifying principle which will reveal the inner and essential articulation of these forms of conduct. As Mackenzie says, Aristotle's list of the virtues is little more than a " collection of specimens of some of the most important types to be found in his age and country." [5]

5. **Other Methods of Classifying the Virtues.**—Many other classifications of the virtues have been made since the time of the Greek moralists. A method frequently

[5] MACKENZIE: *Manual of Ethics*, p. 372.

used is as follows: Certain types of action are recognized as virtuous. These are examined and compared. Points of similarity are noted by which several virtues are associated together and at the same time set off from other virtues which do not possess these qualities. One of these aspects in which groups of virtues differ is selected as a convenient principle of classification. Thus the object of reference of a virtue is often chosen as a handy means of classifying it. Certain virtues are distinguished as self-regarding, like prudence and temperance; others are said to be social in their reference, like justice and sympathy. Or, the faculties which they bring into play are hit upon as a principle for dividing the virtues. We then have intellectual virtues, like tolerance and sincerity; virtues of the will, as courage and self-control; and those of the affections, as kindness, loyalty, etc.

An excellent illustration of this way of treating the virtues is furnished by the classification of Thomas Aquinas, the accepted philosopher of the Roman Catholic church. Thomas first divides the virtues, according to their source, into natural and supernatural. The supernatural virtues, faith, hope, and charity, are produced in man by God. The natural virtues man acquires by the exercise of his own powers. They, in their turn, are divided, according to their source in human nature, into intellectual and moral virtues. The moral virtues are four, *justice, prudence, courage,* and *temperance*. In classifying these four, Thomas uses another principle and distinguishes them according to the object of their reference. Thus *justice,* because it refers to the good of others, is separated from *prudence, courage,* and *temperance,* which are concerned with the welfare of self.

6. **Defects of These Classifications Illustrated by Pre-evolutionary Classification of Living Forms.**—Such a method of classification has grave faults. It is bound to

lead to results largely subjective, because the principle used depends upon individual taste and opinion. The same virtue may belong to an indefinite number of groups, according to the quality or aspect of it chosen for emphasis. Thus tolerance may be classed with sincerity as an intellectual, or with justice as a social virtue, according as we emphasize its source in the individual nature, or the end toward which it is directed. Then, too, a principle of classification so selected for convenience's sake affords no test of the fitness of any activity to be admitted to the system of virtues. Suppose we classify the virtues according to the object of their reference. Then any practice designed to promote the welfare of the self, e.g. *cunning,* might be included among the self-regarding virtues. At least the principle of classification would furnish no obstacle. But these and many other shortcomings have their roots in one fundamental defect,—a principle is employed in classification which is not organic to the field of its application. Hence it follows inevitably that the results obtained are subjective, and room is left for endless doubt and dispute. No necessity attaches to the conclusions because the essential inter-relation of the facts is not observed.

The biological sciences have long since abandoned a method of classification whose results are so unsatisfactory. Before the time of Darwin, however, plants and animals were classified in this fashion. The naturalists of the eighteenth century based their classifications for the most part upon broad and easily discovered resemblances in the external characters of organisms. Such similarities in structure and habit as seemed important to the individual investigator were utilized by him in the grouping of forms. None of the systems thus constructed gained universal acceptance; for all were subjective, and hence artificial. But the advent of evolution changed all this, and put into the hands of the biologist a new and better instrument for the organization of his field. The relation of descent was seen to constitute the natural principle of classification. Living forms which are grouped genetically are not arbitrarily associated by an external tie and a common label; they are organically united by community of descent and consequent identity of nature. By their phylogenetic affinities the various living forms are grouped into an organic system, between the members of which there is essential inter-relation and functional inter-dependence.

7. **Classification of Virtues as Stages in Self-Organization Illustrated by Evolutionary Classification.**—We now ask, can we make such a classification of the virtues, a classification based not on external resemblances but on organic interconnection? Can we apply the organic conception to the moral life, and conceive of the virtues as functions, whose nature and position are determined by the part they play in the realization of the Moral Ideal? This is quite possible if we understand the moral life as a development whose end is the complete organization of human conduct, and the different virtues as necessary steps in this process of organization. Pursuing this method we reach, it would appear, a satisfactory classification of the virtues. It resembles the classification of living forms made by the biologist. Like this, it is a natural arrangement based upon genetic relationship and functional inter-dependence. As the various species of plants and animals are regarded as stages in the evolution of the living organism, so the different virtues are conceived as steps in the evolution of conduct. As the many living species are united by genetic affinities in one great organic system, so the different virtues are united in the complete organization of conduct. As the species are classified according to the part they play in the process of organic evolution, so the virtues are classified according to the office they

discharge in the organization of conduct. Thus our ideal of a principle organic to the field of its application is realized. The virtues are classified within the system according to the function which they discharge in its organization. Temperance and prudence are associated because both are required in the organization of individuality. Justice and benevolence are distinguished from them and classed together because necessary for the adjustment of the individual to society. Finally, it may be noticed that here the principle used in classification is itself a test of the fitness of any activity to be admitted to the system. For it is only through the function which it discharges in the organization of conduct that an activity can be classed among the virtues.

8. **Classification of the Virtues in Accordance with the Method of Self-Realization.**—Adopting the method proposed and following it out along the lines indicated in previous chapters, we recognize first that self-organization for man involves three necessary aspects:

I. The organization of impulses and activities within the nature of the individual.

II. The organization of individual interests within society.

III. The adjustment of human welfare to Universal Reality.

We see further that self-organization in each of the first two aspects (with which alone Ethics is directly concerned) can be achieved only through two subordinate activities of adjustment. These adjustments, rendered habitual, are in truth necessary steps in the organization of conduct. They are as follows:

I. INDIVIDUAL.

a) The adjustment of all natural desires to the material comfort and well-being of the individual.

b) The adjustment of the individual's physical comfort and well-being to those ideals required to satisfy his spiritual capacities.

II. SOCIAL.

*a*) The adjustment of individual interest to the interests of others with whom he comes into personal contact.

*b*) The adjustment of all individual interests to the welfare of all human personality.

Let it be noted finally that each of these habits of adjustment has two sides; a *negative*, in the repression or restriction of constituent activities; and, a *positive*, in the attainment of a more comprehensive end thereby. Such positive and negative sides may be clearly distinguished in any adjustment which is a step in progressive organization and it is not surprising, therefore, to find that in the four or (including the religious) the five adjustments above-named, each side furnishes the basis for a virtue. It is of course a well-known fact that the virtues go in pairs, the members of which supplement and complete one another, as e.g. justice and benevolence, temperance and prudence.

Thus we are enabled to designate and define ten virtues which are necessary steps or stages in Self-realization under the universal conditions of human life.

I. INDIVIDUAL.

*a*-1) *Temperance.*—The habit of restraining single impulses and desires in the interest of individual well-being.

*a*-2) *Prudence.*—The habit of furthering individual comfort and security through the due subordination of single impulses and desires.

*b*-3) *Courage.*—The habit of sacrificing individual safety and comfort in the attainment of a larger and more comprehensive good.

*b*-4) *Idealism* (Wisdom, Efficiency, Refinement).—

The habit of exercising the higher spiritual capacities of the individual at the expense of his material comfort and pleasure.

II. SOCIAL.

*a*-5) *Kindness*.—The habit of surrendering individual interest when this is known to conflict with the interest of another.

*a*-6) *Friendship*.—The habit of promoting another's welfare with disregard for one's own interest.

*b*-7) *Justice*.—The habit of subordinating individual interest, whether of self or of others, to the good of humanity.

*b*-8) *Benevolence*.—The habit of promoting the welfare of all fellow-men, whether in community, nation, or world, by means of individual effort and initiative.

III. RELIGIOUS.

*a*-9) *Reverence*.—The subordination of human interests to the ends of Universal Intelligence.

*a*-10) *Piety*.—The adoption by man of the Universal Purpose as his good.

9. **Advantages of Such Classification.**—The agreement of the classification here proposed with modern evolutionary conceptions is brought out clearly if we compare it with that made by Thomas Aquinas and adopted by Roman Catholic moralists. Indeed, the classification here given is related to that of Thomas much as modern genetic systems in biology are related to those of the pre-Darwinian naturalists. Thus Thomas separates absolutely the supernatural from the natural virtues. The former are gifts of God; the latter have natural causes. In an analogous way pre-Darwinian science separated man from other animal species, believing that the peculiar circumstances of his creation had given him a unique place in the organic realm. We have recognized no such difference in kind between the '' religious '' and other virtues. All are stages in one process

of organization, the religious virtues representing simply the final step in which the individual adjusts himself to Universal Reality. In a like manner, of course, modern science admits of no absolute separation between the human and other species. In his detailed classification of the natural virtues Thomas makes sharp distinctions based upon single features chosen as principles of division, thus separating the intellectual from the moral virtues according to the faculties which they bring into play, rational or appetitive, and among the moral virtues distinguishing two classes according to the object of their reference, social or selfish. All this reminds us of eighteenth-century classifications in biology by means of parts and attributes singled out by the systematist because serviceable to his purpose. On the other hand, the arrangement suggested above agrees with modern evolutionary systems in allowing no arbitrary distinction of forms, but classifying them all according to their genetic affinities in one process of development.

---

The following chapters are devoted to a study of these different virtues which represent, in their orderly sequence, the necessary stages in the life of Self-realization.

## REFERENCES

Dewey and Tufts, *Ethics*, Chap. XIX.
Mackenzie, *Manual of Ethics*, Book II, Chap. III, and Book III, Chap. IV.
Paulsen, *System of Ethics*, Book III, Chap. I.
Alexander, *Moral Order and Progress*, Book II, Chap. VI.
Sidgwick, *Methods of Ethics*, Book III, Chap. II.
Seth, *Ethical Principles*, Part II, Chaps. I, II.
Green, *Prolegomena to Ethics*, Book III, Chap. V.
Aristotle, *Nicomachean Ethics*, Book II (Welldon's trans.).
Plato, *Republic*, Book IV (Trans. of Davies and Vaughn).

PART FOUR

THE LIFE OF SELF-REALIZATION

# CHAPTER I

## THE INDIVIDUAL VIRTUES

1. The Exercise of Volition as the Pre-supposition of All Moral Development. — 2. Temperance. — 3. Prudence. — 4. Courage. — 5. Idealism.

1. **The Exercise of Volition as the Pre-supposition of All Moral Development.**—The human race as a whole has inherited from its animal progenitors certain natural instincts and impulses, such as those of food and sex, of curiosity and acquisition, of sympathy and resentment. These instincts have been developed in the organism as means of adjusting it to the environment; they enable the living being to avail itself of the resources of the natural world and thus to preserve its existence and maintain its strength.

The preliminary condition of all moral development is that the objects of these instincts and impulses, originally pursued from inherited nervous tendency, shall become ends of conscious desire. That the self shall be capable of intelligent volition is the pre-requisite of its own realization. Volition first manifests itself as an organizing agency in the control of action by intelligent desire. In this, the simplest form of voluntary action, an object is pursued because it corresponds to, and contributes to the realization of, an idea already present in the mind of the self. Thus the will initiates that process of expansion whereby the self grows by appropriating from the external world those objects that appeal to it. With the ability to act in fulfilment of desire there appears for the first time in the history of the living organism the possibility of self-expression and self-development. Its advent means the attainment of freedom as well as the assumption of responsibility on the part of the living individual. Hence the ability to satisfy desire through intelligently directed effort must be present as the foundation upon which all further building of personality rests.

Since it is the indispensable preliminary of all personal development,—the first condition of Self-realization with all men,—the ability of volition to achieve successfully objects of desire seems to demand recognition as, in its continuous exercise, the first of the virtues of the moral life. Certainly, the inability to pursue and attain objects of desire would render all moral development impossible; the case of the individual thus incapacitated would be quite hopeless morally. Indeed, the exercise of this fundamental capacity of volition is so necessary that without it the individual could not be regarded as a moral agent at all. Since it is the possession of every normal human being, however, the activity in question is rather taken for granted as the pre-supposed basis of all conduct, than esteemed as a distinct factor in moral attainment.

As its first necessary step forward, Self-realization requires of all men such adjustment of natural impulses and desires as will make them a means to the preservation and comfort of the individual. On its negative side this activity of adjustment is identical with the virtue of temperance.

2. **Temperance.**—Temperance is the habit of restraining single impulses and desires in the interest of individual well-being. Signifying the control of natural instinct by active intelligence it is the fundamental virtue of the moral life. In emphasis of this point Paulsen says:

" Temperance or moderation, the ability to resist temptation to sensuous pleasure, is the precondition of humanization. The animal is essentially blind impulse, in the satisfaction of which its life consists. Man, too, is endowed with an animal nature, but its purpose is to serve as the soil for the higher spiritual life; this soil is prepared by the discipline of the natural impulses." [1]

Our natural desires are thus habitually restrained, but not because they are in themselves evil and ought to be uprooted from our nature. From the Self-realization standpoint, all normal instincts and impulses of man are, on the contrary, good in themselves; moral value attaches only to their expression and never to their suppression as an end sought for its own sake. Goodness belongs only to the affirmation of human nature, never to its negation, except when this is a means to a fuller and more complete affirmation. And it is as a means of securing the fullest satisfaction of our nature rather than of repressing it that temperance is placed in the first rank of the virtues. For the single impulse or desire, if permitted all the gratification which it does on its own account demand, will hinder or prevent the satisfaction of other desires. Hence the greatest possible satisfaction of all desires and capacities makes necessary the habitual restraint of single ones within the limits set by the rightful claims of others.

By temperance we understand, therefore, not abstinence, not repression, but, in general, moderation in all exercise and indulgence. Thus we take the word in the Greek sense, meaning by temperance the *measured* life, the ordered life—the life which observes the '' golden mean '' in all its activities, not refraining from any wholesome pleasure or normal gratification but at the same time scrupulously avoiding excess in every case. But it should be especially noted that true moderation—as Aristotle himself observed of the '' golden mean ''—does not permit of the same fixed amount of gratification to all desires in all individuals.

[1] Paulsen: *System of Ethics,* trans. by Thilly, p. 485.

Interpreted in the light of Self-realization, moderation signifies not the mathematical but the organic mean in the
conduct of life—that each impulse be made, in its expression, a *means* to the promotion of individual well-being.
Now it is manifest that the natural desires differ in strength
with different individuals, as also the conditions under
which these desires may be satisfied vary from person to
person. Hence what constitutes moderation in the gratifying of a desire will be different for every person. It is
then the duty of each person to determine what amount
of restraint the organization of all his activities imposes
upon each single impulse; and in the habitual observance
of this limit consists temperance for him. Moreover, many
individuals cannot indulge certain desires even slightly
without danger of going to excess, frustrating the satisfaction of other desires equally legitimate and introducing
disorder and confusion into their lives. In such cases
temperance, moderation as we have understood it, requires
*abstinence*, complete and entire. The observance of temperance, for instance, compels many individuals to abstain
altogether from alcoholic liquors and others to avoid all
games associated with gambling. Besides these extreme
instances there are in all of us desires especially strong
and eager, apt at all times to slip the leash and work havoc
with our lives; over these temperance enjoins the practice
of strictest restraint.

The rule of temperance extends to all human activities—
prescribing moderation in our amusements, our speech,
our expenditures, as well as our eating and drinking. It
is a fact frequently commented on, that reformers who,
in the name of temperance, zealously wage war upon a
certain indulgence or excess, are often guilty of intemper-
ance themselves in the way of exaggeration and unwarranted assumptions. But while the virtue of temperance
should thus be realized in all fields of conduct, still it

cannot be denied that its chief reference is to a few especially strong desires. Aristotle limited the application of
temperance to the fundamental animal appetites, those of
food and drink and sex,[2] and his judgment in this matter
has been in a large measure confirmed by subsequent experience and reflection. For these three desires or, join-
ing the two former, the two—the desire for food and the
impulse of sex—express the elemental needs of life itself,
in the individual, and the species; hence nature has made
them strong in their appeal and insistent in their demands.
They are often called the " physical appetites " to indicate
their intimate connection with our animal life, an appetite
being well-defined as a " desire with a massive bodily
basis."[3] Now the power and urgency of these appetites
have made them most difficult of all natural tendencies to
control and regulate in the interest of an intelligently
ordered life. Volition has accepted the challenge they
offered, however; and, aroused by the difficulties involved,
and stung by successive defeats, has made with these appetites the supreme struggle for self-control. Hence the practice of temperance in human life still means primarily the
exercise of restraint in matters of eating and drinking and
of the sexual relationship. It will be appropriate then to
take note of some of the implications of temperance when
manifest in these particular departments of life.

The exercise of temperance in the pleasures of eating
may first be considered. The food instinct is, of all instincts, perhaps the most deeply ingrained in the organism.
This is what we should expect; as the activity of the lower
forms of life is for the most part spent in a ceaseless
search for food. Nor is it otherwise with primitive man
who must wage a constant battle with nature to escape
ever-imminent starvation. Thus natural necessity has made

---

[1] ARISTOTLE: *Nicomachean Ethics*, Bk. III, Chap. XIII.
[3] MEZES: *Explanatory Ethics*, p. 222.

the craving for food strong within us,—much stronger than is required by present conditions of life in civilized societies, since for none but a limited class of unfortunates does the securing of sufficient food for bodily sustenance require constant thought and attention. Not only have improved methods of production and distribution increased the available supply of food, but the protection against hardship and exposure secured through better housing, warmer clothing, and easier transportation, for civilized man, has at the same time decreased the amount of food needed to maintain his bodily energies. Add the further fact that man by the possession of intelligence is able to plan and prepare food in such manner as particularly to please his taste, and the situation appears to be plainly one provocative of excessive indulgence. Over-eating is too often regarded as an offense of a trifling character; certainly it is one committed constantly by persons otherwise temperate in their habits and disinterested in their serving of friends and community. But the offense—in its proper designation, the *vice of gluttony*—brings many evils in its train, lessening as it does man's efficiency and increasing his hours of discomfort and misery. It would be difficult indeed to over-estimate the amount of peevishness, discouragement, and bad temper due directly to excess in eating. Here then is a most important field for the exercise of temperance. Temperance calls for the habitual control by volition of the desire for food with a view not to the obtaining of the greatest amount of pleasure out of eating but of maintaining the body in the best possible health and highest state of efficiency. The attention that has recently been given to the subject of food, the manufacture and advertisement of health-foods, the discussion of the merits of various systems of diet, is in its way a healthy sign; for it shows that people in general are awakening to the importance of the careful regulation of diet, especially for those who lead sedentary lives under the artificial conditions of our present civilization. We may expect to derive great assistance from scientific research in this matter of selecting and preparing our food, but obviously much must always be left to the judgment and will of the individual. For no rule can be laid down which will cover all cases. The quality and quantity of food which should be eaten depends both upon the constitution of the individual and upon his environment and occupation. A diet too meager for a man of massive frame, performing exhausting physical labor, will perhaps be too hearty for the brain-worker of light build. Moreover, a change of occupation and surroundings on the part of the same individual may often call for a changed rule of eating, and this alteration of diet is made especially difficult by the existence of previous habits of a contrary nature. Thus the man who as engineer or surveyor has spent years in vigorous exercise out-of-doors and comes to take a desk in a city office, finds that he needs scarcely half the food he consumed formerly while his old habits tempt him continually to eat the same amount. Thus there is constant need with most human beings for self-control in indulging the appetite for food, but the reward of vigilance in this matter is heightened individual efficiency and greater possibilities of personal achievement.

A second appetite which requires habitual restraint if personal development is to proceed unimpeded is that for drink—not of course for food in liquid form, but for intoxicating liquors. So important is self-control in the matter of this appetite that the word " temperance " has been restricted in popular speech to this particular manifestation of it and thus has come to mean moderation or abstinence in the use of alcoholic beverages. The subject of drinking as thus understood has been so complicated by discussion and controversy that hundreds of pages would be needed for its adequate treatment.  Hence it is possible in the present outline only to indicate the general principles which must be applied in reaching a rational solution of the problem.  The first question which arises when the subject is approached from the standpoint of Self-realization is, " Is the appetite for intoxicating or exhilarating beverages a natural or normal one ? "  If it can be proved that this appetite is abnormal or perverted, then, all indulgence in alcoholic liquors is forbidden at the outset.  The truth of this view may appear to be demonstrated by the fact that all fermented drinks contain a poisonous principle —alcohol—and since it seems impossible to regard the desire for what is poisonous as a normal desire, the appetite appears to be condemned as perverted and monstrous.  But unfortunately—for this argument—it applies also to tea and coffee, which contain a poisonous element as well, and few would be willing to condemn tea and coffee drinking on the same grounds.  Moreover the desire for beverages that stimulate and enliven is too widespread among various races and in different times to allow of its being branded offhand as unnatural and perverted.  If, then, as seems more reasonable, we regard this appetite as natural, it is subject to the same rule of temperance that holds in the case of all desires—strict control in the interest of the due satisfaction of other desires, involving moderation for the majority, and abstinence in the case of those who, by individual constitution and special surroundings, are in constant danger of excess.  Only, in the case of the appetite for liquor, the consequences of excess are so disastrous, including the loss of intelligence and self-control, the temporary destruction of that personality itself which is the sole aim of morality to conserve and develop, that an exceptional degree of restraint is imperatively demanded.  In view of this danger which should need no emphasis to one acquainted with the facts of actual life, abstinence is the safer course for a large proportion of mankind. Certainly it is required with the young and with all who have reason to suspect that, because of heredity or on other grounds, they have the slightest tendency to excess. For the rest, the use of intoxicants should be limited to those places and occasions where social and conventional safeguards reduce the danger to a practical zero. Finally, it should be borne in mind that the question of the existence of public drinking-places where such customs as that of treating prevail, is one quite apart from that of " drinking " itself. This latter is a social and not an individual matter and should be settled on grounds of social welfare entirely.

The other impulse of such strength as to be difficult of control is that of sex. Since its satisfaction is the condition of the continued existence of the human species, the demands of this impulse are bound to be imperative with human beings, and it must remain a dominating influence in human society. In Greek Ethics the same rule of temperance is applied to the sex impulse as to the other bodily appetites—the rule of moderation, permitting only such degree of indulgence as would be consistent with the total interest of the individual as a citizen of the state. On this principle, any indulgence injurious to the health of the individual or violating the family rights of a fellow-citizen, would be condemned as vicious excess,—the vice of licentiousness. But we find in this principle no ground for the Christian ideal of chastity which permits this desire to be indulged only under the conditions of monogamous marriage. This ideal of sexual morality professed now by all civilized societies, is based upon the principle first enunciated by Christianity, of the infinite worth of all human personality, Greek or barbarian, male or female, bond or free. For, it should be noticed that the sex impulse differs from the other natural instincts of man in having, not an inanimate thing, but a living person for its object.

Its indulgence is therefore subject to the higher law which governs the relations of persons in an intelligent community—i.e. that human personality should always be treated as an end and never as a means. To treat another person as an instrument for selfish gratification is thus to commit a moral offense of gravest character. In the growth of real reverence for personality is to be found the only solution for the vexed problem of sex-relations, for the " social evil " and other irregularities and excesses.

Reverting to the subject of temperance as manifest in the habitual control of every desire, the growth of this virtue is most effectively encouraged by providing normal and wholesome expression for all our natural impulses. For, whenever through mistaken teaching or unfavorable conditions, any of the desires natural to human personality are denied their normal satisfaction, the result is likely to be either excess in some other direction or a perverted and unnatural expression of the impulse whose rightful satisfaction is prevented. In former times this result was produced by a false asceticism taught in the name of religion; at present it is brought about by unfortunate conditions of life—particularly in sparsely settled and backward rural districts on the one hand, and in the congested urban centers on the other. Because of comparative isolation and inadequate facilities for social intercourse, the country-bred youth is apt to have his natural desire for stirring games, for the relish of eating and drinking in good company, for love-making and courtship, to a large extent denied, and consequently be led into forms of vicious excess. At the opposite extreme, conditions of modern city life, as Miss Addams has convincingly shown in her *Spirit of Youth and the City Streets*, prevent a large proportion of the young from obtaining the wholesome recreation which they normally crave; such conditions offer in the life of the crowded streets opportunities for unwholesome ex-

citement, and, through commercialized enterprises for furnishing pleasures such as saloons, dance-halls, and cheap
theaters, tempt the growing boy or girl to debasing and
vicious indulgence. Hence all efforts to establish play-
grounds, social centers, places of amusement, where healthful recreation may be obtained, particularly by the youth in
both country and city, should be welcomed and encouraged
by all those interested in moral development, as most important aids in fostering self-control and temperance among
our people. " Let us cherish these experiments as the
most precious beginnings of an attempt to supply the
recreational needs of our industrial cities. To fail to provide for the recreation of youth is not only to deprive all
of them of their natural form of expression, but is certain
to subject some of them to the overwhelming temptation
of illicit and soul-destroying pleasures." [4]  In conclusion
it may be added that the best safeguard against over-
absorption in the pursuit of pleasure, even though of a
natural and wholesome sort, is found in such training as
gives efficiency in a chosen line of work—occupation, trade,
or profession—and thus furnishes the individual with a
controlling interest and constant source of pride and satisfaction.[5]

3. **Prudence.**—The limitation placed upon the gratification of various single desires in the exercise of temperance is not an end in itself. It is a means to the maximum
satisfaction of all the desires natural to the human self.
Now, as has been previously pointed out, the amount of
satisfaction permitted to any desire depends upon the inclusiveness of its object—the degree to which it includes
the objects of other desires and provides for their satisfaction. But among these desires there is one whose object
may with truth be said to comprehend the objects of all

[4] Jane Addams: *The Spirit of Youth and the City Streets*, p. 103.
[5] Paulsen: *Op. cit.*, p. 486.

other desires characteristic of man as a natural being. This is the desire for continued security and comfort during the period of natural existence. Itself the conscious expression of the powerful instinct of self-preservation, this desire, we have already seen, constitutes one of the dominating motives of human action.[6] As such, it is an effective instrument in the organization of conduct; since the end which it seeks is of highest importance,—is one whose attainment is necessary to Self-realization. Considered in comparison to larger ideal aims and aspirations, the preservation of natural existence seems an end narrow and poor, indeed. But the maintenance of natural life during the few years of its allotted course, with the enjoyment which accompanies such physical preservation and well-being, is for the human individual the indispensable condition of his participating visibly in the attainment of larger and more comprehensive ideals. Hence physical security with its attendant pleasure is an end of high moral value. The habit of furthering natural well-being and comfort through the subordination of single desires and impulses is identical with the virtue of prudence. Defined in this way, prudence is just the other and positive aspect of temperance, while temperance is the negative side of prudence. The end of prudence is most effectually secured through the attainment of several objects sufficiently general to include, when taken together, practically all the things which man naturally desires. Prudence is therefore practised through the pursuit and attainment of these general objects, adopted as purposes.

## HEALTH

The first of these purposes is to maintain and increase as far as possible, *Health*. The welfare of man as a natural

[6] *Cf.* Part III, Chap. IV, § 2.

being has its foundation in bodily health. Hence of all the " natural " goods of human life this is the greatest and most essential. Health is secured through the attainment of certain objects and conditions which are themselves ends of desire.

The first essential of continued health is *food* and *drink* in proper kind and amount. That the obtaining of food in quantity barely sufficient for bodily sustenance is sometimes difficult or impossible for the human individual—even in civilized countries—is proved by the recent investigations of school authorities in some of our large cities which show that many children are unable to profit by the instruction they receive because they come to school ill-nourished on account of inadequate breakfasts. When the means of the individual are sufficient to provide himself and his dependents with food necessary to life, then arises the further question, to which allusion has been made, of determining its quality and regulating its quantity in a manner suited to individual needs (under, of course, the artificial conditions of human life).—As long as the great majority of human beings were scattered, in their residence, over wide areas it was comparatively easy to secure an abundant quantity of fresh, pure drinking-water. But with the increase of population and the crowding of individuals into cities the sources of water-supply have become contaminated by sewage and refuse. Hence provision for this fundamental physical need, of pure water, is indeed a difficult problem in our centers of population. Yet the need is as important as that of food itself and, as a matter of public hygiene, its satisfaction is also a matter of public morality.

A second necessity of good health is appropriate *clothing*. Clothing is needed to protect the body against the " elements "—cold, wind, sun, rain, and snow—in practically all regions of earth. Clothing of course serves another purpose—that of adornment—and the clothing we wear owes much of its complication to the effort to satisfy the demands both of beauty and comfort. The desire to wear garments that please the eye in texture, color, and shape is certainly legitimate and laudable; still it should always be subordinated to the other, the chief purpose of clothing, to protect the body against hostile influences of air and water and sun. But if it is wrong to sacrifice bodily comfort to considerations of beauty and proportion, what shall be said of the tendencies observable in present societies to risk health, and perhaps to shorten life, in order to follow a vapid succession of senseless fashions in dress!

In the third place *suitable shelter* is required for the preservation of health. In all save tropical climes man must have for his physical security a house closed against rain and snow, and properly heated. Now that the art of house-building gives us, as a matter of course, dwellings which are tight and warm, we must be on our guard lest through their very " tightness " our houses exclude the sunlight and become receptacles for the storing of bad air. Full ventilation and plenty of fresh air are required in any house which is to fulfil the purposes of good health for its inmates.

*Cleanliness* is a fourth essential of good health. The cleanliness needed is not one of body and clothing merely, which of course comes first, but also of house, of grounds, of street, and of all public buildings and conveyances. Cleanliness in this sense embraces all that is implied in modern sanitation—such disposal of all human waste, all refuse and rubbish of all sorts, and such isolation and care of cases of contagious disease, that the micro-organisms which threaten human health shall not multiply or be further disseminated among human beings.

Good health cannot be maintained, in the fifth place, without a moderate amount of *physical exercise* and wholesome *amusement*. The manual laborer receives this exercise—although often of an excessive and unbalanced sort and under most unhealthful conditions—through his daily toil. Those of sedentary occupation, however, must make special provision to secure it in the gymnasium, and through outdoor games and pastimes. Only through such exercise can the brain-worker keep his bodily organs in such healthful tone and his physical functions so vigorous as to permit his brain and higher centers to act with maximal efficiency.

## PROPERTY

A second object whose possession is made a definite purpose in the practice of prudence is *property*. We have just seen that the maintenance of health requires the possession and use of certain material objects such as articles of clothing and means of shelter. Even food, the prime requisite of life itself, must be gathered and stored either by the individual or the society of which he is a member if a quantity sufficient for human needs is to be always available. Indeed we find the ability to provide in the present for future well-being first manifested among living forms in the instinct of animals to hoard food for days to come or even for a season ahead, as when the squirrel stores nuts for the coming winter. Some students of moral evolution look upon the hoarding or acquisitive instinct, which is strongly marked in many animal species, as the basis of the right of private ownership and the institution of property, in human society. No doubt, the idea of acquiring property owes much of its strength as a motive to action, to this instinct which man inherits from the lower forms. But property or wealth considered as an end in moral development has also a rational basis in the principle of use or occupation which enunciates the right of every human individual to possess those material objects which he does or must use, to preserve his own existence and secure his own well-being.

The habit of acquiring, through industry, property sufficient for individual needs, and of protecting and conserving this property when acquired, has come to be regarded as a distinct virtue. This virtue, designated as *thrift* or *frugality,* is usually defined as moderation in the acquisition and expenditure of wealth, a mean which avoids the extremes of *miserliness* and of *prodigality.* It does not surprise us that the practice of obtaining and of safeguarding material possessions should have been raised to the rank of an individual virtue when we reflect that, second to the control of the major animal appetites, there is no more effective means of securing the ends of prudence than that furnished by the ownership of property. It is the best agency which intelligence has devised to offset the radical changes in physical strength and capacity which occur during the course of individual existence, and thus to provide for a life's well-being. Man passes from an infancy of helplessness, through a childhood and youth of limited strength, to a maturity when power and capacity reach their maximum; thence he passes down through stages of decreasing efficiency to a helpless old age. He also has periods of illness and physical disability. During a full third of his life, therefore, the human individual is unable fully to supply his own natural needs. He must then be an unwelcome burden upon the shoulders of others unless during his maturity, when his powers are full-orbed, he is able to accumulate sufficient property to support himself during his old age and also to care for his offspring during their period of helplessness and incapacity, thus squaring himself with society for similar care given to him during his own infancy, and thereby establishing his own economic independence. In a similar manner, through industry and saving, the individual is able to provide for his own support in periods of sickness and enforced idleness.  Hence thrift, though it appears inferior to some other virtues which realize a more comprehensive end, is nevertheless of utmost importance, as one of the foundation stones on which these higher virtues must rest.  A man's first duty to society is to provide for himself and his offspring; the exercise of thrift is the only way to maintain industrial independence and economic integrity.  Without this virtue it is exceedingly difficult to develop the higher personal and social capacities of human nature; the utterly thriftless, as we know, seldom reach any higher levels of moral development. We must always be on our guard, therefore, lest by indiscriminate individual giving or unwise social charities, we deprive any number of individuals of the stimulus and occasion supplied by natural need, for the development of this virtue.

To describe the different kinds of property which man may advantageously possess, to discuss the different forms which wealth may take, would carry us far afield—into the domain of Economics, in fact.  Of material possessions those which have greatest ethical value have already been mentioned.  All human individuals must possess comfortable clothing and adequate, sanitary dwellings if they are to maintain that health and vigor which is the basis of all further achievement.  The ethical value of owning a home is a thing that should be emphasized in this day of restless moving from one habitat to another and of close crowding in tightly packed city apartments.  The possession of house and grounds with which the interest of individual or family is identified and in whose conveniences and adornments the tastes of the owner find expression produces not merely a sense of physical security but also a feeling of personal power and stability to be gained in no other way.  Another class of objects whose possession is necessary to the natural welfare of the individual is that of *tools and instruments*. One of the traits which distinguish man from the animals is the ability to fashion tools by whose use he can avail himself more easily and effectually of the resources of the natural environment. Made at first by the individual for his own use and employed most effectively by their maker, tools were, next to the clothing actually worn, the first class of objects to be recognized as private property. They still constitute a class of private possessions most important to the individual in providing for his own natural well-being. The right of the individual to own those material instruments which are necessary for efficient performance in the special field of his activity, be it physical or mental (and this applies, of course, not merely to mechanical instruments but to books, pictures, musical instruments, etc., etc.), is grounded deep in the conditions of human life and cannot be gainsaid. The invention of machinery and the organization of industry have in a large degree deprived the laborer of this right to his tools—and have also taken from him his rightful share in the product of his labor. That such an industrial system is ethically indefensible is becoming more and more generally recognized, however, and the conviction is growing that capitalism must be superseded by a more equitable arrangement. In addition to these special classes of property, prudence demands, lastly, that the individual possess a surplus in some form of wealth easily convertible into any of the necessities of life, in order that in such emergencies as accident or illness he may have the means of sustenance and be able to secure the necessary remedies.

## REPUTATION

The third purpose is one whose object although not itself material is nevertheless a necessary factor in the material well-being of the human individual. This object is favor-

able reputation in the community—the esteem of one's
fellows. Man is a gregarious animal and from the beginning men have found it advantageous to live and work
together. At first they coöperated for purposes of defense
against common enemies. Then the same coöperation was
found to be profitable in the field of industry—there involving division of labor and exchange of products.
Finally the same principle was extended to the fields of
art and science, of education and invention. But in all
its forms this coöperation has its basis in mutual confidence. Without this confidence the material benefits which
accrue to individuals through the organization of industry
cannot be secured. The man who has entirely lost the
confidence of his fellows cannot carry on with profit any
of those economic activities which are essential to his
continued existence and natural well-being. He cannot
secure a fair recompense for the product of his labor, since
no one will trust the honesty of his work; he cannot buy
the necessaries of life since no one will credit his ability
or intention to pay. In our civilized societies he is frequently unable to secure the opportunity to work at all—
as is shown in the case of ex-convicts who find it impossible
to gain honest employment. He is, in fact, a social rene-
gade, an outcast, and as such is deprived of the means of
natural subsistence. Conversely, in the degree to which
the individual gains good reputation among his fellows,
in proportion as he rises in their estimation, is he able to
procure for himself all the means of comfort and security.
That honesty is the best policy is an axiom universally
admitted in the business world; hence the prudent man
cannot afford to neglect his reputation. Rather, he must
guard his reputation most carefully, making it one of his
chief aims to win and to retain the esteem of his fellows
(if for no other reason) because only through such means
can he secure his own natural well-being.

The objects of the three purposes just described, Health, Wealth, and Fame, as they are sometimes denominated, are often called the three " natural " goods of human life. The value of these three objects as ends of action is so obvious that their pursuit absorbs the minds of the majority of men. Nor is this to be wondered at, for man is first of all a natural being and he must maintain his existence and efficiency in the material world before he realizes his capacities as a self-conscious person; it is not to be regretted that men seek health, comfort, and every other natural advantage, but only that when they secure these benefits they do not use them as means to a larger and more comprehensive good. Intelligence speedily discovers that the three objects under discussion are the most effective means to self-preservation under the conditions of human life, and thus the instinct of self-preservation is called in, and communicates to them great impelling power. The motive-force of the last two ends, property and reputation, which are less closely connected than the first with the preservation of physical existence, is reinforced by the acquisitive and social instincts of which they are, at least in part, an expression. Thus the three ends in question possess exceptional strength as motives. Society avails itself of this fact in discharging its functions of government. Appeal is made to the strength of these motives to secure from the individual, obedience to those laws and regulations which are required for the general welfare. Individuals who break these laws are punished by death or imprisonment, by fine, and by loss of standing as citizens—one, two, and even, in extreme cases, by all of these penalties. The same motives are appealed to, with penalties of course much less severe, by parents in training their children. Punishment, involving physical pain or close confinement, the loss of possessions, disgrace in the family circle, are the penalties commonly inflicted in household and school, to secure that order and discipline which are necessary to individual development and social welfare. When, through an external and artificial system of rewards and penalties, the strength of these motives is thus utilized to support the claims of the larger goods of the social and personal life, they are called the *sanctions* of morality.

4. **Courage.**—While we acknowledge the importance of material comfort and well-being as the condition of further achievement on the part of the human self, still we must not forget that the objects secured by prudence are important *only* as means to the broader personal and social ends of human life. Moral development requires that the natural goods which we have been considering should be strictly subordinated to the more comprehensive spiritual goods. Whenever any conflict arises between the narrower interests of man's physical nature on the one hand and the deeper concerns of his self-conscious personality on the other the moral ideal demands that material well-being shall be sacrificed, that pain, privation, and even death, shall be undergone, in the realization of larger and more inclusive ends. In the words of the formula already adopted, Self-realization requires, as its second step in the individual sphere, the adjustment of material comfort and well-being to those more comprehensive ends through whose attainment the higher spiritual capacities of man gain adequate expression. On its negative side, in the subordination of natural well-being with its attendant pleasures to a greater good, this adjustment is identical with the virtue of courage. Courage is thus the habit of sacrificing individual safety and comfort in the attainment of a larger and more comprehensive good. It is not, like temperance, involved in prudence or to be interpreted as one of its aspects; it rather marks a step beyond pru-

dence and as such is essentially different from, and in some respects antagonistic to, that virtue.

Among the different virtues courage was the first to win recognition and admiration in human history. Primitive societies depended for their existence upon the ability of their members to coöperate in protecting themselves against common enemies. Hence it was natural that an habitual readiness to endure pain and risk death in defending the clan or tribe against ever-threatening foes, should come to be regarded as the whole duty of the individual, both to himself and his fellows. As man's life became more secure and the relations of human societies more peaceable, the field for the exercise of courage was increasingly restricted. The importance of this virtue was lessened and its prestige diminished until in civilized societies of the present it is reckoned as but one and by no means the most important of the many virtues that enter into the moral life. Nevertheless, there is a sense in which courage may still be accounted the supreme and inclusive virtue—identical in essence with goodness itself. Moral development has its source in will and its progress depends upon the continued exercise of this power. But progressive self-expansion through effort of will requires—as has been shown in the foregoing—the constant sacrifice of objects already attained and proved satisfactory, for the sake of larger ends which are new and untried. Moral development is therefore throughout its course a venture; it demands from the agent that habitual willingness to take risks, to endure suffering and privation, in pursuit of remote and apparently inaccessible ideals, which is the essence of courage. Nay, the very will to be a self the horizons of whose life are continually enlarging, which is the basis of all the virtues, is courage—courage of the most fundamental sort. The moral life is throughout a " great adventure " calling for courage, even for heroism, at every stage in its course; and the merely prudent soul which requires to be assured of success before undertaking each new enterprise will never come within sight of the goal.

As man's natural well-being is most effectually furthered through the attainment of health, wealth, and reputation, so the subordination of such welfare to larger ends involves the sacrifice of one or of all of these " goods." Now it is according as one or the other of these objects is sacrificed —whether, that is, health or wealth or reputation, is put in jeopardy—that different forms of courage are distinguished. Courage in its first form, requiring the sacrifice of health, is known as

## PHYSICAL COURAGE

This is the readiness to endure physical pain or risk death in the service of some higher cause. As courage was the first virtue to win approval in the history of mankind, so, among the varieties of courage, *physical* was the first to receive favorable recognition and general applause. Such admiration of courage, particularly of physical courage, along with greatest admiration for the man displaying courage of this type, was inevitable, we have perceived, in view of the conditions of primitive human existence. In the early stages of social development, man lived in constant danger; the element of hazard pervaded the whole of human life. Men were without adequate shelter, or clothing, or tools or weapons. They were obliged to snatch at every advantage which changing circumstances offered them in the continuous battle against ever-present enemies, natural, animal, and (not the least menacing) human. Hence the quality most needed, and therefore most highly prized, in the individual, was the willingness to take his life in his hands in the effort to avert some threatening peril from the tribe or clan. Such bravery would contribute to success, in the hunt, upon exploring expeditions, in warfare; upon the success of its members in these fields does the very existence of the clan depend. So great and so obvious is the social value of physical courage in the earlier periods of human development that as a natural consequence men have come to admire mere daring, the willingness to endure pain, even to risk life, when there is no adequate cause. We in civilized societies share this tendency, although perhaps in a weakened form; for we feel a thrill of admiration almost instinctive over the climb to dizzy heights, or the swim through dangerous rapids, while our reason at the same time may condemn the acts as unwarranted and foolhardy. The readiness to suffer pain or endanger one's life is not itself a virtue, of course; since, as we have just seen, physical well-being is an end of high value and we are justified in sacrificing it only when in this way we attain some larger end. Yet human experience shows that the realization of these larger ideals so frequently calls for the sacrifice of material comfort and well-being that it is not strange that an habitual willingness to place health and safety in jeopardy should come to be regarded as itself virtuous.

As human societies continue and develop, the advantages of leadership and discipline in hunting and in warfare become increasingly apparent. More and more authority is given to chief or sovereign and under his direction a selected group of the strongest and most enterprising men are trained and drilled for purposes of fighting. Organized warfare now becomes possible, and is regarded as the most worthy and admirable of human pursuits. A new theater is thus provided for the display of courage, and of all forms of physical courage, that exhibited on the field of battle is deemed the noblest. In this period of semi-civilized or barbarous society patriotism is thought to find true expression only in *military* courage—in the eagerness of the warrior to lay down his life fighting the enemies of his sovereign upon the field of battle. The battlefield itself with the presence of thousands in disciplined array, the waving of standards, the clash of arms, and the shouts of victory seemed to provide the appropriate dramatic setting for the finest kind of courage. Emotions were stirred by the pomp of military display; imagination was kindled by tales of heroic exploits in battle. The highest praise, the most enthusiastic plaudits, were given to the victorious warriors, while of all weaknesses cowardice in warfare was deemed the most contemptible. Owing to the influences, partly political and partly psychological, which act upon human societies in the period between savagery and civilization, military courage acquired a prestige and importance among the virtues which is quite undeserved. Its presence in an individual served as an ample excuse, even a complete justification for unbridled cruelty, lust, and avarice. Even the clear vision of Aristotle was dazzled by the spectacular and often melodramatic character of military exploits and to the question as to what is the noblest form of courage, he answers not that displayed by facing death at sea or from disease, but on " the noblest occasions, i.e. such occasions as present themselves in war; for that is the greatest and noblest of perils." [7]

The march of social progress at last replaces the militant social organization with the industrial. The individual citizen is now comparatively secure; he is protected in his life and labor by the authorized agencies of society; society requires of him not daring in the chase or upon the battle-field but, primarily, industry, sobriety, and public spirit. Wars have become less and less frequent until now among civilized nations they promise to cease entirely. Does this mean, then, that physical courage is no longer necessary to social warfare and that consequently we may expect it

[7] ARISTOTLE: *Nicomachean Ethics*, Bk. III, Chap. IX.

to disappear from the ranks of the virtues? Many have believed that this is the result towards which industrialism is tending. Some, indeed, have found in this supposed fact a reason for perpetuating war, and for fostering the military spirit; because, they maintain, the kind of courage developed in war—the bravery, the hardihood, the discipline, of the soldier—is one of the noblest qualities developed in man, too good, in fact, to lose. William James disposes of this argument in defense of war, while at the same time answering the question concerning the future standing of physical courage in human societies organized upon an industrial basis in his stirring and trenchant essay on *The Moral Equivalent of War.* He is in the first place a firm believer in the value of the qualities of bravery and hardihood bred by the military life.

"Militarism is the great preserver of our ideals of hardihood, and human life with no use for hardihood would be contemptible. Without risks or prizes for the darer, history would be insipid, indeed; and there is a type of military character which every one feels that the race should never cease to breed, for every one is sensitive to its superiority."

He believes that states pacifically organized, if they are to remain peaceful, must preserve some of the old elements of army discipline.

"We must make new energies and hardihoods continue the manliness to which the military mind so faithfully clings. Martial virtues must be the enduring cement; intrepidity, contempt of softness, surrender of private interest, obedience to command must still remain the rock upon which states are built—unless, indeed, we wish for dangerous reactions against commonwealths fit only for contempt, and liable to invite attack whenever a center of crystallization for military-minded enterprise gets formed anywhere in their neighborhood."

possession of money has proved such an effective means of furnishing the individual with all physical comforts and pleasures—with a luxurious abode, tempting food, skilled and obsequious attendance—is its pursuit and, in many cases, even its possession, liable to be materializing and debasing. For ceaseless preoccupation with money sought always as the price of physical comfort and security, tends to confine the attention of the individual more and more completely to concerns of his own physical well-being, to restrict his gaze more and more exclusively to narrow prudential considerations, rendering him insensible to the appeal of universal principles and shutting him in to the earthy, the prosaic, and the sordid. Moreover, the continued possession and enjoyment of wealth make the pleasures and luxuries it will purchase increasingly necessary; life appears to be unsupportable without them. Thus the individual is made blind to the higher psychic satisfactions which he is missing through his absorption with money-getting, is rendered oblivious to the social injustice which may be involved in his possession of wealth. It is a well-known fact that the ownership of property makes a man more conservative in his attitude towards all proposed changes in social and political arrangements. He inclines to fear political reform, even changes in social convention, lest they diminish the value of his property or interfere with plans he has on foot for augmenting his wealth. Thus there is bred in the individual a spirit of caution essentially inimical to moral development which depends upon the ability of the individual to risk what he has already won for the sake of still larger rewards. In his novel *Open Country* Maurice Hewlett shows, in a picturesque and forcible fashion, how the pursuit and possession of property checks and finally destroys the personal development of many members of modern civilized society. His hero, Senhouse, defines salvation as the " use and perfecting of faculty '' and declares that '' liberty to learn is the only way of it.'' '' Now money, I say, is the one cause of slavery and work our one hope of salvation. Therefore, our civilization as they disastrously term it, is a condition of acquiring slavery easily and of obliterating the hope of salvation.'' '' Civilization is a condition of freedom to use your faculties to their fullest extent; and your faculties are every power of mind and heart and muscle and sense. Very well. Now I say that every sovereign you put into a man's pocket seduces him away from the use of his faculties, and every machine you devise directly deprives him of one of them—and then where are we? Why here; that what is true of a man is true of a million of men and that, so far from being more civilized than the Periclean Athenians, we are actually less so than the neolithic dweller on the South Downs, who hacked up the earth with a red deer's horn and drove his cattle to the dew-pond at sun-down, and back again into an inclosure banked against the wolves. And that's very odd, with art and poetry behind us and before, we might by this time be like the sons of Gods.'' Exaggerated, this is, and largely untrue; but in its statement of the demoralizing influences of the institution of private property, as at present developed, containing more than a grain of truth.

The pursuit of wealth may present a serious obstacle, in some cases even an absolute bar, to the exercise of man's spiritual capacities. It may prevent the individual from seeking truth and power and beauty in his own life, and from laboring to extend these higher satisfactions to the rest of humanity. When this is the case, Self-realization requires that wealth be surrendered. Since surrender involves pain,—the mental discomfort of work and anxiety, and perhaps also physical suffering caused by actual privation and want,—its practice deserves to rank as one of the varieties of courage. It has been distinguished by no special name in ethical reflection; we might, possibly, call it economic courage. But while it has received no distinctive label, this kind of courage is by no means unknown in human society. It has been shown, and is being shown, by all those aspiring human souls who sacrifice all the wealth they possess or all the opportunity they have of ever possessing any wealth of their own, in their devotion to the spiritual well-being of humanity. It is a courage which the well-to-do class needs to exercise, in making those social and political reforms which must come if social justice is to prevail, and all men be given a chance of truly human development. Keen-visioned students of present society see in the women of the propertied classes one of the chief obstacles to needed social reforms, because, while they possess as a rule readier sympathies than men, they are more attached to the comforts and luxuries of wealth, and lack the courage to give them up even to save their fellow-beings from perishing by starvation or by exposure, or from sufferings worse than death. It is just this kind of courage which we may suppose the " rich young ruler " lacked, to whom Jesus said:

" One thing thou lackest yet: sell all that thou hast, and distribute unto the poor, and thou shalt have treasure in Heaven: and, come, follow me. But when he heard these things [conscious apparently of his own fatal weakness], he became exceedingly sorrowful; for he was very rich. And Jesus, seeing him, said: How hardly shall they who have riches enter the Kingdom of God! " [8]

## MORAL COURAGE

The willingness to sacrifice reputation or endure reproach for the sake of a larger social or personal good constitutes a third form of courage. This form of courage

[8] Luke xviii, 22-24.

has been somewhat ineptly named " moral " courage. Reference has already been made to the important influence which the individual's reputation among his fellows exerts upon his own private fortunes. If he stands well in the community, others will look with sympathy upon his efforts to provide for his present and future well-being. Unless his success interferes with their own interests his fellow-men will be glad to see him succeed. Certainly they will not trouble themselves to put obstacles in his path. Let a man lose his reputation, however, let him forfeit his standing in the community, and all this is changed. Other men regard him with ill-concealed suspicion, if not with open hostility. They question his motives; they criticise his actions. His successes awaken jealousy and resentment; his failures are occasions for rejoicing. It is consequently no light thing to sacrifice one's reputation in human society. Such sacrifice entails suffering and sacrifice too severe to be undergone without loss of self-respect and sanity, except indeed as the individual is inspired and strengthened by his knowledge of the greater good which he serves through his suffering. To be sure the suffering is not primarily physical (although physical hardships are likely to follow eventually from social condemnation). But the pain is none the less real because " mental "—the anguish of soul produced by severed friendships, by looks of scorn and contempt, by unjust suspicions and ill-founded resentments. Of this sort is the suffering which has been endured by those individuals of every generation who have remained steadfast in their adherence to unpopular causes. Such men must indeed—as the familiar saying is—have the courage of their convictions. The history of every nation abounds in examples of men who have suffered disgrace on account of their loyalty to righteous causes. The contempt and odium incurred by Abolitionists in many of our communities before the Civil War, is an illustration from American history. Religion, science, art—yes, every great cause, every lofty ideal,—has its heroes who have endured ignominy and derision for its sake.

Steadfast and consistent devotion to principle upon the part of individual members of human society is practically certain to result in a greater or less degree of unpopularity and misunderstanding; therefore those individuals who would organize their lives, and thus realize their larger selves, must be prepared to exercise moral courage. Indeed, this virtue must be cultivated by those who have convictions and propose to follow them. Moreover, the need of moral courage was perhaps never greater than in our modern civilized societies. Not that public opinion exerts a stronger pressure upon the individual than it did in earlier periods of social development. The savage who, on individual initiative, went counter to the customs of his tribe— those of religion or of marriage, for instance—met summary punishment at the hands of his indignant fellows; if he was not killed outright, he was driven forth as an outlaw, to be the victim of whatever hostile force he encountered. But with the organization and complication of life that have accompanied increasing civilization, the range of its influence has been enormously extended, until it now affects the smallest details of daily life touching matters that formerly were regarded as the individual's own concern. Fashion extends her tyrannical rule to every department of our lives—to the utmost minutiæ of our clothing, to the decorating of our homes, to our methods of education, to our art and our literature, even to modes of worship and forms of religious belief. Now it is absolutely necessary for the individual who would preserve the integrity of his own personality, frequently to repudiate this form of social control and assert his right to regulate his conduct and manner of life in accordance with his own convictions. This is not to recommend or even to excuse a foolish contrariety of views or habits, still less a self-conscious eccentricity in word and manner. In matters where no principle is affected or any particular taste or preference involved, it is usually saving both of time and of money to follow the current fashion. But where the individual finds his own principles violated, or his own personal taste seriously offended by a prevailing fashion, it is his duty to refuse to follow it, although the cost may be the derision and dislike of his fellows. For self-development must proceed from within, and no man can build up a self-contained and unified character who is the slave of public opinion.

5. **Idealism.**—The virtue of courage has been explained as the subordination by the human individual of his material interests, whether of health or of property or of reputation, to more inclusive and far-reaching ends. The most comprehensive and therefore the highest ends which can be attained by man in the individual sphere are the ideal objects of his spiritual capacities of thought, action, and feeling. These ideal objects—Truth, Power, and Beauty—are themselves so intimately related that they form, when taken together, an articulated unity, which in its synthesis represents the whole good of the individual self. Now the realization of these ideal objects at the expense of material comfort and well-being, constitutes the virtue of idealism. Idealism is therefore the highest virtue of the individual life; it marks the culminating point in the development of the human individual as a self-conscious person.

The virtue of Idealism as thus understood takes two forms: the combined harmonious development of the three capacities above named, with consequent realization of the three corresponding ideals, producing in the individual the three qualities of wisdom, efficiency, and refinement, which in their union constitute *culture;* and the special and persistent exercise of that one capacity, intellectual, technical, or æsthetic, which is strongest in the particular individual, with resulting *achievement* in an exceptional degree of the end of Truth, Power, or Beauty. Let us consider idealism in each of these two manifestations.

## CULTURE

By culture is meant the unimpeded and harmonious activity of all man's higher personal faculties. It represents, indeed, the complete spiritual development of the human individual. The spiritual capacities of man have their source in the activity fundamental to intelligent personality itself, i.e. volition; but this fundamental activity in the higher stages of its development has three specialized expressions, those of thought, action, and feeling. Hence culture has three departments, the intellectual, the technical, the æsthetic. It consists in the attainment of Truth, Power, and Beauty,—not as three separate ideals, to be sure, but in their organic inter-dependence and unity.

The first essential of culture is the *exercise of thought* in the acquisition of knowledge. Thought is the ability to form ideas which can be verified—that is to say, which are *true*. The work of thought is to interpret the outcome of previous experience in realizing ends, with a view to the guidance of future conduct. The human individual is not limited, however, to the results of his own experience. The results of the experience of past generations of mankind in the realization of objects, may be communicated to him through the medium of language, and thus his mental outlook may be enlarged to include those objects which the conduct of other men has proved real. The effect of thinking on the part of the individual, therefore, in connection with the processes of intelligent instruction, is to furnish him with a world of objects which are possible ends of action. This does not mean that the outcome of education and enlightenment is merely to reveal to the individual the existence of a certain number of objects, to which he is limited in selecting ends of action. On the contrary, through processes of abstraction and comparison, analysis and synthesis, he may work over the results of experience, combining its materials in new ways and thus constructing original ideals, whose reality may be tested in subsequent experiences of pursuit and attempted attainment. More than this, many of these objects are themselves changing, so that each successive moment presents to the agent a situation which, in its totality, is essentially new and thus, for purposes of action, contains many unforeseen possibilities. Never will his knowledge, no matter how great, enable him to predict with absolute certainty the issue of his own conduct; he must nevertheless be willing to advance and prepared to meet many unexpected and surprising developments.

So many ideas have been verified in human experience, so great a body of truth has thus been accumulated, that no individual mind is longer able to contain its detail of fact. The day of the encyclopedic scholar like Leibnitz or Aristotle, who was reputed to be master of every known branch of learning, is now past. All that intellectual cultivation can now hope to obtain is a knowledge of the most important truths concerning each principal class of objects. To this knowledge should be added a firsthand acquaintance with the methods whereby ideas are verified in these main departments of knowledge; for no belief which the individual is unable himself to test through action, deserves to be regarded as a part of his knowledge. The cultivated mind must possess a knowledge of the most important facts which have been discovered concerning inorganic nature, along with some practice in the method of experiment and in the use of mathematics as applied in this field; it must understand the fundamental features of organic life, the structures and functions of living forms, the conditions of their origin and the laws of their growth, besides being somewhat acquainted with the methods of investigation which have brought these facts to light; it must have a comprehensive knowledge of human history—of the origin and development of the human species, and of the characteristics and relationships of the different races of men, and also of the evolution of social and political institutions, recording as it does the achievements of the human spirit in its effort at self-realization—supplemented by accurate information regarding the methods and standards of historical research and criticism; it must know the leading truths from the field of the normative sciences, the world, that is, of values and appreciation, and possess a consequent insight into the demands which human personality makes of the real world, and the resources available to satisfy these demands. Such knowledge will extend the world of the individual beyond the limits of his immediate present, to encompass the experience of past generations of mankind with the vast system of objects which it has shown to be real; such breadth of intellectual vision is perhaps the most distinctive mark of culture.

But amount of knowledge alone does not constitute culture. Ideas as mere ideas are distinguished from reality; they are essentially characterized by their unreality. The idea is of itself therefore *incomplete;* it demands to be realized. The idea is in fact a purpose, which, until it is actually achieved, remains fragmentary and partial. Hence culture can never consist simply in the possession of ideas by an individual, even if the majority of these ideas have been verified in the lives of other men. Culture has frequently been discredited because it has been identified with the acquisition of much information upon many subjects. Now it is possible for a person to possess knowledge in the shape of a great store of ideas, without any ability to put these ideas into practice. He may appear to be embarrassed in action, or even hindered from acting altogether, by the very wealth of his ideas, which causes him at the time of action to be confused by a multitude of inappropriate and irrelevant considerations. Knowledge of this sort is in no sense a real possession of the individual; it becomes real in him only when realized in his conduct. In cases where this does not occur we have that half-culture —or as it is frequently but erroneously called, *over*-culture —which, although it may have been laboriously and honestly acquired, is little better than no culture at all, and which when mistaken for the genuine culture, causes this latter to be depreciated and derided. True culture in contradistinction from such counterfeit is an organic growth, a development of personality through the realization of ideas which are chosen as ends of action. It calls for more than the mere possession of ideas, it requires that they be vitalized in the action of the self, that they be realized in personal life.

Culture then consists, secondly, in *power of action*. It involves the training of the faculty of action in the human individual. The result of such training is technical skill or efficiency. By efficiency or technical skill is meant the ability to realize the ideals of intelligence through the employment of those instrumentalities which the specific situation calls for. The exercise of the faculty of action reveals to the agent what means are required for the attainment of different ends, thus enabling him more effectively to achieve his purposes, and at the same time giving him new knowledge of the inner connection of objects. Despite the indispensable part which action plays in the development of intelligence the exercise of this power has not always been recognized as a necessary element in culture. This is due to the fact that pure thought along with the higher sentiments, such as the æsthetic and the religious, has been supposed to move in a higher plane than that of practical affairs. But recent insight into the dependence of thought upon action for its verification makes such a view no longer tenable. One suspects that this view was possible only because a thorough training in modes and manners of action was assumed to have already occurred in the experience of all those who aspired after the higher fruits of culture; but this is an unwarranted assumption —at least in societies where the opportunity for culture is not limited to a privileged few who are prepared from infancy for its attainment. Now the fields in which the faculties of action may be trained are so many, and the methods so diverse, that it is difficult to give any complete account of them. The home, the school, and finally society and the state, should all furnish technical training.

Of the many kinds of training which it is possible and advantageous to give the faculty of action, a few may be mentioned—with no idea of a systematic classification, but rather of illustrating by concrete instances what is meant by such technical training. From earliest childhood the individual should have experience in handling physical objects, and in manipulating mechanical forces, so that he may acquire skill in utilizing the materials and guiding the processes of nature. Manual training in the primary schools is of great educational value because it subserves just this purpose. Systematic gardening, and the continued care and direction of domestic animals, also furnish the child with valuable technical training—in this case, in the employment and control of the lower forms of life. A thorough training in gymnastics and practical hygiene, received early in life, should give the individual the ability to utilize all the resources of his physical organism down to the last ounce of energy. With such training as a preliminary and preparation, the powers of action should be exercised in those larger fields where alone they can find full and free expression—the social and political. In the local community, the social club, and the state, he may have his technical faculties trained in a multitude of ways, and acquire in result the ability to realize the ends of human well-being through practice of the arts of business, of government, of entertainment, of education, etc. It is only necessary that the individual have the will to act, the initiative to put his own ideas in practice, and then, having acted, that he be eager to learn from his own experience, and the experience of others interpreted in the light of his own, better and more efficient methods of realizing his ends. Only through thus acting, and profiting by the results of his own action, can the individual augment his powers of action and acquire that practical efficiency which is a necessary part of true culture. Useful training in the arts of social and political life is furnished to our young people in high schools and colleges by student societies and enterprises of various sorts—debating and literary societies, journalistic and athletic activities—and for the reason that the experience they furnish is an essential part of true culture, these organizations and activities, when properly regulated, should be encouraged and fostered by the authorities of such institutions.

Our *capacity for feeling* furnishes a third element requisite to culture. Feeling is the response of the self, as subject, to the objective conditions which affect its own existence and development; when pleasant it reflects the strengthening and perfecting of the unity of self-consciousness through the appropriating of new objects. Pleasure thus accompanies all action that is successful in attaining its object, whether this object be particular and limited, like an article of food, or comprehensive and universal, like one of the great causes of social progress. Through such a development of the faculties of thought and action as we have been considering, however, these pleasures of attainment are prolonged and harmonized, since the individual is given a source of permanent enjoyment in the sustained and successful pursuit of a progression of ends, each of which has its place within a single supreme ideal. Culture should therefore substitute for the fitful and conflicting pleasures of the undeveloped self, a lasting happiness and tranquillity. But feeling makes its distinctive contribution to culture in æsthetic enjoyment or the sense of beauty; since in some cases it is possible for the self to feel all the pleasures of an intimate and personal union with an object without actually appropriating it through the usual effort of action. Thus, for instance, we may make a landscape ours and feel possessed of its most essential features through the sense of beauty which it awakens in us, though we do not own, and cannot hope to own, a square foot of the ground which enters into it. Because it does not involve the activities of thought and action which are necessary to give us the pleasure of fulfilled desire, æsthetic enjoyment is called pure or disinterested pleasure. Certain objects have the ability to set our faculties of perception and imagination, or even of judgment and reasoning, in such free and harmonious play as to produce in us the pleasure of immediately possessing them in their inner meaning and significance. Such possession we describe as an appreciation of their beauty. It would be going too far, however, to call the æsthetic experience pure feeling, if by this was meant that it contained only affective elements. Intellectual processes enter, of course, into the representation of the object; technical skill comes in to a degree also in the bodily adjustments made in contemplating a beautiful object. But the æsthetic experience is predominantly an emotional experience, nevertheless; it should be recognized as the distinctive contribution of feeling to our spiritual life. Now culture demands that the æsthetic

sensibilities of the human individual be developed, that his
sense of beauty be quickened and refined. With his feeling
for beauty undeveloped he may find only a brief and occasional pleasure in a bright color, an obvious harmony of
tones, a simple symmetry of figure. His taste must then
be trained and improved until he finds constant and enduring pleasure in more subtle schemes of color, more
complicated harmonies of tone, and more detailed sym-
metries of figure. Not that the real beauty of objects,
which only the cultivated tastes can appreciate, is always
proportionate to the complication of their structure or to
elaboration of detail. But cultivation of taste is accompanied by an increased ability to appreciate the harmonies
which are not apparent upon the surface but, at first concealed by variety and apparent discord, gradually reveal
themselves and, shining through the mass of details, give
them a wealth of meaning and suggestibility that is almost
endless. The result of æsthetic cultivation is thus to reveal
to the individual more beauties in land and sea and sky,
in the social world, and in his own inner life, where the Ideal
in its progressive realization exhibits that beauty which
" never was on land or sea." The objects of æsthetic
appreciation may be divided into three classes, those of
nature, of art, and of social intercourse. In the first class
belong the landscape, the seascape, the starry heavens; in
the second, architecture, statuary, painting, music, literature; in the third, conversation, and manners of speech
and dress. To appreciate beauty in all of these fields
the emotional faculties should be trained, and such training should be deliberately undertaken, wisely planned,
and patiently carried through. There is no more telling
evidence of genuine culture than an appreciation of beauty
in nature, a taste for the best music, the best pictures, the
best books, and a delight in the courtesies and amenities
of social life, in agreeable conversation, graceful carriage,

and attractive dress. Unfortunately, the impression is wide-spread, even in civilized countries, that æsthetic apprecia-tion is an ability belonging to a limited class especially gifted with artistic ability and that the majority of men have no concern with it. This idea is of course quite false and must be opposed in the interest of the higher human welfare. The artist only possesses to an exceptional de-gree powers of selective perception, imaginative synthesis, and emotional response, which we all possess and may cultivate if we will. We may avail ourselves of the work of the artist to quicken our own sense of beauty; he will find in our admiration and enjoyment the inspiration of still finer and nobler works. Only thus through the in-terest and coöperation of the whole community or nation in the encouragement of art and the preservation of natural beauty can the full æsthetic development of individual mem-bers be achieved.

This brief statement of the essentials of culture will have missed its aim if it has not shown with clearness that thought, action, and feeling, are not three independent activities, but only three aspects of the one process through which the self in its spiritual nature develops and expands. Each one of these three capacities involves, and depends upon, the other two. Thought is verified in action and this verification is signified in feeling; action is guided by thought and impelled by feeling; feeling is aroused by an object of thought whose comprehension enlists the powers of action. In true culture, therefore, intellectual, technical, and æsthetic activities blend in the unity of developed personality. The ideal ends of Truth, Power, and Beauty, which are the goals of thought, action, and feeling, re-spectively, are themselves but different expressions of the supreme ideal of complete self-organization sought by the fundamental activity of volition through which self-con-scious personality is itself constituted. The three subordinate virtues of *Wisdom, Efficiency,* and *Refinement,* all merge within the comprehensive excellence of culture.

## ACHIEVEMENT

In addition to culture, idealism or the full realization of the psychic capacities of the human self, demands the prolonged and progressive exercise of that ability, intellectual, technical, or æsthetic, which is most marked in the individual. Such sustained and successful pursuit of the end most in line with the individual's own talent is what we mean by *achievement*. It is an admitted fact that men differ in their abilities—in the strength of one capacity as compared to the strength of others. Indeed, the divergence in this respect is so wide, the resulting combinations of different abilities in different amounts are so many, that the attempt to classify individuals into distinct types or groups on the basis of their predominant abilities appears quite hopeless. Each individual falls into a class by himself, his own particular combination of abilities rendering him different from every other individual. Nevertheless, it does seem possible to divide individuals, roughly, into three groups in accordance with the predominance of in-intellectual, technical, or æsthetic abilities, in their nature. The first and last types appear at first glance to be more clearly marked and hence more easily distinguishable. No doubt there are individuals in whom intellect predominates, men who are " born thinkers " like Kant and Spencer. The æsthetic type or " artistic temperament " is perhaps even more sharply distinguished, its peculiarities are more conspicuous; to this type belong the poets, the musicians, the painters,—the Shelleys, Chopins, and Rembrandts. The third class—the technical or practical—is really so large, occupying so extensive a field and divisible into so many subordinate classes, that it loses all distinctness and seems to have no exact boundaries. Yet it cannot be denied that there are men who are characteristically " men of action." Only this superior technical ability is usually displayed in one province of the practical sphere—in that of mechanics or engineering, as in the case of an Edison or an Eads; in plant- or animal-breeding and control, where men like Burbank show their skill; in medicine and surgery, of which many men in the past century have shown themselves masters; in state-craft and diplomacy where men as widely different as Bismarck and Lincoln show supreme natural ability; in education and religion; in social organization and moral reform; in all these and many other fields as well. According to his type of ability, then, the individual is fitted to achieve *intellecually,* as scholar and investigator, *æsthetically* in the field of art, or *technically,* in practical pursuits,—the world of action being so large, however, that special ability in it is usually confined to one of its provinces.

The difficulty which immediately arises in connection with this subject of an achievement which is necessarily specialized, is its seeming conflict with culture. Certainly the interests of the two do appear to be antagonistic. Culture is many-sided and symmetrical, achievement is one-sided and extreme; culture is extensive and universal, achievement is intensive and particular. How reconcile the balanced and proportionate development of all the faculties of the human self with the exaggerated and disproportionate exercise of a special one? This is the way the problem states itself in the minds of many educators, moralists, and other students of human nature and human life—and as thus stated it is, of course, insoluble. Now the assertion may well appear to be a rash one; yet the truth is that there is really no problem here at all, for the interests of " culture " and " specialization " are not essentially antagonistic when these two are properly understood.

Achievement through the exercise of some special ability in the individual, does not hinder but rather encourages the development of his other powers, provided this ability preponderates in his nature. So far from checking and frustrating the expression of his other capacities, the continued and successful use of this, his special talent, is the most effectual, yes the only, method of enlivening and inspiring his whole nature, so that all his powers may function at their maximum of efficiency. The man who, for example, has marked musical gifts, will not have his intellectual development cut short or his practical efficiency diminished by achievement in the line of his distinctive ability. On the contrary, without the stimulus of this achievement which his nature demands, his powers of thought will languish, his capacity for action will be deadened, and his whole personality be dwarfed and stunted; while on the other hand, if his special talent be given the opportunity for expression it craves, his intellectual perceptions are quickened, his technical skill increased, and his whole nature is vitalized and expanded. This does not mean that his intellectual and technical development will equal his æsthetic achievement; but that inequality is rooted in his own nature and to destroy it would be to destroy the proportions of his own individuality. The case is the same if the exceptional ability is of the intellectual or practical type rather than of the æsthetic. The born engineer or politician will learn most fully to interpret the meaning of the world and to enjoy its beauty, in a life which permits of the special exercise of his distinctive ability; the born thinker will best acquire technical skill and æsthetic sensibility in connection with his special scientific researches. Achievement is consequently not to be regarded as the enemy of culture. As culture is the culmination of individual development, so achievement is the apex and crown of culture, its very pinnacle, where

the individual attains that triumphant mastery of objective
conditions, that complete self-possession, for which the will
that is fundamental within him is ever yearning. It is
true that the individual who exercises to a special degree
an ability which is not strongest by natural endowment will
miss the fruits of culture and develop a one-sided character.
Obviously, this happens often enough. Sometimes it occurs
through careless acceptance by the individual of a certain
pursuit because circumstances make it easy to do so; in
other instances, it follows from a real ignorance in the
individual of his nature and special abilities; in still others
—and these the most numerous of all—economic pressure
forces the individual to engage in an activity inappropriate
to his own nature and hence uninteresting and even distasteful to him. Here of course there is no possibility of
true culture; but neither is there any opportunity for
genuine achievement.

Such achievement as we have been considering realizes
ends of universal value. The pursuit of Truth and Power
and Beauty is a quest in which all human individuals participate in so far as they exercise their spiritual capacities.
In fact, such achievement, if it is to be truly progressive,
requires the coöperation of many individuals—men living
in different places and times, perhaps, but united by ties
of sympathy and mutual understanding through their devotion to common ends. Such coöperation enables the
single individual to profit by the achievements of other
men and then to repay this debt by turning over the
products of his own skill to the uses of his fellow-workers.
As the result of this coöperative effort on the part of
mankind, a great deal has been achieved in the intellectual,
technical, and æsthetic spheres: much truth has been discovered; man's power of control over the objective conditions of his life has been greatly increased; many forms
of beauty have been defined and exemplified. The more

general problems of an introductory character in each of these three lines of activity have been in a large measure solved. But the consequence of this initial step has been to disclose a multitude of special problems demanding solution in each of these fields. To one of these special subjects of study, branches of action, or departments of sensibility, the individual must address himself if he expects to contribute anything to human achievement. This means a still stricter limitation of his activities. The field of knowledge has been divided into the particular sciences, and these sciences have in most cases been again sub-divided; the multiplicity of fields in which technical skill may be exercised has already been alluded to; the æsthetic sphere has also been partitioned off among a variety of special arts. Some suggestion of the different fields which are open to individual achievement in the present state of human culture may be given by the following table, which of course is not exhaustive.

|  |  |  |
|---|---|---|
|  | MECHANICAL | Mathematics |
|  |  | Physics |
|  |  | Chemistry |
|  |  | Astronomy |
|  |  | Geology |
|  |  | Mineralogy |
|  |  | Meteorology |
| INTELLECTUAL (The Field of Thought) |  |  |
|  | HISTORICAL | Botany |
|  |  | Zoology |
|  |  | Anthropology |
|  |  | Ethnology |
|  |  | Sociology |
|  |  | Economics |
|  |  | Politics |
|  |  | Psychology |
|  |  | Logic |
|  |  | Ethics |
|  |  | Æsthetics |
|  |  | Philosophy |

|  |  | Land |
|---|---|---|
|  | INORGANIC | Sea |
|  |  | Air |

TECHNICAL
(The World of Action) ORGANIC

|  |  | Plant |
|---|---|---|
|  |  | Animal |
|  |  | Human |

SOCIAL

|  | Law and Government |
|---|---|
|  | War and Armament |
|  | Production and Manu-<br>facture |
|  | Transportation and Dis-<br>tribution |
|  | Association and Entertain-<br>ment |
|  | Education and Religion |

VISUAL

|  | Landscape and Seascape |
|---|---|
|  | Buildings |
|  | Statuary |
|  | Pictures |

ÆSTHETIC
(The Sphere of Feeling) AUDITORY

|  | Music |
|---|---|
|  | Poetry |

VERBAL

|  | Drama |
|---|---|
|  | Fiction |

from the imitation of others and then interpreting their experiences in terms of his own.

Despite these indubitable facts, the organization of individuality is the condition and pre-requisite of the adjustment of individualities in society. Of the promptings of impulse, of the satisfying of desire, of the forming of ambition, the individual has immediate experience only in himself; upon this experience will therefore depend his ability to enter into the lives of others and to understand their desires and purposes. The individual can only *imagine* the purpose and ambitions of others, while he *realizes* his own and, although sympathy may give warmth and urgency to the other's interests as they are imagined, still the individual's understanding of their character is necessarily limited by the range of his own experience. Evidently, then, the individual must have learned to control his own desires, must have succeeded in subordinating them to some inclusive and unifying purpose, before he can appreciate the presence and supremacy of similar purposes and ambitions in the lives of others. Again we must be on our guard against going to an unwarranted extreme. The human self does not first have to go to the limits of egoism before it can begin the practice of altruism. The view is erroneous which conceives of moral development in the human individual as beginning with the absolute egoism of childhood, passing through the prudential stage of youth, and finally arriving at altruism in maturity. The child is not an absolute egoist. His conduct is not sufficiently organized to permit of the definition of his individuality; he is conscious of no interests as his own, in distinction from the interests of others; he cannot, therefore, manifest a genuine egoism. The child is selfish, however; the *ego* interest is growing more rapidly than the *alter* interest. The conduct of the child is occupied with the satisfaction of a number of desires—only partially

controlled, and very imperfectly adjusted to one another—
in an environment in which other individuals are taken
for granted as necessary and important factors. The child
does not think of distinguishing his interest from the interest of the family; he is absorbed in gratifying his desires in and through the family. But with the organization
of impulse effected through the training of childhood, individuality emerges; clear consciousness of self and self-
interest arises. This result is usually accomplished during
the period of adolescence when the powers of intellect,
imagination, and emotion, are quickened and strengthened.
Then the individual does for the first time become fully
conscious of himself in the uniqueness of his individuality,
and of the interests and ambitions peculiar to his individual
nature. This is the period really favorable to egoism, that
of youth and early maturity, when the young person is
wholly wrapped up in his own plans and either entirely
neglects, or totally disregards, the interests of others. But
this stronger and more adequate consciousness of self gives
the individual his first true conception of individuality
in others—his first appreciation of individual purposes and
ambitions among his fellow-men. Then there becomes possible—and necessary—an adjustment of these different and
conflicting individualities, as the next step in self-organization.

The social adjustment, whose end is the integration of
all individual interests in one inclusive human good, is
effected in two distinct steps or moments. In the first, the
individual adjusts his own interests to the interests of
other individuals with whom he comes into personal contact.
When we emphasize the negative side of this adjustment,
thinking of the self-abnegation which must be practised
if we are to make common interest with our fellows,
we derive the virtue of kindness, the first of the social
virtues.

2. **Kindness.**—Kindness is the practice of subordinating self-interest when this is seen to conflict with the good of others. The " kind " person, in the popular understanding of the word, is the person who is willing to " put himself out " for others; and these words express extremely well the true nature of kindness. A willingness on the part of the individual to suffer personal discomfort, to incur private disadvantage, is the first requirement made of him on entering the life of social relationships. He who is so absorbed in his own plans as to be oblivious of the desires of others, or so bent upon his own ambitions as to disregard the welfare of others, can never hope to enjoy the larger satisfactions of the social life or to realize his own greater social self. Now the actual sacrifice demanded of the individual in adjusting his own to others' interests in the different relationships of the social life, varies in amount from denying a passing desire to violating a life-purpose or endangering a personal ideal. Where the cost to the individual is least, in the sacrifice of present comfort or momentary pleasure—as when, for instance, a man gives up his chance of securing a comfortable seat in order to assist an aged or infirm person in boarding a car—kindness is usually recognized as *Courtesy*.

Courtesy is simply kindness—kindness displayed in the details of social intercourse, and shown in an habitual attention to others' wishes and welfare at the expense of some trouble and inconvenience to oneself. The courteous person is the " considerate " person, the one who constantly considers others' feelings as well as his own. It is true that courtesy usually concerns the minor matters of life. No great interest is endangered, no momentous issue involved; the question is generally one of modes of speech and manners of action, and relates to one's temporary convenience or passing pleasure. Yet courtesy requires effort, nevertheless. It is not easy always to summon the smile of welcome for the friendly caller who comes inopportunely and interrupts the progress of an important piece of work, or to cut short an enjoyable conversation with an old friend in order to say a word of greeting to an uninteresting stranger. Courtesy is exacting in its demand that the individual be always on his guard—always ready by word or by act to assist and encourage his fellows in the many and often irritating details of the daily walk in life. It consequently exposes the individual to vexatious interruptions in the prosecution of his own plans and, not infrequently, to serious disadvantage. But whatever its cost, the value of courtesy in social life can hardly be overestimated. It is the oil which makes the machinery of social intercourse run smoothly, removing causes of friction and thus preventing the parts from becoming so worn and weakened as finally to break and throw the whole machine out of gear. Courtesy adds an element of cheer and encouragement to life, which does much to lessen the nervous fatigue and dispel the discouragement which our modern civilization, with its haste and its complication, produces in many individuals, and thus to increase human efficiency and enlarge the possibilities of human achievement.

But kindness often costs more than temporary inconvenience; it interferes with the realization of our leading life-purposes. Its exercise, in helping neighbor or acquaintance who is in need, requires the sacrifice of time, money, or reputation. Because money as the universal medium of exchange, is convertible into so many benefits, it constitutes in a large proportion of cases the most effective instrument at the disposal of the individual for relieving distress or ministering to the welfare of his fellows. Kindness in this form of the surrender of the " natural " goods of life for the assistance of others, is usually denominated *Generosity.* Of the subordination of wealth to the larger spiritual concerns of life, something has already been said in the discussion of courage; but we were interested there in the sacrifice of wealth primarily as a means to the greater personal freedom of the individual, and here in expending it for the good of others. The obligation resting upon those who have money in excess of their present needs to give at least a portion of their surplus to relieve the distress of others who through illness, misfortune, or even through their own neglect are suffering from lack of the necessities of life, is universally admitted. The amount which one ought in a particular case to give should be determined on grounds of the personal welfare of the individuals concerned. One individual has no right to jeopardize his own personal usefulness and social efficiency in order to give another enjoyments which he cries for but can do without. Nor has any one the right, through his generosity, to avert entirely from another the consequences of his own laziness and self-indulgence, thus preventing him from acquiring the self-reliance and thriftiness which are the foundation of a stable character. Because the generosity of individuals prompted by sympathy for the sufferings of others in distress, often leads to this latter result, it has recently fallen into considerable disrepute; and the proposal is to replace it altogether by systematic charity, organized upon a scientific basis, which aims through a study of social and economic conditions to remove the causes of poverty and make the expenditure of money a means to the real personal betterment of the recipients and not to their temporary enjoyment. But while organized charity promises to do more for the relief of chronic poverty it by no means takes the place of individual generosity. The immediate contact of giver and recipient in the kindly offices of relief affords to both an opportunity for personal expression and a spur to moral betterment which cannot be dispensed with if all the possibilities of our human life are to be realized. The reason why so much well-meant charity fails to accomplish any real good is that it is limited to the bestowing of money, while—in addition to pecuniary relief—advice, encouragement, and even companionship, are needed to put the unfortunate one on his feet again. But—as it may happen—such friendly attention can only be given at the further expense of the agent. The needy person frequently owes his distress to his own indolence, folly, or wrongdoing; in consequence he has incurred the contempt and odium of his fellows. One who would give him the companionship and counsel which kindness demands must cross the social line drawn against him by the community, and be prepared to injure his own reputation for good judgment, if not for good intention. Thus many who are willing to spend their money to help others, are unwilling to go further and risk their reputation. The released convict who needs healthful companionship, sound advice, and hearty encouragement, as he never needed it before, finds that every one shuns him; no one is willing to be seen walking or talking with him; all persons are reluctant to have him live or work in their vicinity. Small wonder that he is drawn back to evil pursuits! Surely that reputation is a cheap and sorry thing, which will be injured if we extend a helping hand to a fallen fellow-man. Kindness demands the sacrifice of nothing that is essential to our own self-realization, when it requires us to subordinate such considerations to others' welfare.

The practice of kindness may involve still greater sacrifices than any as yet described. It may require the individual to neglect his own personal development and the exercise of his higher psychic capacities—to give up his opportunity for continued education or to deny his ability for original achievement—for others' benefit. Here kindness becomes genuine *self-sacrifice*. Fortunately, kindness does not commonly demand such sacrifices; although they are not so rare, perhaps, as we imagine. There is no record kept of the young men who have resolutely turned their back upon college or university with the alluring prospects of professional distinction which they held forth to a youth certain of his ability, in order to support aged or enfeebled parents; of the young women who have missed honorable careers as teachers, or the happiness of wedded life, that they might spend years and exhaust their youth and vitality in caring for a fretful invalid mother or sister; of the ministers and teachers who have denied abilities for scholarly research in their increasing devotion to the welfare of parishioners or students. If such a roll is anywhere kept it is certainly an honor roll. While such instances of self-sacrificing kindness awaken a deep admiration that is akin to reverence in every sober mind, still they present serious difficulty to the student of morality, and particularly to the Self-realizationist. This problem has been already touched upon in the chapter upon self-sacrifice. We believe that those practices which are required for the complete realization of the self are virtuous and, conversely, that whatever is a duty does thus contribute to Self-realization. Now we all recognize that thus to forego the opportunity for personal development in order to benefit others is at times a duty for the human individual—although we may doubt whether we ourselves should have strength to perform it—and consequently we should expect to find it a most effective means of Self-realization. But, is it? Theoretically, we might expect that the very severity of the struggle which preceded such self-sacrifice,— suddenly uprooting plans which had slowly grown and matured during years of time, and tearing down the aims and ambitions whose rearing had taken much painstaking thought and effort—would discover new springs of hope in the individual, and bring to light capacities in himself

whose possession he had never dreamt of; as a great con-
vulsion of nature, rending the rocks and shaking the moun-
tains to their foundation, might disclose new sources of
pure water and lay bare hidden veins of precious ore.
Certainly this is what happens with many individuals when
under such stress of sacrifice; they reveal a sweetness of
temper, a depth of insight, a capacity for achievement quite
unsuspected in them before. Yet in other cases, and they
are not few, the heroic kindness does not seem to promote
Self-realization and cannot be made by any stretch of the
imagination to appear to do so. The unavoidable sorrow
and disappointment over the failure of individual ambitions often leave the person soured and embittered; or the
withdrawal of all stimulus and incentive to individual
achievement renders him dull, prosaic, and commonplace;
or constant association with his own intellectual inferiors
develops a mean, captious, or tyrannizing spirit within
him. What can the Self-realizationist say to such cases,
which are of undoubted occurrence? He cannot pretend
to have a full solution for all the problems here involved.
Two considerations should not be neglected, however, which
when brought to bear upon the difficulty make it appear
somewhat less formidable. In the first place, when the
opportunity for individual achievement is sacrificed in
kindness to another, it should not be forgotten that it is
only the *opportunity to achieve* that is sacrificed. Perhaps
the individual would have failed to succeed even had he
had the opportunity for education, technical training, or
whatever the preparation was which he craved; perhaps he
promised more than he could have fulfilled under any
conditions; his own inherent weakness was merely exposed
by his inability to profit by his resolute and heroic sacrifice for another's benefit. Secondly, while we must believe that such kindness is a means to Self-realization, there
is no reason to suppose that one such deed—as splendid as

it is—will bring Self-realization. The individual must continue to do his duty, to observe the conditions of self-development. Many times this is what he does not do, one fears; instead he allows the temporary exhaustion of his will, after the supreme effort, to become a settled condition or habit, thus sinking into a moral lethargy and permitting his faculties to atrophy and decay from disuse and inaction. Of course the ultimate result is then not Self-realization but self-degeneration.

3. **Friendship.**—When, moved by sympathy or love, the individual sacrifices his own interest, the end sought is the welfare of another. The practice of promoting another's welfare with disregard for one's own self-interest is *friendship*. Friendship is the positive aspect of kindness and one of the most important factors in moral development. As such it has received extended treatment in ethical literature, although it has not always been included in the list of the virtues. There is excellent reason for making it coördinate with benevolence, and considering them as the two positive social virtues, however; because clearness requires us to distinguish two steps in the social adjustment—devotion to single persons or acquaintances, and service of all persons or humanity. It is indeed an evidence of the unique position and surpassing importance of friendship in our lives, that we are accustomed to think of its practice not as a duty but as a rare privilege—one of the priceless boons of human existence.

But friendship is not merely a beautiful ornament of human life; it plays a necessary part in the process of Self-realization. No more potent instrument of self-expansion exists than the practice of friendship, understood as whole-souled devotion to another's good. In such devotion to others there is no question of the individual's overstepping the boundaries of his own life and experience in pursuit of something quite foreign and external to himself. Others' lives and others' interests are already present in his experience, essentially related to his own existence and individuality. The only question is, therefore, shall these other interests and individualities with which he is inseparably connected, remain ill-adjusted to his own, and thus constitute conflicting and discordant elements in his selfhood, or shall he adjust his interest to theirs, integrate their lives with his own, thus increasing the unity of his conscious selfhood and enriching the content of his own personality? Through the promotion of another's plans, the realization of another's purposes, the individual enlarges his own interest, acquiring new ambitions on his own account and discovering in himself hitherto unrecognized abilities. Through such service of others, the individual as it were multiplies his own individuality, finding in the personality of each friend a new self with different interests, fresh enthusiasms, and original aspirations. Moreover, the possibilities for self-development in thus " taking an interest " in another human being seem quite endless; the potency for good of the relation here involved is self-augmenting. Through devotion to my friend my own interests are extended, my own personality enriched; as the result of my self-development I am able more effectively to aid him in realizing the possibilities of his own nature and situation, which in its turn reacts still more favorably upon my own character, and thus, the mutual benefit derived from the friendship grows at a constantly increasing rate. Thus under the influence of true friendship persistently cultivated, the personalities involved develop and expand as plants grow under the warming and vitalizing rays of the sun.

Of course, if friendship is to realize all its possibilities as a means of moral development, it must involve mutual devotion. To the love and devotion of one the other must respond with an equal affection and loyalty. Such is the ideal friendship which has been celebrated in poetry and song, and which is generally regarded as one of the greatest, if not the greatest, blessing vouchsafed by God to man. What then is the basis of such love and devotion among persons? Aristotle believes that it differs in the different kinds of friendship; that in fact friendships fall into three classes, according as they are based on the utility or convenience of the relationship, the pleasure it affords, or the goodness of the persons concerned. The first order of friendships springs from a recognition by the individuals of an advantage which comes to both from their relation, and a desire to preserve this advantage; it is commercial in character. The second is based upon the pleasure which arises from the acquaintance and is best exemplified by the friendships of young people. The third is hence the only one in which the personality is sought for its own sake, in which there is real *personal* devotion. It is grounded upon the '' good,'' upon the personal worth of the individuals concerned, with a recognition of this worth, and consequent reciprocal love and devotion. The last type is, Aristotle admits, the only perfect friendship, and it alone merits our serious consideration as involving that genuine devotion to another's life and interest which is a necessary condition of Self-realization. The first two sorts of friendship may be regarded as types of association between individuals preparatory to true friendship, as forms of social life which lead up to its only perfect and adequate expression in human experience. As a matter of fact, they do indicate in a general way the changes which the attitude of the individual towards his fellows undergoes in the course of moral development. In the first stage of individual development he is interested in other individuals as they serve his convenience or promote his advantage, in his efforts to provide for his own natural wants; reputation is sought as one of the natural goods and a means to comfort and security. Then in the second stage of individual development when the personal capacities find expression, the individual is led by his awakening æsthetic sensibility to take pleasure in the appearance, actions, and conversation of certain others, whose acquaintance he cultivates in order to prolong this pleasure. But through the pursuit of the ideal ends of Truth and Power and Beauty, which are universal in their appeal, he comes to value the human personalities in which he finds these ideals realized, and thus is rendered capable of real devotion to them.

Friendship is based on personal worth; it springs out of the reciprocal recognition by two persons of this worth in each other and leads to mutual love and devotion. In what does such personal worth consist? Our recent study of the conditions of individual development supplies us with the answer to this question. The personal worth of an individual consists in the development within him of the spiritual qualities of wisdom, efficiency, and refinement. It is measured by the extent to which the individual has made his natural existence and resources instrumental to the exercise of his psychic capacities for thought, action, and feeling. To the fact that a single person may realize in an individual, and hence unique way, ends of universal value, is due his worth for other persons. It is this which makes him an end in himself to his fellow-men; for it is obvious that the more such individual expressions of universal reality the human self can include in the system of its own life and interests, the more comprehensive will be its grasp on reality. Now the personal development which gives human individuality its worth and is the ground of friendship has two sides, an extensive and an intensive. It involves the harmonious coöperation and interplay of all the spiritual faculties of man, with consequent extension of interest and increase of ability in every important field of human experience. Such a broad and liberal culture tremendously increases the value of the human individual as an object of friendship. He is capable of varied responses to different situations; his many interests and wide proficiency make him always an instructive and stimulating companion. But the development of character in the person most worthy of friendly devotion must be intensive as well as extensive. He must have so far achieved in some particular field as to give him firm hold on the fundamental principles of this field, on its permanent and abiding truth; since achievement like this is required to give an individual the stability and poise which he needs to make him reliable and trustworthy. And above all others, these qualities are required in persons who deserve our love and devotion. Such complete personal development we cannot expect to find realized in all our friends, to be sure; it is an ideal for others' lives as well as our own. Yet it is helpful to define our standards of personal worth so that we may discriminate intelligently in choosing our friends.

From the nature of friendship itself, it follows that the number of persons to whom the individual can loyally devote himself as a friend, is strictly limited. Grounded on personal worth, friendships take time to spring up, to grow, to reach their full fruition. True friendships in most cases are formed slowly and at the cost of some effort. The personal worth of human beings is not apparent to the eye; it does not reveal itself to the passing glance; it is not made plain by manner of dress or even by facial lineaments. It manifests itself only in course of acquaintance, by word, by deed, by response of feeling, and by countless other tokens. Such revelation of personal character must be awaited, however, before we can even intelligently consider the individual in question as a *possible* friend. For this is a question that should be intelligently considered in every case. We should not be led by chance into our friendships; they should represent our free and deliberate choices. Surely every reason exists to choose slowly and with care, for we make no more important choices in our earthly journey. After having chosen our friends we must be prepared to devote time and labor to cultivating them. Only through continuous personal association and mutual service can the possibilities of any friendship be fully realized. Absence does not make the hearts of friends grow fonder; instead, continued separation will kill all but the strongest and most durable attachments. Constant personal association, in which the two individualities involved are brought into contact at every point, is necessary if the friendship is to yield its full benefit as a means of Self-realization. To the personal intercourse with its exchange of opinion and harmony of feeling, must be added the ready assistance and willing service which friends give to one another, and which must be reckoned as one of the most precious as well as most essential factors in true friendship. When we take all this into consideration we see that a friendship is not a light or easy thing; at its best it is a long, an arduous, and a serious undertaking. There is not time or opportunity in a natural lifetime for an unlimited number of such friendships. To set any number as a limit, however, is of course impossible; the capacity for friendship varies greatly with individuals. The only limit we need observe in making friends is that set by the nature of friendship itself, and every human individual should endeavor to form as many true friendships as he can actually maintain.

Reference has been made to need of taking time and trouble to come into contact with a friend's personality at every important point. Thought and study are required to share in interests which are unfamiliar to us, and appreciate achievement in fields of which we are ignorant. It is one of the beneficial results of friendship that it does thus awaken new interests in us and makes us aware of the value of achievements hitherto unrecognized; thus the narrowing effects of concentrating our attention upon a particular pursuit are counteracted and we are lifted out of the ruts of professional habit and routine into which we tend to sink. Yet the conditions of successful achievement for the individual in his own special line, impose strict limits upon the thought and attention he can give to others' interests, even those of his closest friends. Hence comes the great advantage of a community of interest and endeavor between friends. When the minds of two persons are preoccupied with the same subject, when they are both working to realize the same end, we have conditions most favorable to the rapid growth and firm cementing of friendship between them. No preliminary effort is then required to learn of new things, to understand unfamiliar undertakings. Instead, each individual by pressing forward with his own achievement is strengthening the common interest which binds him to his friend. In such circumstances it is possible for a person actually to cultivate another's friendship while wholly absorbed in the work of his own vocation; for he may derive added inspiration from the consciousness of his friend's eager and constant interest in what he is doing, and the expectation of sharing with that friend the advantages of his discoveries and success. Hence friendships among professional colleagues are natural; with the exception of attachments between husband and wife, parent and child, where there is also a massive common interest, they yield the richest returns. Doubtless it is possible to go too far in emphasizing the advantages of likeness between friends; differences in temperament and ability add to the charm and increase the benefit of friendship. Yet identities of interest and sentiment are more important in making it solid and enduring. An unreasonable prejudice exists to the effect that " talking shop " does not constitute the ideal of friendly intercourse. Yet what is more normal or deeply satisfying than that two friends who have the same trade should spend a social hour discussing the concerns of their common occupation, or that two mothers who are friends should take the evening for an exchange of opinion and information regarding the welfare of their children?

True friendship, Aristotle holds, is permanent; because it is based on virtue, and virtue is a permanent quality. Human thought has generally agreed in finding this quality of permanence in genuine friendship—something of eternal reality which enables it to resist all influence of change and decay, and makes it triumph over death itself. In all ages men have willingly endured death for the sake of their friends, firmly convinced that the friendship was more real than the accident of natural existence, and cheerfully confident of continuing it in a future life. Good reason exists for this belief in the permanence of friendship, if we have correctly described its nature. For we understood it to be grounded in personality, and personality consists in the realization, through a particular individual, of principles and purposes (such as Truth and Beauty, Power and Goodness) which are universal in their scope and permanent in their value. Being thus rooted in universal and permanent reality, the true love of friends abides, unaffected by change in physical appearance, in financial fortune, in reputation among men. Founded upon personality, the only agency which can destroy such friendship is one that destroys personality itself. Aside from death, or mental decay due to physical disease or enfeeblement, the only danger threatening the integrity of personality and hence the permanence of friendship is that of moral degeneration. What should be the effect upon a friendship, of wrongdoing leading to vice, and finally to complete loss of self-control, on the part of one of the persons concerned? Certainly, it will be the duty of a friend to check such a course of wrongdoing if possible at the start and, in later days, to exercise greater forbearance, and make more zealous efforts than any one else to bring about reform. If all such endeavors are fruitless, however, all friendly intercourse must cease. But no matter how low one of the individuals concerned may sink, the bond of friendship is never entirely destroyed. The one fallen must always remain a former friend and, while he lives and the faintest possibility of restoration remains, must receive some thought and care.

Naturally, friendships are first formed within the family-circle. The physical relationships of sex and parenthood are not always accompanied by real love, to be sure; since love or friendship is a personal relation. The reason why so many marriages fail of permanence is that they are based merely on physical attraction which is certain to pass in the course of years. The real love which marriage should but express is a personal attachment which is permanent and bids defiance to the changes and vicissitudes of life. Such love between a man and a woman, with the mutual devotion and self-surrender which it involves, can receive adequate fulfilment only under conditions of monogamous marriage. The principle on which friendship is based—that of treating all persons of one's acquaintance as ends in themselves and never as means of selfish gratification—when observed in one's relations to the opposite sex constitutes the virtue of *Chastity*. This principle of reverence for personality, if always observed, would cure all sexual vice and remove entirely the so-called " social evil " which has ever been a dark blot upon human society.

To the relations of parent and child the same considerations apply. The instinctive attachment which depends upon blood kinship is not enough of itself to produce genuine love. It is necessary here too that the attachment have a personal ground if it is to last. Parents must take trouble to make friends with their children, learning their personalities, sharing their interests, and participating in their experiences, if they expect to have a permanent influence over them and guide their further development.

With all its shortcomings and failures the life of the family as it is organized in civilized countries to-day furnishes the soil most favorable to the growth of true friendship. The existence of the blood-tie pre-disposes the individuals thus bound, to love and serve one another; and the constant association in daily life gives that knowledge of others' personalities which is essential to the formation of friendship. The human individual receives his first lessons in the pains and the joys of unselfish love in his early life with parents and brothers and sisters in the home. Very soon, however, the circle of acquaintanceship begins to widen. Among his playfellows acquaintance progresses and friendships are begun some of which are likely to last a lifetime. In young manhood and womanhood, when the powers of thought and imagination come into play, emotions and enthusiasms are aroused, and the capacity for sympathetic understanding of others greatly enlarged, we reach the period when friendships are the most easily and eagerly formed. The tides of life run high: romantic love and altruistic sentiment are readily awakened. But because personality is not yet organized by any settled purpose or given stability by any continuous or consistent achievement, attachments formed at this time are many of them transitory and uninfluential. Nevertheless, it is probable that some friendship will be formed during—say, the college or university years—which will wield a determining influence upon the life of the individual. When finally maturity is reached, the range of the individual's acquaintance tends to enlarge—through trade union, professional societies, and business associations, religious and philanthropic organizations, clubs for culture and amusement—until it is practically co-extensive with the local community itself, and then by various channels extends to individuals scattered throughout the nation, and even over the whole world. Not that the circle of any individual's friends may be as wide as this. That, as we understand true friendship, would be impossible; a dozen lives would be required to make so great a number of friends. The circle of acquaintance is merely the field in which one may choose his friends. But it is possible throughout the range of the widest acquaintance to exhibit a spirit of friendly devotion and, at opportunity as one moves among acquaintances in the daily walk of life, to say a helpful word or give needed assistance, and receive in passing an inspiring touch of another personality.

But beyond the limits of the widest acquaintance lies the great mass of mankind whose lives are none the less real in their aspirations and disappointments, their thinking and their striving, than those of our nearest neighbors. Into personal contact with these the individual can never come; yet his life may influence theirs—his ideas, his inventions, his achievements, may affect for better or for worse the general human welfare. An illustration of this fact is afforded by the participation of the individual citizen in the government of a democracy like our own. Although he may know but a few hundred of the hundred million people composing this nation, still he may, through his ballot, exert an influence, very slight it is true, upon the welfare of these myriads. Complete self-organization calls, therefore, for a second activity of adjustment within the social sphere: the adjustment by the individual of his own interest, along with those other interests which have become identified with his own, to the welfare of humanity. Here again we must guard against conceiving of the human individual as an isolated being who first defines his own interest and then sacrifices it to a cause quite outside himself—i.e. the general good. Such a view has its root in an entirely false conception of the individual. What Self-realization actually demands to complete the organization of human life, is the integration of all lesser private interests within the larger personal good which all individuals as rational beings share in common. The sacrifice, which is here involved, of the limited and exclusive aims of individuality to the comprehensive good of human personality, as such, is identical with the virtue of justice.

4. **Justice.**—Justice is the habit of subordinating individual interest, whether of self or of others, to the good of humanity. This virtue is the recognition in practice of the right of human personality always to be treated as an end, to which all private interests whatsoever must be subordinated. The subordination in question applies not merely to the individual's exclusive aims and desires but also to those of the family, friends, or social class with which the individual has consciously identified his interest. Often the fact that the individual seeks not his own private interest but the interest of family or friends or class or party, constitutes in his opinion a justification for his neglect of the good of humanity as a whole, or even his violation of general human rights. Justice condemns all favoritism, however; whether it is himself whom the individual favors or a selected group of his acquaintances. Justice forbids men ever to employ human personality as a means to the furtherance of their private schemes and ambitions; it insists upon the duty of making all lesser interests of different individuals means to the promotion of total human welfare.

Justice thus maintains the right of human personality always to be sought as an end and never to be employed as a means. It is negative in character inasmuch as it defends this right by prohibiting any violation of it for private interest or through special privilege. Now to make human personality always an end is to aim at its free development and full expression in the lives of all human beings. As complete Self-realization is man's highest good, the opportunity thus freely to realize his personal capacities is man's moral right. But, as we know, complete Self-realization is possible in human life only under certain conditions—the preservation of bodily and mental health; the possession of some property; the education of the higher faculties, intellectual, technical, and æsthetic; the establishment of ties of family and friendship; the maintenance of a certain position and standing in human society. The same right with which a human individual may demand the opportunity for self-development extends to the conditions necessary for such development. Every man has therefore the right to the possession and preservation of his bodily organism, to the ownership of property, to an education, to family care and friendly love, to citizenship and occupation—in the degree and to the extent required for his own Self-realization. This right, belonging to every human individual as a free person, brings with it an *obligation* also absolute and universal, that of respecting the rights of all other human beings to the conditions necessary for free self-development. Justice defends the ethical right of human personality to develop in accordance with its freedom, by enforcing upon all individuals the moral obligation equally authoritative—that they refrain from any interference with the exercise of this right by others. Hence the demands of justice have naturally found expression in a series of prohibitions: Thou shalt not kill; Thou shalt not steal; Thou shalt not bear false witness; Thou shalt not commit adultery, etc.

## POLITICAL JUSTICE

The end of human society is the fullest possible development of the powers of human personality in all its members —in other words, the realization of the highest human good. To this end it aims to establish the conditions requisite to Self-realization among human beings. But since these conditions—health and security, private property, education, etc.—can be made *conditions of self-realization* only through the volition of the individuals concerned, the primary function of society is the protection of its members from any interference in the exercise of this, their right to avail themselves of the means necessary to their own personal development. The state, or body politic, is society acting as a unit in defense of the rights of its members, through the use of physical power; it is society exercising force in the attainment of its end, which is the promotion of the highest human welfare. With the means at its disposal, i.e. force, the state cannot directly affect the wills of its members and produce either the intention to exercise the right of self-development, or the acknowledgment of the obligation to respect this right in the case of others, All it can do is to remove hindrances to self-development by protecting its members from interference or encroachment while exercising this right. In thus " removing hindrances " the state is compelled again to act in an indirect and negative way. It cannot force its members to respect each other's rights; but by the inflicting of penalties it can interpose obstacles which effectually hinder all violation of others' rights through outward action. Thus Professor Bosanquet [1] finds the function of the state most adequately expressed in the principle of " hindrances to hindrances." This phrase well expresses the limitation imposed on all state action, as long as it

[1] *Cf.* BOSANQUET: *Philosophical Theory of the State.*

acts through the instrumentality distinctive of it, physical force. For force can only determine outward action. This does not mean, of course, outward movement alone, since all voluntary actions proceed from intention. But the state can only enforce such intention as is necessary to bring about compliance with requirements stated in terms of outward movement; it cannot make sure that the action will be performed from a motive that would give it moral value. Thus the state can produce in the minds of individual citizens the intention to keep hands off others' property; it cannot, however, make sure that such honesty will proceed from a regard for others' welfare; in the case of many individuals it will be due to a fear of the law's penalties. Hence there are decided limits to the profitable use of force by the state in the promotion of human welfare. No one would think of enforcing by law the finer expressions of courtesy, loyalty and devotion to friends, courage in the defense or rescue of the weak and afflicted; for to appeal to the lower motive in the case of these actions would tend to prevent their performance by the higher motive, the one which gives them greater moral value. Thus it has been said that only those acts should be enforced by public power which it is better to have done from any motive, than not to have done at all. Even though we adopt the principle of '' hindrances to hindrances '' as expressing the distinctive function of the state in the moral development of man, if we understand its ultimate aim to be, not the happiness of separate individuals but the highest personal development of humanity, the sphere in which it may legitimately exercise its power remains, nevertheless, a large one. As human societies grow in experience and intelligence they gain an ever increasing insight into the essential conditions of personal development. In consequence, they are able in a growing degree to secure for their members an opportunity for Self-realization, by removing the ob-

stacles which have hitherto deprived them of this opportunity, either as a whole or in part. Thus it is apparent
that sufficient food and proper training in childhood are
necessary to the later development of the distinctively
human faculties, and it is now seen to be the duty of the
state to provide care and education, if need be, at the public
expense. It is obvious that if working men are to enjoy the
benefits of a truly human life, they must be guaranteed as
much safety in their work as the character of their occupation permits, with the added assurance of support for self
and family if injury results in occupations particularly
hazardous; nations are now enacting laws by which these
fundamental human rights are secured for workers largely
at the expense of those who profit directly by their industry.
And indeed when we consider the work of the state in the
large—its office in furthering the highest human good—
the line we have drawn between a negative activity in
the hindrance of hindrances and a positive work for human
betterment, seems abstract and artificial. While it is true
that the state in enforcing its laws can only determine
external actions, still the existence of laws and the machinery for their enforcement tend to create a social sentiment and public opinion, both of which act as a direct stimulus to moral development.

The human individual, who is a citizen of a state, has
therefore *legal* in addition to *moral* rights. A legal right
is a claim upon the public power to be protected from
interference in free personal development. These legal
rights are enforced by the state and represent the conditions
of Self-realization in so far as the social community is able
to secure them for its members. In the strict and impartial
enforcement of all laws enacted to maintain the rights
of citizens, consists, then, political justice. Of course, the
human individual has moral rights which extend beyond
his legal rights. He has a moral right to the com-

panionship and sympathy of his fellows which he, as a social being, craves, yet this is not and cannot be a right enforced by law; to recognize and observe this right must remain for the higher sense of justice in his fellows. But in gaining legal rights the citizen also incurs legal obligations. He is bound to respect the rights of others as these are defined by the law; in thus complying fully with the law he meets the demands of legal justice. Justice as a moral attribute, however, requires that he respect the rights of his fellows out of a genuine regard for their welfare and not from fear of the penalties of the law; the law may nevertheless influence him in his conduct towards other men, by making clear to him their rights, and bringing home to him his duties towards them. But moral justice must necessarily go farther than legal justice in its requirements; man's full duty to his fellows' welfare cannot be enforced by law. As Paulsen says: " A legal system attempting to enforce the complete realization of the idea of justice in the acts of men would, as may readily be seen, necessarily lead to a most intolerable state of insecurity and tyranny. Hence the legal order confines itself to enforcing that minimum of righteous acts without which the human social life would not be possible. It thereby of course leaves a wide margin for injuries and unjust assertion of individual interests at the expense of those of others." [2] The law forbids murder and assault but it does not forbid the renting at a profit of unsanitary and flimsily built houses which cause the death of their occupants by disease and fire. The law forbids robbery and burglary, forgery and embezzlement, but not sharp business practices which deprive men of their honest savings and hard-won financial standing. The law forbids libel and slander but not malicious gossip and mischievous tale-bearing, which ruin reputations and produce discouragement and despair.

[2] PAULSEN: *Op. cit.*, p. 633.

The law forbids the violation of the marriage vows and seduction of the youthful and unexperienced, but not the secret disloyalties of mind and heart nor the pollution of immature minds by improper plays, stories, and conversation. But these latter actions as well as the former—and they are, of course, only examples—the practice of justice as a virtue prohibits as a matter of course, since they hinder the development of human personality.

## CORRECTIVE JUSTICE

The state enforces its laws enacted to maintain the fundamental rights of citizens, by punishment of those who transgress them. This exercise of force in defense of its enactments is a right belonging to the state, representing as it does the general will and common interest of its citizens. Punishment in a civilized state takes the form of fine, imprisonment, or, in extreme cases, of death. Now since the ultimate aim of that system of rights enforced by the public power is the self-development of humanity within its boundaries, it is clear that the aim of punishment is the promotion of human welfare. After the offense is committed punishment is necessary to conserve that social order and security which are required for further human development. This end it subserves primarily by hindering others, and the criminal himself, from committing such offenses in the future. In the second place, it contributes to the same end, of social well-being, by bringing home to the criminal the serious and self-destructive character of his act and thus turning him back into the paths of useful citizenship and personal rectitude. All this is so clear that it seems strange that any other view of the aims of punishment should have arisen or gained currency. Yet the reason for this becomes plain in its turn if we consider the origin and development of the institution of public justice in course of social evolution.

Methods of corrective justice have their natural root in an instinct possessed by animals as well as men. When injured, or threatened with injury the animal instinctively defends itself by retaliating upon the aggressor and seeking to inflict similar injury upon him. Such instinctive resentment or retaliation is at first man's only means of defending his life, person, and property, from attack. The evolution of justice as a social institution begins when individual injuries are taken up by the clan or tribe of the injured individual, which revenges itself not upon the offender alone but upon his tribe or clan. The "blood-feud" being defined and regulated by custom grows into a recognized social institution but in its purpose remains entirely retaliatory. When society becomes sufficiently organized to have chiefs or sovereigns of admitted and permanent authority we have the beginnings of justice administered by the public power. But justice as meted out by the sovereign in his decrees is at first altogether retaliatory; for the sovereign punishes offenders not because they have violated the rights of their fellows but because they have transgressed his authority—have violated the "king's peace." [3] Gradually the idea gains ground that the political authority in inflicting punishment is not wreaking private vengeance but is acting for society and is defending the rights of subjects or citizens. But still the idea of retaliation survives and lingers; for the punishment of the criminal is looked upon as the just retaliation upon him of the social order which he has injured, as the retribution which his fellows, acting through the duly constituted political authorities, have a right to exact from him. This view that the first purpose of punishment is retribution still prevails among many, probably the majority of people,

[3] HOBHOUSE: *Morals in Evolution,* Vol. I, Chap. III.

even in civilized countries, and is subscribed to by not a few political theorists and moralists.[4]

According to the retributive theory punishment in its primary function does not look forward to social progress which it aims to promote, but backward towards the offense which it aims to requite. The suffering of the offender when punished is conceived as something that he owes to the social order which he has injured, as a debt which he is obliged to pay. In harmony with this view it is further believed that punishments should be graded in their severity according to the gravity of offenses. The hold which the retributive theory has on the popular mind is not difficult to explain; it gives articulate expression—and ethical justification—to the instinct of revenge which is still a part of our nature; nearly every one of us feels the instinctive craving for vengeance when a particularly cruel and cowardly crime is brought to his attention. But the influence which this view still has among intelligent students of human life and society—an influence which is growing steadily less—is due mostly to the influence of several great modern thinkers who have sought to find an ethical or even a metaphysical justification for retributive punishment. Most notable in this connection are the views of Hegel. According to this philosopher a crime, while it is actual as an external event, possesses no positive reality; rather it is essentially naught, the negation of the real will, the true self, of the wrongdoer. The realization of his true will, then, his own right in fact, demands the negation of this negation. This is what occurs in punishment and therefore punishment is logically necessary—made so by the crime itself. Even capital punishment is, in extreme cases, owed by society to the criminal as his own right. An element of truth may be recognized in this conception

[4] *Cf.* SHARP: "Popular Attitude Toward Retributive Punishment," *International Journal of Ethics,* Vol. XX, p. 341.

of punishment, without at the same time admitting any truth in the retributive theory. No doubt the criminal does by his own act negate his own larger self; but punishment is not needed to establish this fact. Nay, the less conscious he is of his own guilt, the more insensible to the suffering he has inflicted, the more completely self-destructive is his act. It is undoubtedly necessary, furthermore, to bring home to the criminal consciousness the nullifying and self-destructive effect of his act upon his own character as a social being. But this is necessary as the condition of his reform and not as the consequence of his crime. Thus we are brought around again to the teleological theory of punishment, which has as its aim always the self-development of humanity.

If punishment is to accomplish its true aim the first object which must be sought by the society which inflicts it, is the prevention of crime. The degrees of punishment prescribed and inflicted for different offenses must be determined with a view to this object. It is a mistake to think, however, that the severer the punishment the more efficacious it is as a deterrent to crime. The experience of past ages has shown—ages when the direst penalties, even death itself with torture, were inflicted for what appear to us now as minor offenses, such as, for instance, the picking of pockets or the stealing of horses and cattle—that when the severity of the punishment is increased beyond a certain point it tends to defeat its own purpose by breeding among those individuals of the populace who have criminal proclivities a spirit of recklessness and indifference to their own life and safety, as well as to the life and safety of others. Much more important than severity of punishment in the prevention of crime is the speed and certainty of detection and conviction whenever crime is committed. But besides the office of prevention punishment has a work of reformation to accomplish. Aiming as it does at the highest human good, punishment cannot neglect the personal well-being of the offender. And by forcing upon the criminal's attention the seriousness of his offense from the standpoint of the society of which he is a member punishment may be, as we have seen, a most effective instrument of reform. In this reformative work, however, our present methods of punishment are most inadequate. Our prisons and penitentiaries are in all too many instances schools of crime instead of true reformatories. This is particularly true in the case of youthful offenders. Close confinement and enforced inactivity have further checked the normal development of capacities for achievement, and association with older and more hardened criminals has contributed to a further corruption of character and perversion of motives of action. That prisons should become institutions of reform does not mean, however, that they shall be converted into pleasant sanitariums or schools of moral instruction. The convicts in such institutions need to gain new ideals of conduct, to be sure. But more than preaching they need training—more than new conceptions of life they need new habits of living, habits of industry and application, and perseverance. And the continued effort which is required for the learning of a trade or the development of a capacity is none the less beneficial because exceedingly irksome and distasteful. Often it is because the individual, through weakness of will or unfavorable surroundings, has been unable to endure the tedium and drudgery incidental to learning a legitimate trade, that his activity has been turned into evil channels and he has been prevented from becoming a useful citizen. That deficiencies in early training should thus be remedied by the teaching of trades in our penitentiaries, and that additional incentives to faithful effort in this direction should be provided in the way of opportunities for further development and of earlier release, seem to be in every way wise and salutary. Many new and promising methods of reformative work in prisons have been devised in recent years and their prompt and thorough trial should be encouraged by all those interested in human welfare. There is certainly no field where humanitarian zeal may be more profitably exercised than that of prison reform.

## DISTRIBUTIVE JUSTICE

Human societies are concerned with the distribution not only of penalties, but of " rewards." By rewards, in the present connection, we mean external possessions and pre-rogatives, such as wealth and public recognition, whose use and enjoyment in some degree are necessary to the human individual if he is to attain Self-realization. To the extent in which wealth and fame are required as means of Self-realization, their possession is of course man's moral right. And if the supply of these " goods " were unlimited we might, conceivably, leave it altogether to the conscience of the individual to decide how much effort the interests of his own personal development would allow him to devote to the pursuit and enjoyment of them. As we well know, however, the quantity of wealth available for man's use and the amount of honors which human societies can bestow is *not* unlimited; the supply is in both cases so far limited that such amount as is appropriated by any one individual for his own exclusive use is thereby withdrawn from the quantity available for others. In these circumstances human society, in the pursuit of its own proper end, cannot afford to overlook the question of the distribution of these rewards among its members; it must endeavor through its authorized agencies to secure such distribution of wealth and honors as will most effectually further the development of human personality. But this task is by no means easy; it is beset with many difficulties, both theoretical and practical. Indeed, we encounter radical disagreement among authorities at the very outset—in respect to the principle upon which this distribution should be effected. This disagreement is at present most clearly seen in the conflict between the principle generally accepted by European thought since the time of Aristotle, that reward should be apportioned to individual ability and accomplishment, and the " socialistic " principle which has lately gained wide acceptance that external goods should be distributed among men according to their *needs* which are fundamentally alike, leaving superior ability and greater efficiency to be their own reward.

That the private ownership of property is, under the conditions of human life, a means necessary to man's Self-realization, can scarcely be disputed. The value of the institution of property as an instrument of self-development in enabling the individual to provide for his own material well-being, present and future, and thus encouraging him in the exercise of forethought, industry, and self-control, has already been shown. The possession of wealth contributes to Self-realization also by enabling the individual to provide himself with the tools and equipment necessary to the advantageous exercise of his abilities. But the ownership of property even in excess of the amount needed to supply all these wants now and to come—property which belongs to the individual to dispose of at will in the realization of his purposes—seems required for complete self-development. How is the total wealth available for human use to be distributed in order that these fundamental rights of human personality shall be fully observed? What principle of distribution is prescribed by the ideal of Self-realization? To this question we may answer with some assurance that Self-realization would distribute wealth among men in accordance with what is needed to make their individual capacities most effective in promoting human welfare. To make clear the meaning of this principle, let us indicate in a word what it does *not* admit as a just basis for the distribution of external goods among human beings. In the first place, it does not propose to distribute wealth among individuals in accordance with their differences in native ability. The possession of superior capacity by certain individuals constitutes no rightful claim to superior reward. It is certainly the height of injustice to increase the advantages which some individuals possess by giving them a larger share of the fruits of labor; extraordinary ability *is* certainly its own reward. Nor, on the other hand, is it proposed to apportion the amount of reward to the value of the service which the individual renders society. It is practically impossible to determine the comparative value to society of the various human activities. Indeed there is reason for holding that all human capacities honestly exercised have equal value to society; since all are factors equally necessary in the development of human personality. Who shall say that the work of the miner has less value to society than that of the artist, the work of the navigator less than that of the lawyer or merchant? But our principle does recognize differences in the amount of wealth which must be expended in the training and exercise of different human capacities if they are to attain full development. The achievements of house-builder and architect are equally necessary and valuable to human society, yet the training and exercise of distinctive capacities of the latter require the expenditure of much more money in study, travel, and equipment. Instead of the words " if they are to attain full development " we might with the same truth have said " if they are to be of greatest social service," since we may assume that the various capacities of man receive their full development only when they contribute most to the personal well-being of humanity. In fact, the principle which Self-realization prescribes for the distribution of rewards is difficult to grasp because of its very concreteness which forces us to consider at once the many aspects of the human situation—the amount of reward which the individual is to receive being determined not solely by the degree or kind of ability which he possesses, nor alone by the value of the service he renders to society, but by the requirements which the exercise of his particular capacity makes, if it is to be of largest service in the personal development of man.

Justice requires that rewards be so distributed among men that all individuals shall be given an equal opportunity for self-development. In the expenditure of public money to provide facilities of education and training the needs of all individuals should receive the same consideration. This does not mean that all individuals shall be given an education equally costly, a training equally prolonged; but rather that the kind of education provided for each individual shall be determined by the character of his distinctive abilities, as these abilities are manifested in his early development. When the preliminary period of training and education is past and the individual is put in full possession of his personal powers, wealth should be distributed among individuals in accordance with the demands which their different capacities make if they are to achieve their utmost for human welfare. It is obvious that different "callings" equally honorable and alike necessary for human well-being require for their successful pursuit the employment of widely varying amounts of wealth. For the work of both diplomat and teacher, for example, a preparatory training prolonged and costly is required but the activity of the former, when his career is actually begun, makes much larger demands in the way of external emoluments than that of the latter. Certain important positions in human life, if they are to be so filled as to contribute their utmost to social welfare, require the expenditure of wealth far above the average, in securing for their occupants freedom from material discomforts and inconvenience, the opportunity for leisure and travel, and the intellectual stimulus which congenial companionship affords. To such positions should attach incomes proportionate to their needs. An equitable distribution of incomes would be based, as a recent writer has said, upon '' the individual necessities of livelihood (essentially the same for all men) and the added needs which the position itself imposes.''

This principle of distributive justice which seems to be implied in the Moral Ideal gives to us, to be sure, no formula for calculating precisely what the incomes of different men in different walks of life shall be. It partakes of the nature of an ideal, very general in character, and whose application to particular cases is difficult to see, because of the many and perplexing details which must be considered. Yet it affords us a standard by which existing economic systems may be criticised and their justice estimated. And when we measure our present system of distributing wealth by this standard it falls far short of the requirements of justice. Doubtless the system of free competition which now prevails in civilized societies is much more just than the system which preceded it, by which the opportunity of personal development accorded to the individual as well as that of sharing in the fruits of human industry was strictly limited by his hereditary status. With the injustice of the older system fresh in memory it is not strange that men believed that if they were accorded the liberty to labor in a chosen field in competition with others, and to dispose at will of the products of their labor, the ends of justice would be attained. But the system of '' unlimited competition, unlimited accumulation, and unlimited inheritance '' has, in actual practice, been attended with great injustice. Free competition in business and industry has bestowed upon a certain few capacities having but a narrow range—those of technical proficiency in one or two departments of practical life—a reward far in excess of their own demands for fulfilment, or of the contribution they are able to make to human welfare. An artificially high premium has been set upon shrewdness, foresight, and enterprise, when exercised in the manufacture and distribution of material commodities. It has permitted the accumulation of wealth in the hands of those possessing these qualities which, privately owned and employed as capital, has given them such enormous advantage as practically to deprive others of the right of free competition which on theoretical grounds they possess in equal degree with the capitalists. Finally, unrestricted inheritance of vast sums of wealth and its further use as capital by those who receive it, gives this great and unfair advantage to individuals who cannot claim even to have " earned " it by the exercise of any personal capacity whatsoever. The result of all this has been the growth of monopoly, the concentration of wealth in the possession of a few, and the comparative impoverishment of the many. No wonder cries of protest are raised against the social injustice of such a system; and that men are everywhere seeking a new principle for the distribution of wealth which shall remedy these abuses. Flagrant examples of the injustice of the present system come to attention daily. In the reports of the death of a real estate agent recently published in the newspapers of his city it was stated that his income had frequently reached $50,000 a year owing to the special ability he possessed of closing large " deals " in real estate which had for long been pending but not brought to the point of decision. Surely a large reward for the capacity exercised; yet the present system is responsible for just such cases as this! The capacity for shrewd prevision along with the possession of some capital enables certain individuals, through the buying and selling of houses and land, to reap profits so huge from the labor of others in the up-building of cities and the settling of localities that they are led to pay commissions proportionately large and undeserved to all the intermediaries in their transactions. A railway official was lately quoted in protest against the review and revision, by a state officer paid $2,500 a year, of rates fixed by a railway traffic officer paid $25,000 a year. Certainly the ability requisite for reviewing and adjusting railway rates in the interest of all the inhabitants of a state demands for its training and development the use of as much wealth, and in its exercise makes as great a contribution to human welfare, as that required to fix charges with reference solely to the profit of a single corporation. There is no questioning the fact that if the ends of democracy are to be realized and every individual is to be given an equal opportunity for self-development, a new and truer method for the distribution of wealth and the adjustment of incomes must be put in practice.

5. **Benevolence.**—The end which is sought through all the various restrictions imposed upon individuals by the practice of justice is the development of human personality itself, recognized wherever and whenever it exists as an end of absolute moral worth. The habit of promoting the well-being of all fellow-men in the community, in the nation, and in the world, through individual effort and initiative, is the virtue of benevolence. Benevolence is, therefore, justice with emphasis laid upon the positive end towards which this latter virtue is directed. It is a more comprehensive and hence a higher virtue than friendship; in the ideal which it sets before the human individual it indicates the goal of self-organization in the social sphere.

The duty which benevolence imposes upon us is the service of humanity. This means the human self *as such*, humanity as a whole, with no limitation of age or sex, race or nationality, time or place. There is no blinking the wide and sweeping character of the obligation which the Moral Ideal lays upon us as the final step in Self-realization. It demands the development of the capacities of human personality *universally;* it will brook no discrimination or restriction whatsoever among individuals or among peoples. It includes the most unattractive individuals, the most unpromising peoples. Benevolence, in fact, is humanitarianism in practice. To insist upon this point may seem to some minds to be discrediting benevolence; for humanitarianism is often compared unfavorably with less comprehensive virtues like patriotism and ridiculed or denounced as vague, impracticable, and hypocritical. If pretensions of humanitarianism are used as a cloak to hide a lack of neighborly kindness or sympathy, or if ineffective and foolish methods are employed in efforts to further its ends, surely these faults are not to be charged to the account of the ideal itself. The truth remains that complete self-organization requires the adoption and pursuit of an ideal no less comprehensive than that of total human welfare. If, therefore, the individual is justified, from the ethical standpoint, in cultivating especially a few chosen friends and in failing of the same devotion in case of all other human beings it must be, and is, because the development of his own capacities for human service, under the conditions of human existence, make such limitations of his activity necessary. Or if a man strives for the good of his own country and neglects, by comparison, the well-being of other nations—if he consents to the continued development of the more civilized at the expense of the less civilized peoples,—it must be because he understands in the former case that the good of his own country includes the performance of a helpful office in the family of nations, and believes in the latter case that the uninterrupted development of the civilized peoples is necessary to the best interests of future humanity. Doubtless, in case of such judgments, too, there is a peculiar danger that self-interest may lead to self-deception or insincerity, yet man's short-sightedness or the impurity of his motives should not be allowed to reflect discredit upon the ideal whose realization is required for the complete and permanent satisfaction of his will.

If we are to understand aright what the " service of humanity " means we must guard against a prevalent misconception of social well-being in its relation to individual interests. A misunderstanding on this point may cause the ideal of benevolence to appear as a mistake and an absurdity. If human society be conceived as an aggregate of individuals each of whom has his own private and exclusive good, then such service of others, as benevolence contemplates, must mean that every individual shall deny to his own nature the satisfaction it craves, and devote himself to the fulfilment of others' desires. Suppose benevolence to be practised universally and we have all individuals abandoning their natural pursuits and occupied with the interests of others, each of whom is likewise busy with the affairs of *his* neighbor rather than with his own individual interest. Such a social life would of course be quite empty and worthless. That " life of humanity " whose development is the end sought by benevolence is something altogether different from this. It is truly conceived not as a sum of individual lives and interests but as a spiritual whole of which individual selves are the differentiations. It is an organization of personalities in which each individual may perform his peculiar function in effective adjustment to all the rest. The development of this, the personal life of humanity, is the end whose attainment is required for the complete satisfaction of the human will. It is the comprehensive ideal which underlies and correlates all lesser interests. As Hobhouse says: " That the individual is member of a spiritual whole with a common life and a general interest, is the axiom which gives the needed coherence to the multitudinous sympathies, susceptibilities, reluctancies, that guide the moral life of the unreflecting man.'' [5] The inclusive social well-being to the furtherance of which benevolence is directed is, therefore, not a monotonous and empty round of futile self-sacrifice; it possesses content inexhaustibly rich and infinitely varied. It consists in the maximum development of all the personal capacities of its members exercised in complete organic adjustment.

But how shall the individual with his limited range of acquaintance and influence, affect for better—or for worse —the well-being of humanity? Is not this end, through the vastness of its range and the magnitude of its content, so far beyond the scope of any individual's action as to cause whatever effort he may devote to its realization to be entirely wasted, and, as withdrawn from lesser interests nearer at hand, to be positively injurious in result upon his life? Is not the humanitarian ideal an impracticable dream? The best answer to all these really perplexing questions in regard to the method whereby the end of benevolence may be realized, is found in the idea of *vocation*. The individual best serves humanity who most faithfully and fully develops the capacity that is greatest within him, in effective coöperation with the efforts of his fellows to realize their distinctive capacities. One who does this may rest assured that his achievements, although they make no apparent difference to humanity are nevertheless real contributions to human progress. In the present age, moreover, with its improved methods of transportation and communication the value to all existing humanity of productions of the individual need not remain a matter of faith with him; he may hope to see his original achievements appropriated by all his fellow-men and made means to general human betterment. By railway and steamship, printing-press and postal-service, telegraph and telephone, the individual's illuminating idea, his life-saving remedy, or his labor-saving invention, are in the course of a few days, or months, or years, made the property of humanity. This idea of vocation, by which is meant the call to each human individual to make, through the exercise of the capacity most marked in his nature, his own unique contribution to human development, is of utmost ethical importance. For the " welfare of humanity," as we have seen, is not an undifferentiated mass, a great sum-total of happiness, say, homogeneous in character. It resides rather in the union and communion of personalities, each different, each in fact unique in the combination of abilities which it possesses. The development of such spiritual system takes by a necessity of its nature the form, not of an obliteration of distinctions between its constituent members, but of further differentiation accompanied by increasing organic inter-dependence. It is now a commonplace of social philosophy that the progress of human society depends upon growth in organization with an ever more complete division of labor among the individuals involved. Thus every person will achieve what he is best fitted to achieve, dedicating to the use of humanity the products of his labor; he will in the meantime avail himself of a share in the achievements of all other individuals in their respective fields of action. The physician contributes his skill to the relief of his sick and suffering fellows; he enjoys during his career the better methods of government devised by legislators and administered by executives, the superior educational opportunities provided by teachers, the conveniences and comforts originated by inventors and engineers, and so forth.

From these facts it follows that the choice of a vocation is a momentous event in the life of the human individual. So fraught is it with possibilities of good and ill that its significance cannot be exaggerated. Such choice should be based upon the knowledge which the individual has of his own capacities, and also upon a consideration of the different kinds of activities which are recognized by men as contributing to human welfare. Most important certainly is the knowledge which each person alone possesses of his own abilities and of that which, because strongest and most urgent in its demands for expression, holds forth the greatest promise of achievement. Much assistance is given to the individual in thus sounding the depths of his own nature, however, by a study of the various pursuits which have acknowledged social value. For the occupations and institutions of society are but the objective expression of the powers of human personality itself; in them the individual may see realized on a larger scale the capacities of his own nature. Hence it may well be that his own distinctive ability will be revealed to him by the compelling attraction of some department of social service rather than by the stirrings of some special potency within him. Besides these fundamental criteria which should govern the individual in his choice of a profession, are minor considerations of a practical nature which must exert a varying influence in different cases. Mr. Rashdall, who, in his profound and penetrating study of the moral life,[6] gives an important place to the idea of vocation, mentions a number of such practical considerations which, he holds, must set limits to the requirement of the Ideal [7] that each person should choose the most useful and laborious calling. These practical considerations are in substance as follows: [8] (1) A person should hesitate before embarking under the influence of high motives upon a course of action calling for

---

[6] RASHDALL: *Theories of Good and Evil.*

[7] The Ideal of Social Welfare, when conceived abstractly, i.e., as requiring the individual to sacrifice his own preferences and enjoyments altogether, in the service of his fellows. *Op. cit.,* Vol. II, p. 121.

[8] *Ibid.,* p. 122 ff.

severe labor and constant self-sacrifice when he is not sure that the inspiration to carry it through will be forthcoming. (2) Certain social functions require to be performed in a certain *spirit* which cannot always be summoned at will. Unless the individual possess the qualities of mind and heart that produce this spirit he should avoid such pursuits. (3) As a general rule a man cannot hope to do well, and hence is not qualified to perform successfully, a work for which he has not a natural liking. (4) All men cannot engage in the most altruistic and self-sacrificing pursuits; consequently it must be the duty of some men to continue in the more worldly and self-profiting occupations. (5) Some men require more ease and amusement than others if they are to work to best advantage in any line; they have a right to consider this fact in choosing a vocation. (6) A person's own happiness is part of that social good which he should aim to promote through the discharge of his vocation; it ought not, therefore, to be sacrificed to promote a less amount of it in others. (7) That differentiation in modes of life which is necessary to social progress must lead to inequalities in the amount of luxury and enjoyment possible to different individuals; this fact may in certain circumstances justify the individual in choosing the easier and pleasanter career. (8) Some kinds of work which call for less self-sacrifice are as socially useful as those which call for more; thus a moral justification exists for choosing them.—These considerations contain much truth and practical wisdom, and it is without doubt helpful to bear them in mind. Yet whatever truth they contain seems to have been already comprehended in the principles we have adopted to govern the choice of a vocation—that the individual should choose that line of activity in which he is best fitted by his distinctive capacity to achieve permanent results, considering the actual state of human society and the existing division of labor within it. In accordance with these principles, having chosen a vocation as the most effective means of promoting human welfare, the individual is constrained by all the force and authority of the Moral Ideal to prepare himself as thoroughly and perfectly as possible for its discharge and then, when preparation is complete, to devote all his strength and ability to the fulfilment of this, his vocation.

The choice and practice of a vocation by no means removes all the difficulties, it must be confessed, from the path of one who sincerely desires to realize the larger possibilities of his nature in the service of humanity. Innumerable perplexities remain regarding the relation of legitimate individual interest and the social well-being which the individual is bound morally to promote. No one can pretend that every actual, and apparently necessary, occupation in our social economy is a true vocation, or that every genuine human capacity can find satisfactory expression in some acknowledged form of social service. We can only hope that the further diversification of activities which must accompany continued social progress will make some place for the talents of those individuals for whom the world seems at present to have no use, and that industrial progress will so alter methods and conditions of work as to make the occupations of machine operatives, domestic servants, and " day laborers " truly human vocations—which, in too many cases at present, it must be admitted with regret, they are not. Allusion has already been made to the hard fact that, at present, economic pressure, by driving individuals forth in search of the means of subsistence before their faculties have had development or training, prevents many from discovering what their distinctive abilities are, and prevents others who are aware of their own aptitudes, from entering those occupations in which alone their special capacities can find realization. It is a demand of simple justice that these conditions should be removed which deprive our fel-

low-men of their fundamental moral right—the opportunity
to attain Self-realization through participating in the personal life of humanity.   But these reforms await the coming
of a clearer vision of the larger social welfare, a more sincere devotion to the self-development of human personality,
a stronger feeling of the essential unity of all intelligent
beings within the one universal life.

At the end of the previous chapter an outline of the
various fields of human activity was given, based upon that
classification of the capacities which has been followed in the
present book.  In connection with this outline a list of
human vocations may be made which, though it can make
no pretensions to completeness or finality, may be useful
for purposes of illustration.

| | | | |
|---|---|---|---|
| INTELLECTUAL | NATURE | | Scientist |
| | MAN | | Humanist |
| | UNIVERSE | | Philosopher |
| TECHNICAL | INORGANIC | Land | Mining Engineer |
| | | | Mechanical Engineer |
| | | | Civil Engineer |
| | | | Electrical Engineer |
| | | Water | Navigator |
| | ORGANIC | Plant | Farmer |
| | | Animal | Breeder |
| | | Human | Physician |
| | | | Surgeon |
| | | | Dentist, etc. |
| | SOCIAL | Law and Government | Statesman |
| | | | Diplomatist |
| | | | Lawyer |
| | | War | Soldier |

|  |  |  |
|---|---|---|
| | *Industry* | Manufacturer |
| | | Distributor |
| | *Education* | Teacher |
| | *Religion* | Clergyman |
| | VISUAL | Architect |
| | | Painter |
| | | Sculptor |
| ÆSTHETIC | AUDITORY | Musician |
| | VERBAL | Poet |
| | | Dramatist |
| | | Novelist |

# CHAPTER III

## THE RELIGIOUS VIRTUES

There is a third feature characteristic of the life of man which adds another aspect to the process of Self-realization that we have been studying—the presence in human experience of universal reality. This essential feature of our lives necessitates a third adjustment, the adjustment of man to the universe, the integration of universal reality within the life of the human self. This, the final step in the organization of conduct, is an affair of religion rather than of morality. The conception of religion which it suggests is not unfamiliar,—it is most common at present, although differently expressed by different thinkers, according to each one's philosophical bias, as the " final synthesis of subject and object " or the " feeling of harmony between ourselves and the universe," or a " faith in the ultimate conservation of values." But when understood in connection with the theory of moral development just outlined, this conception of religion as an adjustment of man to the universe is illuminating, both as to the development of the religious consciousness and the relation of religion and morality.

If we thus regard religion as the final step in Self-realization, it is possible to distinguish three stages in its evolution and also to show why these three stages are directly dependent for their specific character upon the degree of moral development attained by the self. The first two adjustments, which belong properly to the field of morality, are logically prior to that of religion; since the final adjustment of the self to the universe can be attained only when its capacities have been fully realized in its natural and social environment. But notwithstanding the fact that such a relation of dependence exists between these different steps in the process of Self-realization, they do not occur in strict temporal sequence. Thus religion does not delay its appearance until moral development is complete and the individual thoroughly socialized. We find the religious adjustment attempted in the lowest stage of human culture. The universe presses in upon the individual and forces him to take towards it some attitude. It is inevitable that the attitude taken should vary with the character of the self. The form of belief required to adjust man and the universe will depend upon the needs and aspirations of the human self and the view which it takes of the universe. Thus religion while distinct from morality is still dependent on it, and its successive stages are determined by the successive epochs in moral development.

At the lowest stage the self consists of a medley of different impulses, unregulated except by those customs which have grown up as conditions of social survival, and whose significance is not understood by those who obey them. Anything like a controlling aim or life-purpose is entirely absent from the consciousness of the self at this stage. The universe is regarded as an aggregate of objects or agencies capable of ministering to the desires of man, or of inflicting upon him dire calamities. Religion at this stage takes the form of belief in divinities which, in response to human appeal, have power to influence the objects and forces of nature so that they may minister to human needs. As there are many impulses and many objects, so there are many gods. Each main source of food supply has its divinity, so have springs and wells. There is a god of the chase and one who controls procreation. The leading attribute of deity at this stage is *Power*. This power is neither exclusively physical nor mental but something of both, the two not being clearly distinguished. The worship of such divinities takes the form of an endeavor to placate them by offering and sacrifice. They are assumed to have the same desires as man, and their favor is sought by gifts of food and drink. Within this stage fall the various forms of religion usually regarded as primitive, from animism, through the different forms of nature-worship, to polytheism.

In the second stage we find the self in possession of a well-developed individuality, the result of subordinating the many conflicting impulses to a few controlling aims and ambitions which represent the interest of the self as a unit. The universe is consequently looked upon as a factor influencing the fortunes of the individual. The form of religion needed to adjust individual interest and the universal order, is belief in a power able to guarantee to the individual who fulfils certain stated conditions, the realization of his own ambitions. Hence the tendency is at this stage to conceive of God as a conscious individual possessing the attribute of *Justice* in addition to the power possessed by the divinities of an earlier stage. He is regarded as one who rewards or punishes men according to their deserts. As the human individual has his own interests and ambitions, so God is believed to have his own designs and purposes. These are expressed in laws and decrees supernaturally revealed. The man who obeys these divine laws is rewarded with happiness and the fulfilment of his ambition while he who disobeys is punished by misery and deprivation; for God is not only Legislator but Judge of all the world. The reward of those who obey the divine commands is at first supposed to come within the limits of earthly existence. But experience proving that fortune does not discriminate between the deserving and the undeserving in this present world, the reward of the individual who serves God is postponed to a future life. This stage includes types of religion from organized polytheism through henotheism to monotheism—at least such monotheism as makes God sharply individual and separate from the world.

Finally, in the third place, we have the social or ideal self more or less fully developed, as the result of the adjustment of individual interest to the welfare of society. Man seeks to realize, now, not narrow self-centered ambitions which are different from, and opposed to, the good of others, but those larger ends which embrace the well-being of humanity. He looks upon the universe, not as deciding his fortunes as an individual, but as determining the destiny of man and the reality of those ideals, social and intellectual, which are being slowly and painfully realized in the course of human progress. The kind of belief required to adjust the individual, thus socialized, to the universe, is faith in the existence of a universal principle of such character as to conserve the highest human welfare and guarantee the reality of those values to which man attributes supreme moral worth. Now man, at the height of his moral development, regards the complete social life, —the recognition of brotherhood, the feeling of sympathy, the practice of coöperation,—as the object of supreme worth in human life. Hence the religion that gives reality to those values which man holds highest, is one which finds the nature of God, the universal principle, most completely expressed, not in power, not in justice, but in *Benevolence*. Faith in such a God who is the expression of infinite benevolence, gives to those altruistic qualities and habits which the social life demands, a foundation deep in the nature of reality. The individual who sacrifices health and possessions and even, in extreme cases, physical existence itself, in the service of others, receives from such a faith the assurance that he has not lost but gained reality thereby;

for such a life approaches most nearly to the absolutely real. At this, the culminating stage in the evolution of the religious consciousness, man adjusts himself to the universe, not by sacrifice offered to win the favor of a capricious divinity, nor by obedience to a law externally imposed by a deity who has his own ends to attain, but by faithfully discharging his duties in society and devoting his life to the service of his fellow-beings. Thus the claims of religion and morality are brought into perfect harmony, and man, by the performance of earthly duty, identifies himself with Universal Reality. This final form of religion may be called theism (if we contrast theism with deism) or, as has been suggested, spiritual pantheism.

The existence of a Universal Purpose which is striving to adapt the natural world to the needs of a society of free, self-developing persons has, to be sure, not been demonstrated. Complete proof of the working of such a Universal Purpose whose aim is the welfare of all intelligent beings, will be given only when this purpose is itself realized. The realization of the purpose awaits the fulfilment of the process of Self-realization which is being accomplished in the moral development of man. But faith in the existence of a universal principle which makes for righteousness is being justified, belief in a God of universal benevolence is receiving verification, in the power which it has given, and is giving, to man of organizing his life and adapting the conditions of his existence to the demands of a free personal life. Indeed, this is all the proof we should expect since, as we have seen, man's personal development at every stage depends upon the exercise of faith—a faith which is justified only through the success which it gives to the human self in attaining a larger and more comprehensive life.

The religious adjustment is the basis of two further virtues whose place and importance in the moral life is generally recognized. It requires, first, the subordination of all the particular interests of the human species to the ends of universal intelligence, or *reverence*. Reverence for God is thus an expression of the reverence which we owe to the Moral Ideal itself—when this ideal is defined and personalized. Second and finally, self-organization requires that man employ all distinctively human abilities in the realization of the Divine Purpose, and this is to practise *piety*.

# INDEX

Achievement, definition of, 363; *vs.* culture, 364 f.; fields of, 367

Action, capacity of, 20 f., 177 f.; in culture, 357; aim and method of, 358, 359

Addams, Jane, 331

Æsthetic capacity, nature of, 24 f., 177 f.; in culture, 359; development of, 360 f.

Alexander, the Good some form of conduct, 92; individual *vs.* social adjustment, 218

Altruism, place in Self-realization, 186; maxim of, 229; *vs.* egoism, 272 f.

Amusements, importance of, 330

Angell, 3

Antisthenes, founder of Cynicism, 113

Aristippus, founder of Cyrenaicism, 97

Aristotle, on the pre-eminence of reason in man, 117; the "mean," 185; courage, 253, 345; self-love, 281; happiness, 298; classification of virtues, 311; temperance, 323, 325; forms of friendship, 380

Arnold, Matthew, contrast of Hellenism to Hebraism, 202 f.

Asceticism, moral value of, 124; injurious effects of, 125

Attention, effort of, necessary to voluntary action, 10, 91

Authority, of conventional morality, 49, 50; of conscience, 55; of moral law, 61; of *summum bonum*, 70

Baldwin, on development of action, 138, 141

Beauty, as ideal, 179 f., 353

Benevolence, definition of, 406;

problem of, 408; solution through idea of vocation, 409 f.

Bosanquet, theory of the state, 391

Capitalism, injustice attendant upon, 338, 404 f.

Categorical Imperative, Kant's theory of, 67; criticism of Kant's theory, 69; attaching to the *summum bonum*, 70

Character, in relation to conduct, 93

Chastity, 386

Chesterton, 231

Christianity, in relation to Hebraism and Hellenism, 207 f.; as a theory of Self-realization, 207 f.; conception of Providence, 295; conception of God, 419

Citizenship, duty of, 222 f.; education for, 267, 268

Classification of virtues, desirability of, 308 f.; historical, 310 f.; defects of historical, 313; according to Self-realization, 314 f.

Conduct, meaning of, 3; human, as subject-matter of Ethics, 12; Ethics considers whole of human conduct, 13 f.; in relation to character, 93

Conscience, not special faculty, 38; identical with moral judgment, 39; influenced by feeling, 43; Intuitional and Empirical theories of, 44 f.; rational basis of, 50; *summum bonum* as ground of, 51; Self-realization as supplying standard for, 214 f.; supreme importance of, 54

Consequences, not always in